Faith, Philosophy, Scripture

FAITH, PHILOSOPHY, SCRIPTURE

James E. Faulconer

NEAL A. MAXWELL INSTITUTE
FOR RELIGIOUS SCHOLARSHIP

BRIGHAM YOUNG UNIVERSITY
PROVO, UTAH

Neal A. Maxwell Institute for Religious Scholarship
Brigham Young University
Provo, UT 84602

Library of Congress Cataloging-in-Publication Data
Faulconer, James E.
  Faith, Philosophy, Scripture / James E. Faulconer.
     p. cm.
  Includes index.
  ISBN 978-0-8425-2778-1
  1. Philosophical theology. 2. Philosophy and religion. 3. Church of Jesus Christ of
Latter-day Saints—Doctrines. I. Title.
  BT40.F37 2010
  230'.9332—dc22
                          2010036663

CONTENTS

About the Author

James E. Faulconer was born in Missouri and raised as the son of an Army officer. Because of his father's work, he grew up in Japan, Arkansas, Germany, Texas, Korea, and Massachusetts. Faulconer joined the Church of Jesus Christ of Latter-day Saints as a teenager in San Antonio, Texas. After serving a mission to Korea he married Janice K. Allen of Herlong, California. They have four children and eleven grandchildren. Faulconer obtained his BA in English from Brigham Young University and his MA and PhD in philosophy from Pennsylvania State University. He has taught in the Philosophy Department at BYU since 1975 and is a holder of the Richard L. Evans Chair of Religious Understanding. He is the author of *Scripture Study: Tools and Suggestions* and a forthcoming study on the first eight chapters of the book of Romans. Faulconer has edited several philosophy books and published articles in philosophy books and journals.

INTRODUCTION

My father was an Army officer, so I spent at least half of my childhood outside the United States, graduating from high school at the Department of Defense school in Seoul, Korea. At the end of my father's tour of duty in Korea, we were flying across the Pacific Ocean: he and the rest of the family headed to Fort Devens, in Ayer, Massachusetts; I headed to Brigham Young University as a first-year student. At some point in the flight, my father handed me an envelope containing a letter. In it he gave me advice about the life I was beginning by leaving home. Among other things, he said he hoped that I would think about becoming a teacher.

I had never considered teaching. I liked many of my high school teachers—such as Mr. O'Brien, my art teacher, and Mr. Smith, my English teacher—but I couldn't imagine myself doing what they did. I thought I wanted to practice medicine. However, years later, after studying at BYU, serving a mission, and marrying—and for much of that time no longer knowing what I wanted to do—I realized that my father knew me better than I knew myself. I wanted to teach. So, I went to graduate school in philosophy and, in 1975, came back to BYU as a professor.

Professors have three primary duties: teaching, scholarship, and participation in the organizing and overseeing work of the university and their profession. For me, each of the second two flows from the first. Scholarship is a way of preparing to teach more and a way of extending my teaching; doing the work of the university and profession are ways of supporting teaching. Teaching is what I do. The other things are

Faith, Philosophy, Scripture

what I do so that I can teach. Being a good university and professional citizen is necessary, though occasionally drudgery. Being a scholar is hard work, and often very intellectually stimulating. Neither, however, gives the kind of personal fulfillment that teaching gives.

Thus, the ten essays in this book are the result of my profession as a teacher, the work I do, of course, but more importantly that which I *profess* as a teacher. I am a profess-er, so I profess, and these essays are about the most important things I profess: faith, philosophy, and the scriptures. My faith has been central to my life since my conversion. The scriptures were important before that and have become more and more important as I have studied. In fact, graduate school was a turning point in my study of scripture, for it was there that I came to understand fully the scriptures' power to teach and the blessings to be had by studying them carefully.[1] Philosophy has been important in my life because, of course, it is how I have earned my living and supported my family. But it has also been important because it has been a way of life.

For many of the ancients, philosophy was a competitor with religion because it offered an alternative way of understanding what it meant to be a human, how we are related to each other and to the cosmos, and what is expected of us. For me, however, philosophy has the same relation to religion that it had for those such as the fourth- and fifth-century Catholic thinker Augustine of Hippo: it is a supplement to rather than a competitor with religion. The confidence of my faith, a confidence that came by revelation, has allowed me to hear the questions of philosophy without fear, and philosophy has never asked me to give up my faith, though it has asked questions about it. Those questions have often been of great help in refreshing my understanding of the gospel, in helping me see it with new eyes. I offer these essays so that others might see how these three—faith, philosophy,

---

1. For an account of one of the experiences that has been pivotal in my in learning about scripture study, see "Studying the Scriptures" in my *Scripture Study: Tools and Suggestions* (Provo, UT: FARMS, 1999), 1–15.

and scripture—can be part of a whole life, each helping make sense of the others, with faith as the ground and center of them all.

To make a more or less coherent whole of this collection, each of the essays has been revised, some of them lightly, some more heavily. The first essay, "Remembrance," reflects on the importance of remembrance to my life as a Latter-day Saint.[2] I argue that memory and conscious recollection are not the same, and that we remember by means of signs, symbols, tokens, institutions, acts, rituals, memorial objects, and many other things. Often we are not engaged in the conscious recollection of that which we remember—as when we wear a wedding ring—yet even when we are not, we remember. Or, as I suggest, it might even be appropriate to say that those signs, tokens, objects, and rituals remember for us. In our relation to us, they always remember for us that which we sometimes bring to explicit memory. By doing so, they make those explicit memories possible. Explicit memories of profound faith-events put us back in touch with those events, safeguarding our faith, but memory keeps them ready for recollection even when we are not recollecting them.

"Room to Talk: Reason's Need for Faith" was originally written as part of a Festschrift for Truman Madsen.[3] I have great respect for Professor Madsen. I had my first experience with university teaching when I worked as his assistant in 1971, grading papers and leading discussion groups. Responding to Truman Madsen's work as something that created room for Latter-day Saints to talk about their faith, I argue that the tension between faith and reason is, ultimately, not real, for faith is the foundation of reason.

During the 1994–95 academic year, David Paulsen, a professor of philosophy and a specialist in the philosophy of religion, as well as a previous holder of a Richard L. Evans Professorship of Religious

---

2. "Remembrance" was first delivered as a devotional address at Brigham Young University, 23 June 1998.

3. It was published in *Revelation, Reason, and Faith: Essays in Honor of Truman Madsen*, ed. Donald W. Parry, Daniel C. Peterson, and Stephen D. Ricks (Provo, UT: FARMS, 2002), 85–120.

Understanding, brought a variety of theologians to BYU's campus to speak of their views on theological topics. A Latter-day Saint scholar was asked to respond to each. Paulsen gathered the presentations together and, with Donald W. Musser, eventually published a book, *Mormonism in Dialogue with Contemporary Christian Theologies*. That volume contained not only the initial presentations and responses, but also additional responses. I wrote one of the additional responses to the Catholic theologian, David Tracy: "A Mormon View of Theology: Revelation and Reason," chapter 3 in this collection.[4]

Professor Tracy's essay asks how Latter-day Saints understand the relation of revelation and reason and the relation of the two to theology, and I respond by arguing that there are a variety of views among us, but that few do what would count as academic theology. I give three reasons for that absence, reasons that figure importantly in later essays: continuing revelation, the nature of scripture, and the fact that religion is a matter of practice more than it is a matter of belief.

In the same volume, I contributed a response to the work of the Protestant theologian, Langdon Gilkey: chapter 4, "Myth and Religion: Theology as a Hermeneutic of Religious Experience."[5] Gilkey's argument is that science and religion can coexist. However, we live in an age that is fundamentally secular, so scriptural language is no longer truly meaningful. Gilkey sees the job of the theologian to be to help make religion once again meaningful. Doing so means using the language of secularism against itself to "translate," as it were, the religious understanding of the world into secular terms. My response is that Gilkey has misunderstood the conflict between religion and the secular by privileging the secular. We cannot, as he proposes, rewrite the truth of religion in secular terms. Neither of the two languages is reducible to the other. But we can use the truth of religion to create a "space" within the secular world for religious understanding. To show

---

4. "Response to David Tracy: A Mormon View of Theology: Revelation and Reason," in *Mormonism in Dialogue with Contemporary Theologies*, ed. Donald W. Musser and David L. Paulsen (Atlanta, GA: Mercer University Press, 2007), 468–78.

5. Faulconer, "A Mormon View of Theology," 423–34 and 445–48.

that possibility, I argue that we can understand, philosophically, how the sacred manifests itself in the world. However, that sacred is manifest mostly in the lives and practices—the way of being—of believers.

The fifth essay, "Why a Mormon Won't Drink Coffee but Might Have a Coke," deals with the problem of why Latter-day Saint doctrine is often difficult to explain.[6] I say:

It is a matter of curiosity to many and an annoyance to a few that it is sometimes difficult to get definitive answers from members of the Church of Jesus Christ of Latter-day Saints to what seem like straightforward questions—questions of the form "Why do you believe or do *x*?" Latter-day Saints subscribe to a few basic doctrines, most of which they share with other Christians (such as that Jesus is divine) and some of which differentiate them (such as the teaching that Joseph Smith was a prophet of God). They also accept general moral teachings, the kinds of things believed by both the religious and the nonreligious. Apart from those, seldom can one say without preface or explanation what Latter-day Saints believe.

I answer the question of why it is difficult to know what Mormons believe using the same three themes that I suggest in chapter 3: continuing revelation, the nature of scripture, and the priority of practice over belief. I give an extended argument under each topic for why theology is dangerous and conclude that there are nevertheless kinds of theology that are more likely to avoid those dangers.

"Rethinking Theology: The Shadow of the Apocalypse,"[7] chapter 6, argues that, in spite of the arguments in chapter 5, arguments

6. First delivered to a conference, "God, Humanity, and Revelation: Perspectives from Mormon Philosophy and History," Yale University, 29 March 2003. A slightly edited form was later published in *Element: A Journal of Mormon Philosophy and Theology* 2/2 (2007): 21–37.

7. First delivered for Brigham Young University's Harold B. Lee Library House of Learning Lecture Series, 25 January 2007. This piece was published in the *FARMS Review* 19/1 (2007): 175–99.

that conclude that systematic theology is more dangerous than other types, the kind of theology one does is not as important as whether that theology testifies of the nearness of the kingdom of God. Though Latter-day Saints have no official theology except the scriptures and the declarations of modern prophets, and though I think that theology can be dangerous, it does not follow that we should avoid all theology. Food can be dangerous, but it does not follow that we ought not to eat. Instead of avoiding theology altogether—which is probably impossible—we must be aware that our theology can be dangerous and be sure to avoid that danger. Theology can do that if it understands itself as a kind of testimony.

In chapter 7, "The Writings of Zion,"[8] I argue that the point of scripture reading is to be called to a different way of being-in-the-world, the way of Christ. I argue that the way to hear that call is through an appropriative reading—through making the scriptures our own, in Nephi's language, likening the scriptures to ourselves—and I show that historical meaning is not only not irrelevant to an appropriative reading, it is often important to it, though never primary. I argue for a particular understanding of what it means to liken the scriptures to ourselves, seeing our lives as types that are prefigured in various ways in scripture and the scriptures as teaching us, through those types, how to live in covenant with the Father and the Son, and therefore with one another. In the end, the most important meaning we find in scripture is that revealed through the Holy Spirit, a revelation that occurs, most often, if we liken the scriptures to ourselves.

The longest and probably most difficult essay in the book is "Scripture as Incarnation," chapter 8.[9] In it I ask what it means to say that the scriptures are literally true, and I argue against the usual understanding of that claim: they do not necessarily give us a description of what one would see were one to see a movie of the life of Abraham

---

8. The first version of this piece was given as an address at the annual meetings of the Association for Mormon Letters, Brigham Young University, Provo, Utah, 8 March 2008.

9. Originally published in *Historicity and the Latter-day Saint Scriptures*, ed. Paul Y. Hoskisson (Provo, UT: BYU Religious Studies Center, 2001), 17–61.

or Moses or the ministry of Jesus. Instead, the scriptures are literal in the root sense of that word: they mean what they say "by the letter." The problem with the usual view of scripture is that it uses the canons of modern, scientific history to judge the meaning and veracity of scripture, but doing so is anachronistic, for the books of scripture were written by people with a different understanding of history. I explore the difference between the premodern and modern understandings of history, and I argue that the premodern understanding has a great deal to teach us (though we cannot merely return to it). As I explain it, the premoderns understood history as an incarnation—the entry into historical "flesh"—of a divine order of meaning. On this view, the divine order of meaning shapes and gives meaning to the events of human history. This means that whereas for moderns religion is one sphere of life among others in which we can participate and which we can investigate, for premoderns it was not a sphere among others, but that which makes sense of all the various spheres of our lives. Scripture is the multivocal expression of that order; its incarnation in words.

Chapter 9, "On Scripture, or Idolatry versus True Religion,"[10] asks what idolatry means in a contemporary context, argues that we often think about that question naively, and contends that some contemporary thinkers give us tools for thinking about what it means to live non-idolatrously. Nevertheless, more than those thinkers, the scriptures can bring us to repentance and true religion if our reading of them is an event in which we hear the preaching of the gospel, an event in which we are called. Chapters 2 through 9 make an extended argument for the importance of reading scripture in an appropriative way, making it one's own by likening it to oneself, but not interpreting in a merely subjective manner. So chapter 9 ends with examples of the kinds of readings of scripture that can be done, readings of the story of Adam and Eve and of Abraham and Isaac.

---

10. An earlier draft of this piece was published in *Discourses in Mormon Theology*, ed. James M. McLachlan and Lloyd Erickson (Salt Lake City: Kofford Books, 2007), 247–64.

The final essay, "Breathing," concludes the book with a meditation on the last half of Romans 7 and the first half of Romans 8.[11] That
meditation centers on the role of the Holy Spirit in the change that
occurs when, having found ourselves unable to live the commandments, we are inspired—literally "breathed into"—by that Spirit. As
an appropriative reading of scripture, I think it is a fitting end to the
book because it brings together the themes of the preceding chapters:
faith, reason, and scripture.

I have arranged these essays in an order that I think will help make
my arguments more clear. Indeed, in general, chapters 2 through 8
move from the simpler to the more difficult, with chapter 9 providing a
transition from the more academic back to the more general, and chapters 1 and 10 providing "bookends" for the discussion between them.

Of course, a person need not read the essays in the order in which
they occur here. Each began its life on its own and can continue to
stand independent of the others. Nor should anyone feel obliged to
slog through all of the arguments in a particular essay if he or she does
not have an interest in the intricacies of the argument. Some of these
pieces were originally addressed to audiences of lay members, others
were addressed to Latter-day Saint philosophical audiences. Even with
editing, those differences remain.

What I say may be confusing or difficult in places, sometimes
because I have not expressed myself as well as I ought, sometimes
because the material itself is difficult. I am tempted simply to quote
the twentieth-century German philosopher Martin Heidegger.[12] He
began a lecture, "Time and Being,"[13] by remarking that if we were to
see two pictures by Paul Klee painted in the year of his death, "Saints
from a Window" and "Death and Fire," we would want to stand before them for a long time, and we would not be bothered by the fact

---

11. An early version of this essay was first delivered to the Sunstone New Testament
Lecture Series, in Salt Lake City, Utah, April 1991.

12. For more on Heidegger, see chapter 2, note 62.

13. Martin Heidegger, "Time and Being," in *On Time and Being*, trans. Joan Stam-
baugh (New York: Harper & Row, 1972), 1–2.

that they were not immediately intelligible. Similarly, if we were to read a great poem (he suggests Trakl's "Siebengesang des Todes") or to have it recited to us, we would want to hear it more than once, and we would not think it should be immediately intelligible. Or if Werner Heisenberg were to present some of his work in theoretical physics, at most two or three people in the audience would be able to follow him. No one would offer it as a criticism that his work is not immediately intelligible. In each of these cases, we would be satisfied to listen, to listen carefully and more than once before we made our criticisms.

The same thing is not true of philosophy. Those who do philosophy are supposed to offer "worldly wisdom," and it is supposed to be immediately intelligible. Everything is supposed to be clear and distinct; nothing should be difficult. If philosophers do not make themselves immediately intelligible, then they, not the subject matter or the audience, are assumed to be at fault.

But Heidegger's remark will not do for me—partly because I am not yet presumptuous enough to compare myself to Klee, Trakl, Heisenberg, or Heidegger, more because ultimately my subject matter is not philosophy, but the gospel of Jesus Christ, and in some sense that must be immediately intelligible (though I would emphasize the words "in some sense"). Nonetheless, I doubt that everything I say will be immediately intelligible to most readers.

There are at least several possible reactions to that difficulty: one is that of the naive, and I mean that word to have positive connotations. The naive are of two types, those with childish faith and those with more mature childlike faith. Those with childish faith will find what I say difficult because it makes the obvious difficult. They are likely to be bored or, at best, indulgent of me, and their reaction is the right reaction. I have nothing to say to those who are naive in a childish way because anything I say would be superfluous. Those with more mature, childlike faith have moved from their initial naivete to one that knows the obstacles to faith and has faith anyway—not necessarily *in spite of* those obstacles, but aware of them and able to cope with them.[14] Often those who have a second naivete are aware of the problems but do not find them problematic, though perhaps once they did. It is as if they do not care because their faith has made them secure. I especially like to read the work of those in their second naivete, or listen to them speak, but what they say is not philosophical. If it were, it would not be naivete. The second kind of naivete is better than philosophy since philosophy is more like adolescence than childhood.

Another group of readers may find what I say difficult because it invokes difficult concepts and calls the ordinary way of thinking and speaking of things like faith and scripture into question, offering a different vocabulary, and they are afraid to have their ordinary concepts and vocabulary questioned. Those in this group have a dangerous naivete. In the face of the difficulties any child soon encounters, in the face of evil and indeterminacy, they have given up their childish faith and turned to "what everyone knows." Sometimes what everyone knows is what everyone in church knows. Sometimes it is what everyone in a particular culture knows. Sometimes it is what everyone in a particular profession knows. There are many ways to succumb to "what everyone knows."

Those with this kind of naivete assume the values and ideas of their history and culture without question, though they sometimes pride themselves on questioning, especially if the "everyone" who "knows" is a professional or academic community. Unaware, they mingle scripture and the philosophy of men—the ideas that most people in our time and culture take to be true. They are fish that do not know the water they swim in. For them, perhaps Heidegger's quotation would be appropriate if it were not for the fact that I am sometimes one of them.

A third group may find what I say difficult mostly because of my shortcomings. I may have made the simple unnecessarily difficult. I may

---

14. See Paul Ricoeur, "Religion, Atheism, and Faith," in Alasdair MacIntyre and Paul Ricoeur, *The Religious Significance of Atheism* (New York: Columbia University Press, 1969), 58–98, for a discussion of this second naivete, though he does not use the term in that essay.

not express myself as well as I should. If you are among this third group, please bear with me and forgive. I have not done so intentionally.

Given the various audiences to which these essays are addressed and the difficulties some may encounter in them, readers should feel free to skim those parts which they find either irrelevant to their interests or more philosophical and academic than suits their tastes. Pick out the conclusions and move to the things that interest you more. Just as not everyone needs to be a scientist to enjoy learning about science or an art critic to enjoy looking at a painting, a person need not be an academic philosopher to read these essays. Philosophy is not to everyone's liking, and those who do not like it should feel free to ignore the more technical parts in order to focus on that which they—and I—find more important.

Finally, I owe thanks to so many people that I fear that in naming any I may inadvertently exclude someone important. My wife, Janice, and my family (children, in-laws, and grandchildren) have been and continue to be of enormous support to me. Only a few of them have much intellectual interest in the things that I do (though they have powerful intellectual interests of their own), but for many years they have unfailingly put up with my shortcomings and idiosyncrasies as well as my philosophical interests and the absences those interests have sometimes caused. I cannot tell how important their love and support has been and continues to be.

Outside my family, the number of people to whom I am in debt is staggering, but I should name a few and apologize profusely to those I overlook. My oversight is not a reflection of the value of their contributions. Some to whom I am indebted and whose names come to mind are Brant Bishop, Grant Boswell, Sabrina Clifford, Robert Couch, Alison Coutts, Elder Henry B. Eyring, Stephen Goldman, Daniel Graham, Ralph Hancock, Paula Hicken, Paul Hoskisson, Jeff Johnson, Bruce Jorgenson, Brenna King, Keith Lane, Adam Miller, Paul Moyaert, Nathan Oman, Noel Reynolds, Shirley Ricks, James Siebach, Joseph Spencer, Brandie Siegfried, Carl Vaught, Rudi Visker, Mark Wrathall, ... Thank you all.

CHAPTER ONE

REMEMBRANCE

Ido not know when children begin to remember, but I know that
my earliest childhood memories are an important part of who I
am even though I do not have a good memory for things that I really
should remember: people's names, things that happened to me, important events. For example, I was fourteen when I was baptized, but
I remember only a few details of what happened, though I remember
vividly some things surrounding my conversion. Perhaps it is true that
you do not remember what does not matter to you or what is painful,
but I do not think so. I remember relatively little about my childhood,
but I know that it was a happy one. I remember relatively few details of
when Janice and our sons and I lived in Pennsylvania while I went to
graduate school, and that was one of the most important and happiest
times of my life.

In spite of my poor memory, some memories stand out. One of
my earliest is a game that my mother and I played: she chewed gum
and blew as large a bubble as possible, and I tried to break the bubble
before she could suck it back into her mouth. I also remember the
interior of my Grandfather Sammon's car. It was dark and warm, and
I especially remember the seat covering—gray, rough, and musty but
pleasant smelling. Was it made of horsehair or wool? I do not know, but
once in a great while I smell the smell again, though I can never quite
decide just what I am smelling. In new-car showrooms or dry-goods
stores I often sniff the air, unsuccessfully searching for that smell.

I remember riding in the back of that car with my mother—my
grandfather driving while she pointed at the telephone poles going by

outside. I think she was counting them, and we pointed to animals in the fields: "Look, a horse" or "See the cow?"

These two shadows of memory come together in one vivid memory. While my father served in General MacArthur's honor guard in Japan during the Korean War, my mother and I lived sometimes with and sometimes near my grandparents in central Missouri. I remember riding with my mother one afternoon, probably in the fall—my mother on the right and me in the middle of the backseat, and my grandfather in the front, driving. Mother blew an especially large bubble, and this time I won, exploding the bubble before she could pull it back. When it burst, it was all over her face and in her hair, and she laughed. But Grandpa did not laugh. I think he was probably afraid we would get gum on the upholstery of his car.

I also remember my first experience with death, though I did not know that was what it was. The house where my grandparents lived when I was young is gone now, torn down after both had passed away because it was dilapidated. I am told that the large room in the northwest corner at the front of the house was the bedroom for my mother and me when we came back from Colorado after my father left for Japan, but it was not until many years later that I remember being allowed in that room, a sitting room. In the early days its large double doors were kept closed, and I had to be quiet when around them. At that time my Aunt Betty, Uncle Ermon's first wife, slept in the room behind those doors. In fact, she was confined there with tuberculosis—which I only learned when I was quite a bit older.

I remember nothing about Aunt Betty except being kept from her, but I remember standing in the front yard one day, north of the yard gate across from where the chicken coop was later built, watching Uncle Ermon carry a small woman wrapped in a light-colored blanket or quilt out to the car, her head on his right shoulder. My mother and grandmother stood watching from the porch. My grandfather got in the front seat to drive.

The memory ends there, but my mother says this must have happened when I was about two years old, perhaps on a visit, because by the time we returned to Missouri to wait for my father, my aunt was dead.

I also remember well the first time my father talked to me about baptism, several years before we joined the Church of Jesus Christ of Latter-day Saints. I was in the fourth or fifth grade, and we lived in Munich, Germany.

One day, I suppose it was a Saturday or Sunday, my father took me for a walk. We crossed the two-lane highway (now a freeway) west of our apartment building, and we walked along the forest paths with others out for a stroll. The sky was clear and bright, and the green and black of Perlacher Forest contrasted beautifully with the light of the sky. My father talked to me about whether I wished to be baptized, and I consented. I only vaguely remember being baptized by the Protestant chaplain, but I remember well the event of our conversation. In a certain way, that walk in the Bavarian woods, talking with my father about serious things on a beautiful day, has come to define my experience in Germany.

Such memories have played a large part in shaping who I am. I do not believe in what many refer to as "the unconscious," at least not as it is usually described. I cannot make sense of what is said about it. Nevertheless, it is obvious that there is much about myself that I cannot bring to explicit consciousness. Memories such as those I have mentioned are the tips of icebergs floating in my consciousness; they indicate places where matters of considerable weight can be found, even if I cannot explicitly name or bring them to consciousness. They reveal not by exposure, but by suggestion.

As the title of this essay suggests, I want to think about memory here, partly because it is a professional interest of mine, most of all because memory is so central to the gospel that we covenant to remember every time we take the bread and water of the sacrament.

Philosophers have had quite a bit to say about memory. Reading and teaching philosophy, I have learned to distinguish between recollection and memory. The former is a psychological phenomenon that is a subset of the latter. Memory includes the things I can recollect, but it is not limited to it.[1]

You may ask, "What in the world can he be talking about? What could memory be *except* a subjective psychological phenomenon—what I call to mind?" To think about that, consider an example.[2] Like most married people in our culture, I wear a wedding band, and it cannot be reduced to its economic value as a piece of gold or even to its instrumental values. That is because, beyond having economic or instrumental values, my wedding band is a symbol of my marriage. As a symbol, it is obviously connected to memory. However, though it serves to remind me that I am married, it is more than just a reminder.

What more could it be? First notice that if my wedding ring were only something for reminding me, then I could also have chosen to tie a string to my finger. However, though I can create such reminders—putting yellow sticky notes on my computer monitor or remarks in my daily planner—a wedding ring "works" differently than such things.

My wedding ring is more than a reminder at least because my wife, Janice, gave it to me. It is different from a reminder because it has a physical relation to her and so mediates my physical relation to her. However, when I wear the ring, it is not that, by doing so, I touch Janice in absentia. The ring is not a substitute for my wife. Though the ring *can* remind me—it can cause me explicitly to think about my marriage—most of the time I wear it without explicitly calling my wife or marriage to mind. And yet it continues to do its work, as I notice quickly if I have taken it off to work and forget to put it back on. I am more conscious of its absence than its presence, so I cannot ex-

---

1. Recall is a psychological event. Memory is what we share and participate in. As such, it gives us direction (intention) beyond our subjective intentions, often intentions we do not know. It also creates expectations of us that are beyond our will but are part of who we are.

2. My thinking about memory is heavily influenced by the Belgian philosopher Paul Moyaert. For more on these issues, see chapter 8 in this volume.

plain its work by the way in which it is, sometimes, explicitly present to thought.

Thus my wedding ring is a memorial of our relation because it does something for me in spite of myself. Even if I am not thinking of my marriage, the ring demands a certain attitude toward the world, a certain reverence and respect for Janice; it connects me to Janice even when I am not explicitly thinking of her. My wedding ring makes possible certain relations in the world by embodying those relations.

Said another way, my wedding ring gives order to my world: an order that relates me to my wife and to the rest of the world, an order that cannot be reduced to an intention to remember my marriage. Though it is odd to say, *it is as if my wedding ring remembers my marriage for me.*[3] Not only does the ring not usually refer to or represent Janice, it does not take her place. In a very real sense, it takes my place rather than hers. My ring can serve as an explicit reminder because it remembers all the time, while I recollect only sometimes.

We encounter the same phenomenon in many things other than wedding rings—for example, in other physical symbols, in sacred objects, in ritual practices, in a variety of institutions. I mentioned the sacrament earlier, perhaps the most important of such event-symbols in Latter-day Saint experience, but we can also see the phenomenon in other, more mundane places. Perhaps all symbols remember for us rather than merely reminding us.

The university is an institutional repository of memory. As an institution, it remembers a great deal for us: making our explicit recollection of many things possible, giving our lives a particular character, and creating possibilities for us that we have often not yet envisioned. The university is a memorializing object and institution, not only in the library collections but also in its organization and influence, in such things as our academic regalia and other traditions (recognized or unrecognized), in our folklore and style of gossip, and in courses

---

3. Remember that I distinguish memory from recall. Though the ring remembers for me, it does not always or even usually recall for me. Probably it never does.

such as the civilization courses or American heritage classes. We often see the university as a place from which we look to the future—a place where we prepare for jobs, where we produce knowledge that will have effects in the future. But it is equally important to recognize that, as an institution, the university is a place of remembrance and memorial.[4] In fact, I suspect that a university can be oriented toward the future only because it is an institution of memory. As a Latter-day Saint institution, Brigham Young University is the repository for one particularly important memory, that of the restoration as it enlightens the academy. That memory orients us to the world and the future in a unique way.

At the personal level, memory resides not only in my subjective recollections, but also in things I may seldom notice, such as the ways I speak—ways that sometimes betray my origins, as when I say "Missouruh" rather than "Missouree." More broadly, that I speak English rather than Korean or Swahili or Romanian as my native language is a memory of my cultural inheritance. The ways that I interact with others are memories of the interactions of my family and childhood as well as the accumulated results of countless human interactions in ages past. When I joined the church, such things as our pioneer heritage became part of my memory, as did a uniquely Latter-day Saint vocabulary and various social practices. Most important, by joining the church, the memory of the prophets became part of me, as did the atonement. Though I was raised a believing, Bible-reading Christian, through my conversion a vast storehouse of memory was added to my being, an important part of which is latter-day revelation.

While studying the scriptures a few years ago, I was impressed by the importance of memory when I read a passage from the Book

---

4. This should make us wary of sudden or drastic changes in the university. Revolutions, whether cultural or political, rarely succeed because they propose to cut themselves off from the very memory that makes them possible and meaningful. Progress can be important (though we often overrate it), but it rarely, if ever, requires what have come to be called, in a mistaken understanding of the philosophy of science, "paradigm shifts": Even when it does, such shifts are events that happen as we work and learn but that we can rarely, if ever, engineer.

of Mormon. At the end of 1 Nephi 1, the prophet tells us that he will
abridge the sacred record that his father, Lehi, kept, and he will give
an account of his own life. He then tells us that Lehi prophesied to the
people of Jerusalem, but they refused to listen. Instead they mocked
him and sought to kill him. Then, having set the context and the
mood of his message, Nephi says, "I . . . will show unto you that the
tender mercies of the Lord are over all those whom he hath chosen,
because of their faith, to make them mighty even unto the power of
deliverance" (1 Nephi 1:20).[5] As I read this sentence, it struck me that
we might take this to be Nephi's "thesis statement" for the Book of
Mormon: Nephi and the other Book of Mormon prophets give us to
remember the tender mercies of the Lord so that we can be delivered
according to our faith.

As I reread the Book of Mormon with Nephi's statement in mind,
I was struck by how often the prophets begin by calling us to remember the Lord's mercy.[6] However, given that the Book of Mormon ends
with the annihilation of the people of Mormon and Moroni, we may
find this thesis startling. How does a record that ends in disaster and
genocide show us the tender mercies of the Lord? Moroni's answer
is clear: By showing us that the Lord has, over and over again, been
merciful to his children, the Book of Mormon, like the Bible, gives
us hope, even when we are in what would otherwise seem a hopeless

---

5. Nephi's language seems to be influenced by Psalms. See Psalm 25:6: "Remember,
O Lord, thy tender mercies and thy lovingkindnesses; for they have been ever of old." We
find similar language in other psalms.

6. The Book of Mormon as a whole begins with such a call. Its preface tells us that the
book was provided: "to show unto the remnant of the House of Israel what great things
the Lord hath done for their fathers; and that they may know the covenants of the Lord,
that they are not cast off forever—And also to the convincing of the Jew and Gentile that
Jesus is the Christ, the Eternal God, manifesting himself unto all nations."

Lehi's descendants will learn what the Lord did for their fathers, and the Jew and
Gentile will be convinced that Jesus is the Christ by seeing that God has revealed himself
to all nations. In other words, by seeing what the Lord has done for the descendants of
Lehi as well as for those in Jerusalem. Moroni's preface confirms Nephi's thesis statement: In the Book of Mormon we are reminded that the tender mercies of the Lord are
over the faithful to their deliverance.

situation. In Moroni 10:1, Moroni begins his final exhortations. To the remnant of the Lamanites he says:

> Behold, I would exhort you that when ye shall read these things, if it be wisdom in God that ye should read them, that ye would remember how merciful the Lord hath been unto the children of men, from the creation of Adam even down until the time that ye shall receive these things, and ponder it in your hearts. (Moroni 10:3)

And he follows this exhortation to remembrance with an exhortation that those who receive the Book of Mormon should ask the Father whether it is true. In other words, they should ask the Father about the truthfulness of the record of God's mercies in the Book of Mormon. In verse twenty-four Moroni turns from the descendants of Lehi to the rest of us, exhorting us, too, to remember the things we have read—namely, the account of God's tender mercies to his people, tender mercies that "make them mighty even unto . . . deliverance" in faith.

As do the psalmists, Nephi and Moroni see a close connection, perhaps even an identity, between remembering the tender mercies of the Lord and repentance. Without such memory, we seem unable to repent; if we repent, remembering those tender mercies is always part of our repentance. Over and over again we find this theme in the Book of Mormon: conversion and reconversion come by remembering; dedication, sacrifice, and covenant are one with memory. Sermon after sermon begins with a prophet reminding his listeners or readers of what the Lord has already done for them. They remind us of the flood (Alma 10:22), of the exodus from Egypt (Mosiah 7:19), and of the journey across the ocean (2 Nephi 10:20). Ammon converts Lamoni by rehearsing these stories to him, beginning with the story of Adam and Eve (Alma 18:36).

Once I noticed this theme of remembering God's mercy, I saw it everywhere. The Lord announced himself to Moses by calling himself "the God of Abraham, the God of Isaac, and the God of Jacob"

(Exodus 3:6), a common appellation and a name that reminds us of the mercies that he showed to Abraham, Isaac, and Jacob, particularly as those mercies are manifest in his covenant with them (see Leviticus 26:42).

Occasions for memory are found not only in the scriptures. Each Sunday we renew our covenant with the Father by taking tokens of Christ's body and blood in remembrance of that flesh and blood and by promising always to remember him. I understand the Word of Wisdom as an ongoing memorial of who we are and what we have promised.[7] One of the most obvious sites of memory is the garment worn by those who are endowed, reminding us of the covenants we have made; we wear sacred memory on our bodies day in and day out. Like my wedding ring, the garment remembers for me, calling me to recollection when need be, but ordering my world even when I do not have it explicitly in my consciousness. Because I wear the garment, I am in the world differently than I would be if I did not.[8]

In my own life, the memorializing objects and practices of the church continue to make my spiritual life possible. When I remember the Savior not only in my recollections, but especially in my practices and relations with others, I bear witness of his saving relation to me, and, as promised in the sacrament prayers, I receive the Spirit. To the degree that I do not have memory—from the readily identifiable and seemingly mundane culture that Latter-day Saints all over the globe

---

7. The Word of Wisdom may also direct our attention to the coming of Christ. Since anticipation is a form of memory, it may call the second coming to our remembrance. The Savior says: "But I say unto you, I will not drink henceforth of this fruit of the vine, until that day when I drink it new with you in my Father's kingdom" (Matthew 26:29). Perhaps by ourselves not drinking of the fruit of the vine now, we remember the Savior's promise that he will drink with us when he returns.

8. Noticing the power of memory and its difference from recollection is, I argue, an important part of renewing our spiritual life. However, sometimes memory has the opposite effect, deadening us to what is spiritual. An example would be vain repetitions in prayer, repeating phrases because they are so much part of our memory that we need not recollect them in order to say them. In such cases, conscious recollection can be a powerful tool for bringing power back to our memory. (Thanks to Brant Bishop for reminding me of this problem.)

share, to my obedience to commandments even when I am not thinking of them, to the mysteries and blessings of the temple—I am not
part of the body of Christ, I am not one of his adopted children.

Sometimes I find myself slipping from the memory into which I
entered through my conversion. I have doubts about my testimony.
Something happens that I do not understand, and I wonder whether
the church is true. I may chafe at commandments or policies. I might
think myself better than others—sometimes because of education,
sometimes because of social status, often for who-knows-what reason.
I may criticize instructors and leaders in the church, wishing (not out
loud and rarely even to myself, but wishing it anyway) that they had
more "training for the ministry," that they were better at getting my
interest—shifting the burden of my spiritual life to them. Occasionally
I find myself bored with the talks in sacrament meeting or quietly and
self-deceptively scornful of the testimonies borne on fast Sunday. In
other words, though I may be able to *recall* my covenants, sometimes
I find myself no longer *remembering* them, no longer remembering
(whatever I recollect) that at baptism I promised to "mourn with those
that mourn; yea, and comfort those that stand in need of comfort" so
that I would "stand as [a witness] of God at all times and in all things,
and in all places" (Mosiah 18:9).[9] In spite of having so promised,
sometimes I do not even learn with those who would learn or testify
with those who would testify, much less mourn or comfort. Whatever
I may recall, whatever I may repeat consciously, at such times I have
begun no longer to remember the tender mercies of the Lord; I have
begun to slip out of the ongoing process of repentance. (I hope that
you will recognize a version of yourselves in my self-description, not
because I hope you share my failings, but because I assume that I am
not the only one who finds himself slipping on occasion.)

---

9. Notice that Alma makes bearing witness (recollection) dependent on our relation with others (memory): "mourning with" and "comforting" make testimony possible,
suggesting that it is not truly possible without such relations to our fellows.

Such events do not characterize most of my life in the church, but they happen often enough that I must consider how to deal with them. My answer is recollection. Though memory cannot be reduced to recollection, when I begin to fade and falter, the answer is to explicitly recollect a few events in my life that have brought sharply to my attention what living my life memorializes. Recollecting the visible tips of the largely invisible icebergs of memory helps resituate me, bringing me back to who I am, putting me back into the larger context of memory. Let me finish with a few of those recollections.

I share them with some trepidation. Sacred experiences are not to be shared easily, like political slogans or loose change. One should be careful about sharing them, for sharing them too often or under inappropriate circumstances strips them of their sacred character. They become commonplace rather than sacred. Nevertheless, there are times and places when we can share sacred recollections with each other to strengthen the testimonies of both those who testify and those who hear the testimony. I pray that this is such an occasion.

The first experience I recall is that of my conversion. My father met the missionaries through a friend at work, Robert Clark. I met them through my parents when my mother cajoled me into taking part in a "cottage meeting" at our house. Though I began reluctantly, once I started listening, I was hooked. I enjoyed the missionary discussions and liked the missionaries, and I enjoyed learning what they taught. To be honest, I did not read the Book of Mormon, and I did not pray about the church very much. However, after several months of discussion, with the rest of my family, I wanted to join the church.

Since we had not been to church yet, the missionaries arranged for us to attend the next Sunday so that we could be baptized the Saturday after that—the first Saturday of February, 1962. Sitting on the left side of the chapel, about one-half to two-thirds back, watching the meeting begin, I was not particularly impressed. It looked very much like the Protestant services I was accustomed to, except that there were more people on the stand, the table for communion—what Latter-day

Saints call the sacrament—was to the right of the room rather than in the middle, those to say the prayers over the sacramental elements were surprisingly young, and when the meeting began, it was almost shockingly informal and unpolished. Though I had decided to be baptized, as yet I remained a curious onlooker more than a convert. As the sacrament was blessed and passed, the bread came to me. In my former church, the Disciples of Christ, we believed that everyone present should take the sacramental emblems, and though the missionaries had told my parents that this was not the Latter-day Saint practice (at that time), no one had told me. As the bread tray came around, I took a piece and put it in my mouth.

As I placed the bread in my mouth, I was overcome by the most intense spiritual experience I had ever had. Instantly I knew something of what Paul had experienced on the road to Damascus. Without being especially worthy of it, without having sought it any more than superficially, I had been touched by the Holy Ghost. My entire soul—body and spirit—was electrified and on fire. Now, rather than thinking that it would be a good idea to be a Mormon, that LDS theology was interesting, and so on, *I knew* that I had to join this church. I was no longer a spectator. I knew that what I had learned from the missionaries was true. I knew that what I would learn later would be true. I knew that Joseph Smith was a prophet, as was David O. McKay, the prophet at the time. Though I had as yet read only a passage here and a passage there in the Book of Mormon, I knew it was the word of God. Though I had believed in Christ all my life, for the first time I knew that Jesus Christ had died for my sins and I understood something of what that meant.

With that experience, I suppose there was a sense in which I could still choose not to be baptized. Nevertheless, there was a more profound sense in which I no longer had any choice. I knew that my life from that point on would be inextricably bound to the Church of Jesus Christ of Latter-day Saints. I did not know what that entailed, but I knew it was true.

I do not know why I was privileged to have such an experience when others are not. I cannot explain what happened. I only know that the experience has provided an anchor for my soul, something to which I can return in recollection when I begin to falter, something that returns me to the ordering of the gospel and the order of the church. This is a recollection that returns my memory to me and returns me to it. It is something for which I am deeply and eternally grateful.

That first taste of the sacrament has been the most important spiritual experience of my life because it *converted* me, changing my life. On the whole, since then I have lived a relatively mundane life; though spiritual experiences are common, they are rarely dramatic. I do not regret that. It is important to learn to see the spiritual in the mundane, to find spirituality even when not emotionally wrought, to recognize that the Spirit usually brings peace and speaks quietly (John 14:27). That is more important than having dramatic experiences, and we must be wary of equating our emotional and our spiritual lives. Nevertheless, my first experience with the sacrament was not the only such emotionally powerful spiritual experience.

A few months after we were baptized, my father was assigned to the Korean Military Advisory Group for the South Korean Army and was allowed to take his family to Korea with him. We were privileged to grow up in the church while in Korea, to be taught and guided by such families as the Terrys and the Hogans, and to be inspired by wonderful Korean Saints like Han Insang, Rhee Honam, and Kim Cha Bong. In those days in Korea we did not have stake or district conferences for people in the armed services. We had "servicemen's retreats," occasions when those who could get time off could go to Seoul and spend two or three days meeting and sharing testimonies. Elder Gordon B. Hinckley was the visiting General Authority for Asia, and he was often able to attend our retreats, so they were a special occasion for us.

One year, during late fall or winter, we had a retreat in Seoul, and Elder Hinckley attended. We started on Friday and ended on Sunday, and as we met in our final meeting, a testimony meeting, many bore their testimonies, including my younger brother. I recall nothing said in those testimonies (though President Hinckley had such a prodigious memory that decades later he could tell what my brother said), but I felt the Spirit as strongly then as I had when I first received my testimony. I particularly remember Elder Hinckley bearing his testimony, telling us that the Spirit in our meeting was as strong as he had ever felt it, as strong even as he had felt it in meetings of the Twelve in the temple. He said that there were angels in the room witnessing our testimonies.

I knew that what he said was true. I could see no angels. Tears were streaming down my face so heavily that I could not see anything, much less angels. But I knew, absolutely knew, that he was right. I knew what I had learned with my first experience with the Spirit: the church is true; the priesthood is real, and it is the power of God. I had a feeling that I take to be a premonition of what it means finally to be sanctified, for like King Benjamin's people, for a short time I had "no more disposition to do evil, but to do good continually" (Mosiah 5:2). I could not and did not want to separate myself from the church that made such an experience possible or from the gospel taught in that church, pointing as it does to salvation in Jesus Christ. That experience with the Spirit in the presence of one of the Twelve became another anchor for my soul.

The Lord has not ceased to give me such anchors. One of the more recent was in August of 1994. My second son, Matthew, was to return from his mission to Pôrto Alegre, Brazil. He asked that his mother and I meet him and do some traveling, but we could not do that. However, we compromised, and I went to Pôrto Alegre to pick him up. Matthew and I stayed in Pôrto Alegre for a few days and then set out to São Paulo by bus. The day we were to leave for Curitiba, we discovered that we would have to wait until late afternoon to get the bus, but we had already checked out of our hotel and did not have anything left that we wanted to do in Pôrto Alegre.

Matthew had the idea to take a bus to some point midway between Pôrto Alegre and Curitiba, spend the day there, and then catch the bus to Curitiba as it came through our stopping point at night. He asked the woman selling tickets to tell us a good place to go. "Rosario," she said. "It is a nice resort town with a beach." We bought our tickets and headed to Rosario.

When we stepped from the bus in Rosario, we were surprised. There were mountains, but no beach. We were obviously inland and rather high. We decided to get some lunch and see what Rosario had to offer. If worst came to worst, we could sit in the bus station and read.

As we turned the corner of one of the first streets we passed, two boys, one a teenager and the other perhaps eleven, came running down the street shouting, "Elders! Elders!" Matthew stopped and talked with them, explaining that although I was wearing a white shirt and tie, only one of us was a missionary and that we were to be there for only a few hours. They were excited anyway, not caring that I was not a missionary as long as someone was. We must go to see their mother. The older boy ran off to find her, and the younger boy led us toward her. As we came around another corner, a middle-aged woman came running down the street, tears flowing, also crying, "Elders! Elders!" Again Matthew explained that he was the only missionary there and that we would be there only a short time, but that was irrelevant to her. Her prayers for missionaries to come to Rosario had been answered. She pled, "Have family home evening with us, please."

We could not refuse, so we agreed to go to their home early that evening for family home evening. We spent the afternoon in the town wandering around, buying some presents for Matthew's sisters, and sitting in the park, reading and talking. Then we went to their house. We visited with them and sang a hymn. Matthew taught a lesson, and we prayed with them. As we were finishing, the sister told us that we must visit a young man in town who was inactive. (I was not sure how one knows that another is inactive when there is no branch or church activity in a town, but she knew—and she was right.)

We walked across the small town to the highway where this young man owned a truck stop. He fed us a gigantic, definitely non-vegetarian dinner and talked at length with Matthew. As Matthew later explained to me, the young man had a dream the night before. In the dream the missionaries came to visit him and told him that he must return to church—and there we were. (He could attend church in a neighboring city by hitching a ride with truck drivers, but he had stopped doing so.)

I was thunderstruck. I could not believe the faith of these people. I could not believe how desperately they hunger for what I take for granted. I could not believe how much the Lord loves them as individuals. I could not believe that he had used our seemingly chance wandering around Brazil to bless a few of his children. As I sat on the bus that night, I had difficulty sleeping, not because the bus was uncomfortable (which it was), but because I was so overcome with a vision of the love that the Father and the Son have for us, of the need for missionaries in places like Rosario, of the beautiful faith of people like those I had just met, of my own unworthiness in comparison to theirs, and of my ingratitude for the blessings I have received.

Those few hours in Rosario, Brazil, gave me a deepened appreciation for the love of God. I was reminded that his love is not a general love but a love for each specific person. Though what we brought to the Saints in Rosario was relatively little, that we could be instruments for bringing it renewed my understanding of the Lord's power to save—to save from difficulty, from oppression, from loneliness, and especially from sin. It made me ashamed of taking for granted the access I have to the church and the temple, to inspired leadership and instruction. It showed me why the missionary effort is so important and must expand, for here was a group of ten or fifteen Saints to whom the church could not yet come because, in spite of the large numbers of young people who serve missions, there are still not enough missionaries in the field. Like the previous experiences, those few hours in Rosario became another anchor for my soul, something I recollect as a way to continue to remember the covenants I am part of and the obligations that have come to me.

I live in a world that gets its significance from memory: memory manifest in wedding rings and garments and sacramental emblems, in ordinances and practices and customs, in speech patterns and names and literature, in universities and libraries and classes. I have learned that I live not on my own breath but also on that of the Spirit, without which there is only recollection at best and no memory, without which, ultimately, emblems, ordinances, and society are dead and hollow shells. Memory—manifest in my speech, our customs and habits, our relations, our ordinances and commandments—transcends and encompasses me, making the world I live in possible by giving it meaning and structure.

Recollection, calling various things to mind, is not memory. Nevertheless, recollection can resituate us in memory. As I recollect—re-collect—my experiences with the Spirit, I take my place again in the memory that makes life possible and good, that strengthens and continues my testimony. Most people have experienced moments of spirituality to which their souls are anchored. Those who have not will—sometimes in answer to prayer, sometimes unbidden. My prayer is that, when you face doubt or difficulty, you will re-collect your souls by recollecting those anchoring experiences. And, though I have no authority to offer spiritual promises, based on my experience, I promise that if you will so recollect, you will continue not only to recollect but also to remember the everlasting gospel, the covenants you have made, and the holy name of Jesus Christ.

CHAPTER TWO

ROOM TO TALK:
REASON'S NEED FOR FAITH

Truman Madsen's slim volume, *Eternal Man*,[1] had a profound effect on me and, when I ask others who were students in the late
sixties or early seventies about it, I find that it was equally important
for them. The book was not academically profound, but then it had no
pretensions to be. As Madsen says in the introduction, its chapters were
intended "as a kind of 'midrash.' . . . The goal has been to clarify rather
than to verify, with little room for argument, except an implicit appeal
to introspection."[2]

The result of that goal was that one can find much to challenge in
the book: Must we understand the doctrine of preexistent intelligences
to imply that we have existed eternally as individuals? Does Madsen
not create straw persons in his descriptions of orthodox Christian
and other beliefs? For example, is it true that religious existentialism,
such as that of the nineteenth-century Danish philosopher, Søren
Kierkegaard, is "utter pessimism"?[3] And does Madsen not assume
that being is a thing rather than a process or event—does he not reify
it—when he argues against the dualism of traditional theology by dis-
missing its concerns for nothing and for being?[4] Does he not dismiss
too easily some of the traditional problems of theology and the philosophy of religion, such as how it is possible to speak meaningfully

1. Truman Madsen, *Eternal Man* (Salt Lake City: Deseret Book, 1966).
2. Madsen, *Eternal Man,* viii.
3. Madsen, *Eternal Man,* 29.
4. Madsen, *Eternal Man,* 31–32 and 44.

of a being who transcends our mortal finitude?[5] How does defining freedom as self-determination remove all of the problems of freedom and determinism?[6] It would not be difficult to add to the list.

But adding to the list would be beside the point. It would mean refusing to recognize the book for what it claims to be and is: a primer to aid us in introspecting about the intellectual strengths of our belief in the premortal existence of spirits. If, as such a primer, the book raises these questions and more, it fulfills its function, inducing us to think about its topic. Perhaps it will some day even goad one of us to provide the promised "tome which is not pressed [as Madsen's was] for abbreviation"[7]—a tome that one wishes Madsen himself could have found the time to offer, all the while recognizing that his life continued to be busy enough to make that difficult.

But for those like myself, *Eternal Man* was important not so much because of the problems with which it dealt or the positions that it took on the questions of the eternality of individuals, divine omnipotence, the materiality of the Divine, human freedom, and so on, but because of what it did. More than teaching a particular doctrine or suggesting any particular solution to a philosophical or theological problem, the book gave its readers permission to think about these kinds of problems, to read the books listed in its many footnotes and books like them. *Eternal Man* said, "It is good to think about and deal with these issues." It gave those of us in college and graduate school in the late 1960s an alternative to the two most common positions taken with regard to such things: "One position assumes that they [the ideas about preexistence] are so remote and incomplete that a 'practical man' avoids thinking about them. The other assumes that by mere reference to preexistence one can 'explain' all events and eventualities."[8] By writing *Eternal Man*, Truman Madsen said to me—and, I believe, to many others—"Take seriously the admonition from the Prophet

---

5. Madsen, *Eternal Man*, 35.
6. Madsen, *Eternal Man*, 66 n. 9.
7. Madsen, *Eternal Man*, viii.
8. Madsen, *Eternal Man*, 14.

Joseph Smith that introduces chapter two: 'When things that are of the greatest importance are passed over by weak-minded men without even a thought, I want to see truth in all its bearings and hug it to my bosom.'"[9] Reading *Eternal Man* made me not want to be one of the "weak-minded." The book gave me an intellectual goal and told me that my new goal was not only commensurable with my faith, but an expression of it.

Reminding us that Joseph Smith described the gospel as requiring "careful and ponderous and solemn thoughts,"[10] Madsen said, "A related kind of authority is needed in this realm. It is what, in the vernacular is called 'room to talk.'"[11] By suggesting the possibility of taking our faith seriously while also understanding the writings of scholars, of thinking about both without being ashamed of or frightened by one or the other, Madsen opened such a room and many entered.

Given today's hypersensitivities of various kinds, such room to talk is as difficult to come by as it ever was. Some, recognizing that current trends of thinking are not consonant with the gospel (as if they ever were), think that we should shut our eyes and ears to such things and that, especially, we should not speak of them to the young for fear of corrupting them. Others think that it is enough merely to repeat conventional wisdom about the gospel or, perhaps, even merely to repeat the truths of the gospel. For them, repetition without investigation is enough to answer all questions. A few others, convinced that this or that seemingly newfangled notion is, at last, the answer to our problems and questions, would either ignore the gospel or twist it into a shape that fits better their newfound intellectual faith. But all of these kinds of problems respond to the difficulties of the intellect with one kind of dogmatism or another. They shut the door on any room to talk.

---

9. Madsen, *Eternal Man*, 23.
10. As quoted in Madsen, *Eternal Man*, ix.
11. As quoted in Madsen, *Eternal Man*, ix.

In this paper, I will address the relation of faith to reason. I doubt that I will add new insights to the discussion of that hoary subject. Rather than do so, I intend to say a few things that I hope will, in imitation of *Eternal Man*, use the topic to open and leave room to talk. I will argue that faith and reason are commensurable. I have heard persons whose ideas I respect suggest otherwise. Nevertheless, I think my conclusion is one that most Latter-day Saints would agree with.[12] In making this argument, though I argue for what I believe to be true, I leave open the possibility that I am wrong. That is one reason that philosophers offer arguments, to make it possible for others, by seeing the steps of their reasoning, to show them where they went wrong.

Besides arguing for the commensurability of faith and reason, I will go further. I suggest that faith is fundamental to reason, though I do not more than sketch an argument for that suggestion.[13] The full argument for that claim would take at least another paper and probably a book. Neither of the positions that I outline is novel and, in some circles, they may even be ordinary. But the marvel of the ordinary and wonder at that marvel is sometimes itself not so ordinary. In fact, I think it has become so *in*ordinate in our day that we often need to be reminded of quite ordinary things. So, I offer here some musings and reflections on the relation of faith to reason, with an argument or two, in the same spirit as that we find in *Eternal Man*—namely as points for reflection and provocations for thought more than as a philosophical treatise.

In particular, I want to suggest that faith is fundamental to reason, but let me begin my reflections on that claim with a story, for my reflections have their genesis in an experience in the spring of 1993. I think the story illustrates that rationality cannot be reduced to sets of propositions or beliefs related to each other by implication relations. Instead (and I will argue that this is true of every kind of rationality),

---

12. Of course, arguing for a conclusion with which most already agree may be a problem: we often overlook the deficiencies in the arguments of those with whom we agree.

13. A sketch can create room for discussion by suggesting a topic and outlining an approach to that topic worth considering, while leaving the details and even the decision about the ultimate value of the approach to be worked out in further discussion.

rationality must begin with something outside of such sets and relations, as I think the experience I will recount suggests.

My oldest daughter had been an officer for one of the Utah chapters of the Future Homemakers of America, and they held their end-of-
the-school-year banquet in Salt Lake City. I was going through all the
usual hoopla politely but condescendingly. I was there to do my duty as
a father, though I would have much preferred to be elsewhere. Chicken
dinner for 750 accompanied by speeches and awards for a large group of
fourteen- through seventeen-year-olds was not my idea of a great way to
spend my Saturday afternoon. Sitting next to me at the table for parents
was a couple of about my age, both of whom were obviously enjoying
what I was merely tolerating, from the food to the entertainment. When
I asked where they were from, he said, "Wayne County."

"Where in Wayne County?"

"Just Wayne County."

"How far away is that?"

"About a four-hour drive."

It quickly began to be more difficult for me to condescend. Their
four-hour trip made my forty-five minute one look like a walk across
the street, but I was the one who was slightly irritated about having
to make the trip. Had I stopped to reflect (although I did not), I could
have explained their enjoyment of the occasion geographically: such
things might look good in comparison to the pleasures of Wayne
County. Our conversation continued:

"About what time will you get back tonight?"

"About 11:00."

"Well, at least tomorrow is Sunday. Maybe you can sleep in."

Stupid me. I assumed that all people have five-day-a-week jobs,
Monday through Friday, and work from eight to five.

"Well, it's lambing season and one or the other of us has to get up
every hour to check the ewes. We trade off, so we can sleep about two
hours at a time."

Condescension turned to humiliation: this man and woman loved their daughter more than I loved mine. Though, unlike me, they actually had to sacrifice to be at the banquet, they were pleased to be there, enjoying what happened, not because they were so intellectually blighted that they thought that seventeen-year-olds have much of importance to say and certainly not because they liked the food on the menu or found the pleasures of Wayne County so abysmal. They were there because they loved their daughter and they enjoyed seeing her enjoy herself and be honored. I love my daughter too, but what I saw as an inconvenient and mildly irritating responsibility that is consequent on loving that daughter, they saw as part of that love. That experience *persuaded* me in a moment that they were right and I was wrong. Their lives were right in a way that mine was not, and I came to that understanding by seeing a small part of their lives.

The couple next to me did not—almost certainly would not have thought to—offer me what philosophers recognize as rational arguments, and they almost certainly did not have the training to do so in a way that I would acknowledge as philosophical. In spite of that, their behavior did bring me to a conclusion, the conclusion that one should enjoy such events. They did not intend to do so. I certainly had no impression that they were trying to teach me anything—certainly not that I was wrong. Nevertheless, being in their presence did persuade me. They *were* something like evidence; they did not offer it. I would have had to have been unreasonable to deny the conclusion that their behavior persuaded me to accept. What was the nature of the experience I had in seeing what their lives revealed? How did that experience make it possible for me to be persuaded, to come to a rational conclusion, immediately and without a chain of reasoning (deductive or inductive) from assumptions to conclusion?

How did seeing them and talking with them make possible a rational belief that I was wrong (the *conviction* that I was wrong, if I can use the word in both of its senses) without any chain of reasoning? What I saw in them was neither an axiomatic truth nor a truth deduced from axioms. It was not a "bare empirical fact" (granting, for the argument, that there are such dubious things). It was not an objective truth.[14] But neither was it merely a subjective opinion. My judgment of myself was rational. Some evidence that is was a rational belief rather than a merely subjective one is that others, hearing the story, know its conclusion before I tell it; they are able to adduce the same conclusion from the story that I did from the experience. The behavior of the couple from Wayne County was like evidence for a rational conclusion, but it did not require that I begin with a belief and then come to a conclusion based on that belief in order to be persuaded.

Before trying to give an account of why the kind of knowledge I acquired that afternoon was rational, let me be clear about what I am saying: Seeing the couple next to me and listening to them talk about their daughter was sufficient to persuade me (in a sense of the term that I will leave open) of the inferiority of my love for my daughter when compared to their love for theirs. That is not to say that I could not have been wrong about that belief. It is only to say that the belief to which I came was rational. It had sufficient grounds and could not be explained solely in terms of my previous beliefs. It was not just subjective. This is also not to say that persuasion cannot take other forms. It is only to suggest that this event raises important questions about rationality, particular questions that may help us think about rationality as a whole. Careful readers may worry that I wash over important distinctions: rationality cannot be reduced to a response to relevant information; giving reasons for a belief is not the same as

---

14. The phrase *objective truth* gets used in many ways. In common usage it means little more than something like "real truth." The strict, philosophical sense of the word *object*, however, is "that which stands at the other end of a perceptual or mental directedness or of a possible directedness." On this understanding, there are objects that are not physical objects (such as mathematical and other ideas) and there can be existing things that are not objects (such as things to which no one is presently directing any awareness). In the strict sense, to be objective is to consider things simply as standing at the other end of a perceptual or epistemic directedness and, therefore, to ignore other possible relations to that which one considers. I here use the phrase *objective truth* in this more strict sense: the truth as it pertains to objects of that sort.

being evidence for a belief, and so forth.[15] Nevertheless, recognizing
the legitimacy of that worry, I will proceed. I am not arguing that response to relevant information and rationality are the same, and I do
not think my argument requires that they be the same. Instead, I am
looking at a particular kind of case—the case in which I find myself
persuaded of something based on something that our ordinary meta-
talk about reason seems to exclude or at least to render problematic,
as in the example of the couple from Wayne County. That kind of case
is sufficient for the purposes of this paper, namely to raise questions
about our understanding of reason that will allow me to argue that
reason and faith are commensurable and to sketch an argument that
reason requires faith.

I will suggest that faith and reason are commensurable by arguing
that reason always requires something outside the chain of reasons
(such as my experience of that couple). In addition, as mentioned, I
will sketch what I think may be an argument that the relation of reason to what is outside itself is a matter of faith. If that is the case, then
at least one way in which faith and reason are commensurable is that
the latter requires the former.

Before I make my case, however, let me briefly take up another
way in which faith and reason are commensurable: not only does reason need faith, faith needs reason. If, as it is often defined, faith is understood to be belief or even knowledge in the absence of compelling
reasons, then it is obviously true by definition that faith and reason
are mutually exclusive. When we are asked to talk about faith, if we
are not careful, we almost always slip into our semiphilosophical or
theological mode and, when we do, we are likely to say something in
which faith is defined in this way.[16] Although this response is com-

---

15. My thanks to Mark Wrathall for helping me see the importance of this problem.

16. Although most people would not think of themselves as philosophers or theologians or even think of themselves as ever doing philosophy or theology, most still use the
methods and concepts given to them by philosophy to talk about various matters, including the nature of reason. It is natural to use that kind of thinking when we talk about certain subjects. The problem is that, when we do so, we almost always unconsciously use the
ideas, concepts, and methods of reasoning that we have inherited, without reflection, in

mon, I think it is seriously mistaken. The American philosopher Alvin Plantinga has argued—brilliantly, I believe—that we should reject that definition: compelling experience may be sufficient for knowledge, even in the absence of compelling beliefs.[17] Faith is best thought of, not as belief in the absence of reasons, but as fidelity to something that one has been given, such as an experience or covenant, or trust in someone, such as God. That is how it seems most often to be used in the scriptures.

Besides appealing to Plantinga's argument, I have additional reasons for rejecting the common separation of faith from reason. For one thing, to think in that way is to confuse faith with opinion (though even opinion has its reasons and evidence, often, but not always, poor ones). If we confuse faith and opinion, we should not be surprised when arguments showing the insufficiency of opinion and the necessity of moving from opinion to knowledge grounded in reason also work as arguments against faith. But it is a mistake to define faith as belief without reasons.

Paul is explicit about faith being a matter of evidence: "Now faith is the substance (*hypostasis*; meaning "reality" or "realization") of things hoped for, the evidence (*elenchos*, meaning "proof" or "argument for"[18]) of things not seen" (Hebrews 11:1). Nephi and Lehi, the

---

our common language and culture. Since these are "natural" to us as part of our "common sense," it is not surprising that we use them to discuss philosophical and theological problems, whether or not we recognize that we are doing so. But since these ideas and concepts are also unexamined, we often make mistakes when we use them, including the mistake of introducing ideas that are incompatible with other ideas that we hold. (This natural and understandable reversion to common sense is my understanding of the phrase that speaks of mingling the philosophies of men—in other words, their common sense—with scripture.)

17. For the details of Plantinga's views, see Alvin Plantinga, "Reason and Belief in God," in *The Analytic Theist: An Alvin Plantinga Reader*, ed. James F. Sennett (Grand Rapids: Eerdmans, 1998), 102–61; Plantinga, *Warrant: The Current Debate* (New York: Oxford, 1993); and Plantinga, *Warrant and Proper Function* (New York: Oxford, 1993). Plantinga argues for a number of conclusions regarding reason. For my purposes, the only one that is relevant is that it is possible to have grounds for belief that are not, themselves, beliefs.

18. I am grateful to James L. Siebach for first pointing this out to me, as well as making me think about its importance to our understanding of the relation between faith and reason.

son of Helaman, convert hundreds to faith by offering them "great evidence" (see Helaman 5:50). Several years later, Nephi, the son of Helaman, tells the people that their unbelief is unreasonable, a rejection of convincing evidence (see Helaman 8:24). Faith has reasons and requires them; at least part of what is wrong in the supposed confrontation between faith and reason is that a poor definition of faith is used. Since I will assume that most of the audience of this essay consists of practicing, faithful Latter-day Saints, however, this argument needs little development. They already know, at least in their hearts, that there is more to faith than belief without reason; that faith is essentially trust and fidelity rather than belief, though beliefs will result from trust and fidelity; and that when they do, they will have their reasonable ground. Thus, my primary focus will be on the nature of reason and its relation to faith.

Aristotle says that to be human is to be rational.[19] Along with most people, I'm willing to accept that assumption without further proof, but the assumption cannot mean that to be human is to offer and listen to arguments. Aristotle's claim is not that human beings are all philosophical in the conventional sense of the term. At best, Aristotle is making the weaker claim, that all human beings are capable of using reason. But what does that mean?

In its essence, the problem of reason is simple: does reason have a reason, and if it does, how do we think that reason? How do we establish certain knowledge when reason seeks for its foundation? René Descartes—one of the most important fathers of modernism, a seventeenth-century philosopher to whom we owe much of our contemporary, ordinary understanding of reason (our "common sense"), and the author of the oft-repeated and much misunderstood sentence, "I think, therefore I am"—assumes that reason has no reason: it begins from principles that are intuitively known to be true without reference to anything else, and proceeds logically from step to step, establish-

---

19. *Nichomachean Ethics* 1097b24–1098a3.

ing knowledge as certain when it reaches its end.[20] In contemporary philosophical jargon, he is a foundationalist: according to Descartes, there are self-certifying, rational foundations to reason.

It is true that Descartes must know there is a God in order to know that there really is a world that can be the object of his ratiocination, but though the existence of the world and our knowledge of that existence require God, reason does not. If it did, Descartes believes, we would never get to a knowledge of God's existence or even our own, for it requires reason to know either. Thus, Descartes' methodological doubt can get us to the conclusions he reaches only because, for him, reason is self-grounding and complete. It is the only thing without reason; it is its own reason. Despite the fact that much twentieth-century philosophy on both sides of the Atlantic has devoted itself to a critique of the Enlightenment notion of reason, and even with the introduction of such things as probability theory, studies of induction, and new theories of logic, I think that many—certainly most nonphilosophers—continue to think of reason in terms that are ultimately Cartesian: reason is self-grounding and, in principle, eventually capable of giving a complete description of the world. Certainly this is the implicit view of many who advocate reason as the solution to all problems and science as the ultimate example of reason.

But I see only two possible consequences of the claim that reason is self-grounding and complete: radical skepticism or totalitarianism. The eighteenth-century Scots philosopher, David Hume, an important critic of the Cartesian understanding of the world, shows us the first of these: if we accept Descartes' foundationalist position and reject the proof for God's existence (as we most certainly can when we confine our thinking to what can be demonstrated by reason unaided),

---

20. For perhaps the best place to see Descartes' discussion of reason, see his *Discourse on Method*. Of course, Descartes' view is not created out of whole cloth. It has everything to do with the tradition from which he comes, and it remains the dominant way of understanding science—knowledge—for a long time. See Barry Gower, *Scientific Method: An Historical and Philosophical Introduction* (London: Routledge, 1997), 1–108, for a good overview of both the importance of this view of science and how it changed.

then we are reduced to the tautologies of pure logic and to reporting the fact of immediately present experience (which may not be able to be plural without losing its immediacy). Even memory of very recent events cannot be trusted.[21] On the other hand, if we find a rational way around Hume's argument, a way of speaking about the world rationally (or if, as many have done, we ignore Hume's argument), then we accept Descartes' assumption that reason is ultimately adequate to the world: it is in principle possible to make a list of the true propositions that give a complete description of the world at any given point in time and to relate those propositions to one another by logical implication alone.[22]

In the last half of the twentieth century a Lithuanian born, Jewish, French émigré, Emmanuel Levinas, argues that such an understanding of reason is not just mistaken, but eventually amounts to totalitarianism, even political totalitarianism, and, in the end, the horror of Auschwitz.[23]

As extreme as that claim is, I find it plausible, although I can here do no more than give a précis of an argument for it. As moderns, we assume that reason makes us masters of this world. To use Francis

21. See David Hume, *A Treatise of Human Nature.* I believe that Hume gives this argument, not because he is a radical skeptic, but because he is radically skeptical about rationalism. I take his argument to be a *reductio ad absurdem* of the rationalist position. But that does not change the point I am making here.

22. You find the culmination of such a view in Ludwig Wittgenstein's famous phrase, "The world is everything that is the case" (*Tractatus Logico-Philosophicus* [New York: Routledge], 31). Notably, Wittgenstein later repudiated that view in *Philosophical Investigations* (Malden, MA: Blackwell-Wiley, 2001). Wittgenstein, Austrian-born but later a British subject, was one of the most important philosophers of the twentieth century.

23. See, for example, Emmanuel Levinas, *Totality and Infinity: Essay on Exteriority,* trans. Alphonso Lingis (Pittsburgh: Duquesne University, 1969), 21–25; and Levinas, *Otherwise than Being or Beyond Essence,* trans. Alphonso Lingis (The Hague: Martinus Nijhoff, 1981), 4–5, 118–19, 159–60, and 177. Notably, almost every person in Levinas's family was executed by the Nazis during World War II. Though perhaps shocking, Levinas's conclusion is shared by other contemporary European thinkers. See, for example, Jean-François Lyotard, *Heidegger and "the Jews,"* trans. Andreas Michel and Mark S. Roberts (Minneapolis: Minnesota University Press, 1990), and Edith Wyschogrod, *Spirit in Ashes: Hegel, Heidegger and Man-Made Mass Death* (New Haven: Yale University Press, 1985).

Bacon's phrase, "knowledge is power" (rather than virtue, as it was for Plato and other ancients). Given the modern view, the world, including other persons and ourselves, is a set of objects subject to rational investigation. If Bacon is right that knowledge is power, then the search for absolute knowledge (knowledge without limits) is the same as the search for absolute power (power without limits). In our century, that search for power in the form of knowledge, loosed from its traditional mooring in the search for the Good (as it must be loosed if we accept Bacon's erasure of virtue with power, and the resulting identification of knowledge and power), has cost millions of lives and caused unspeakable horror and suffering.[24]

But even if one were to reject Levinas's claim as exaggerated, the modern understanding of reason contains an irony: the attempt to fulfill our desire to give a complete description—to say "the last word"—can only result in continuing babble and never in the last, controlling word for which the search for power hungers. In *Metaphysics*, Aristotle argues that without something outside of the chain of explanations, there can be no actual explanation.[25] I think that is an argument whose power is often overlooked. Aristotle calls this something the *archē*, the origin. (This Greek word is the root of English words like *archaeology* and *architect*, as well as "archangel" and "patriarch.") It is tempting to think that the *archē* is either the first in the series of efficient or other causes or to think of it as the first instance in a chain of rational explanations. To understand it in either of these ways is a mistake, however, for these two ways of understanding the *archē* are of a piece. Each reduces the *archē* to something that has the

24. This is not to deny that previous eras have also been guilty of horrors and holocausts. It is only to point out the connection between modern philosophy and the modern versions of such horror.

25. Aristotle, *Metaphysics* 994a1–20. Of course, not all rationality consists in creating chains of reasons. That is irrelevant to this argument. Aristotle's point, that chains of reasons require a ground, applies equally to any other form of rationality. So the point I make here with regard to chains of reasons applies equally well to other forms of reasoning. For the purposes of this paper, I do not believe that the difference between chains of reasons and chains of explanation is important.

same way of being as any other moment in the chain of explanation or account, the only difference between the *archē* and any other moment in the series is that, mysteriously, the *archē* is the first of those moments. Understood that way, Aristotle's argument makes no sense.

But, as we see in Thomas Aquinas's use of Aristotle's argument in the proofs for God's existence,[26] that is a misunderstanding of the argument. As I think Aquinas's use shows, Aristotle's point is that there must be something outside of or beyond or prior to any chain of reasons to ground the chain in question or there will be no real reasonings.[27] There must be what the late twentieth-century French philosopher, Jacques Derrida,[28] calls "the supplement," though the name itself indicates that one speaks from within a chain of reasons rather than from any external point of view. One speaks of what is beyond reason from within reason because there is no alternative.[29]

Expanded, Aristotle's point is this: potentially every chain of reasons, every reasoning or explanation, is infinitely long. No matter

---

26. Thomas Aquinas, *Summa Theologiae: Latin Text and English Translation*, 61 vols. (New York: McGraw Hill, 1964–1976), Q.2, A.3.

27. I have sometimes also argued, though not in print, that the belief in the *archē* is at the root of the problem of the common understanding of reason. Here I may seem to contradict that claim. I think that my claim that the *archē* is behind the standard view of reason is true, though there is not space enough here to lay out the difference in the two conceptions of *archē* that are at work, both philosophically derived from Aristotle. Suffice it to say that the problematic view of the *archē* is a view that takes it to be the first in the causal or logical chain, a reified originary point for explanation—precisely the position I here argue against.

28. For a readable and accurate discussion of Derrida's work (and accuracy is something often missing from those discussions, whether pro or con), as well as its relation to some kinds of religion, see Kevin Hart, *The Trespass of the Sign: Deconstruction and Philosophy* (Cambridge: Cambridge University Press, 1989).

29. The claim that there is no alternative outside of reason may seem too strong, but it will do for the purposes of this paper. But I take quite seriously the idea that there is a kind of speaking that is an alternative to the narrow, Cartesian understanding of reason. Of course that is not an alternative that is external to reason. The alternative to reason narrowly conceived is something that Martin Heidegger (an early-to-mid-twentieth-century German philosopher) sometimes called *poetry*. He had poetry as we understand it in mind, but he also understood poetry to include much more, such as other forms of imaginative thinking. See my later discussion of Kierkegaard and irony for a first suggestion of how we might understand this alternative. (For more on Heidegger, see note 62.)

where I stop, in principle someone could ask, "And what explains that?" Nevertheless, our chains of reasoning do *not* go on to infinity. Something stops them; something makes any particular stopping point of an adequate chain of reasoning the appropriate place to stop. That which constitutes the adequate stopping point of a chain of reasons, however, is itself not part of that chain. The reason for the explanation is outside the chain. (It could be, and often is, something as straightforward as a state of affairs, "the way things are.")

The real origin or first cause of any chain of reasons, is not the point at which we stop saying "A because of B because of C," but something that is not itself part of the chain of reasons, something that we do not account for in our chain of reasons or causal account. The *real* beginning of the chain is the *archē* that gave rise to the chain (and can, therefore, also give rise to a chain with only one link, the conclusion). That which gives rise to a chain of reasons is something that cannot itself be explained; it is an "uncaused cause," to use the traditional terminology, and cannot be included in the chain of reasons, since it could be said to be the cause of the chain rather than a link in the chain.[30]

Of course, as I pointed out earlier, in principle it is always possible to give an account of whatever we can point to, and, on reflection, we can always point to the origin of a chain of reasons. But when we do so, we remove it from its status outside the chain of reasons. It ceases to be the origin of the chain and becomes one of the things in the chain, namely, its first element. The problem is that this means something new has taken its place as the origin of the chain of reasons, as the supplement—in other words, as the ground of explanations and

---

30. As used here, "uncaused cause" is not the contradiction that it appears to be. It is a way of pointing to that which initiates the chain of reasoning, in other words brings it about or causes it, but that is not itself part of that chain, and so, not named as a cause in the chain. Much use of this phrase and of this argument confuses reasoning and explanation—in which there must always be an "an uncaused cause"—with what is, where it is not obvious that there must be such a cause. Such thinking moves from epistemology to ontology without the resources for doing so. Being outside the chain of reasons, the "uncaused cause" is not a cause, a reason, in the same sense as any of the items in the chain. That is the substance of Aristotle's point.

reasons that is not itself part of the chain of reasons. Thus, if we take the Cartesian understanding of reason seriously, if we assume that the origin of reason is not supplemental to reason, that there is nothing outside the process of reason because reason is self-grounding, then we will have no way to stop giving reasons in any particular case.[31] Without a supplement, an *archē*, every chain of reasons will go on to infinity and so will not do as a chain of reasons. An explanation that cannot come to an end is no explanation at all. If explanation requires a last word rather than a supplement, then the desire for the last word is implicitly the desire for garrulousness, not understanding.

This observation that the use of reason depends on something external to that use is a matter of common sense. As always, philosophers argue for what ordinary people know without having to argue it. In addition, many more philosophers have known this than have not. Medieval Christians certainly knew that explanations require something beyond them and their processes. The various sorts of empiricists also knew it, as did the Romantics. Marxism knows that reason has a "supplement" and, like Christianity, reminds us that ignoring that fact is seldom innocent. Plantinga gives us perhaps the best explanation in analytic philosophy of this truth that we all already know.[32] Deconstruction begins with the assumption of this need for something more and then tries to show places in texts and philosophies at which that dependence on what is beyond reason shines through the text. Feminism allies itself with Marxism, though sometimes only implicitly, in recognizing both that reason is not self-grounding and

---

31. Descartes tells us that first principles are things that we see to be true without further reflection. It is possible to understand that declaration as itself recognizing the need for a supplement. In fact, his recourse to the proofs of God's existence (see *Meditations*), can be read as just such a recognition. (For a reading of Descartes along these lines, see Levinas's interpretation of Descartes in *Totality and Infinity*, 210–11 and 48–52.) Nevertheless, the standard way of reading Descartes, and, so, of understanding reason, has been much as I describe it in the body of the text and that is what I find fault with. Note, too, that I equivocate here on "reason" and "explanation," but recall note 25. Every explanation is an exercise of reason and prototypical for what it means to exercise reason. I do not think that the equivocation damages my argument.

32. See the works referenced in note 17.

that the claim that it is, is not innocent. Every ordinary member of the church knows that something more than reason is needed. But in spite of the fact that "everyone" knows at least implicitly that reason requires a supplement, I think it is also true that few people recognize this fact when they reflect on reason or faith and fewer still recognize its implications or the questions it raises.

Having argued that reason requires a supplement, let me now turn to that supplement: what can we say about its character, if anything? and what is its relation to reason? For our purposes, these are the same as the question of how we can reasonably talk about what falls outside reason, so I will treat them as one question. On the face of it, we seem to be faced with a dilemma:

In order to speak reasonably about something, it seems that it must be within reason.

The supplement of reason is outside reason.

So, we cannot speak reasonably about it.

That conclusion at least raises doubts as to the tenability of the second premise, the premise for which I have argued. The argument seems to imply a self-contradiction: It is reasonable to say that the supplement of reason is outside of reason *and* we cannot speak reasonably about what is outside of reason.

To deal with this problem, we need to consider a way in which we talk about the supplement of reason that is not helpful. When we hear people talk about faith and reason in church talks or classes or serious conversations about serious matters, they often use the language of Romanticism: there are things to be known and things to be felt; things to be explained rationally and things that defy rational explanation but are known by means of some other faculty. We sometimes use the word that the Romantics gave us for that other faculty, *intuition*; sometimes, instead, we speak of feeling; sometimes we associate the promptings of the Holy Ghost with the Romantic faculty for knowing. Those who take this approach see the problem of the realm of reason as we usually understand it, and they try to solve that problem by supplementing reason's realm with another, that of feeling, a realm that goes beyond our ability to conceive and that gives unity to the whole of experience.

But there are philosophical problems with Romanticism.[33] Having created two realms of knowledge, those who think in this way find that they have doubled their problems. The problem with reason is that it cannot answer the question of how we can know things like the supplement of reason. It is not clear how creating an additional realm of knowledge, the realm of feeling, solves the problems of the first, the realm of reason. In fact, it is unclear how having two realms of knowledge and two faculties for knowledge undoes the problems that follow from relying on reason alone. If I know by intuition or feeling in one realm, why can I not know that way in the realm of reason? Additionally, if reason and intuition are separate realms, why doesn't one of the two realms end up encompassing the other? And if one does not encompass the other, how can I speak of knowledge in both realms? What do the two have in common that allows me to speak of knowledge in both without there being some way of bringing them together, something in common with both of them? If reason and intuition are distinct ways of knowing, what holds them together so that I, an individual, can make sense of each? With Romanticism, not only are human minds caught in the clutches of Enlightenment, foundationalist reason, we are also hopelessly and essentially schizophrenic.

My final objection to the Romantic solution to the problem of reason is that, by moving everything that could not be understood by Cartesian reason (such as religion and art) into the realm of feeling, Romanticism deprecates those things. Without intending to, Romantics make any talk of knowing the objects of religion metaphorical, at

---

33. Though I am not a Romantic, the position for which I argue has a number of parallels with philosophical Romanticism. That should not be surprising since both are attempts to respond to the problem posed by Immanuel Kant's metaphysics, in which it is impossible to speak meaningfully of that which transcends our immanent experience. However, I am not speaking of philosophical Romanticism here, but of its contemporary, popular manifestation. To avoid clumsiness, I will refer to popular Romanticism as Romanticism, without the qualifier.

best, thereby robbing important parts of our lives, such as religious and aesthetic experience, of their ability to give us genuine knowledge.[34] Their approach to knowledge creates a dilemma: I cannot know the truth about the most important things rationally, and I cannot know what the other way of knowing them is unless I have already experienced it.

Given these problems with Romanticism, though religious people and artists often use the language of Romanticism to talk about the relation of their concerns to reason and to explain their experiences and knowledge, Romanticism will not do. Whatever the relation between reason and its supplement, that relation must be understood from within reason or it will fall into the abyss of irrationalism or, at best, the whim of subjective sentiment (which is where Romanticism ends up, in spite of itself, by cutting itself off from reason). Whatever the relation of reason and its ground, we must understand reason in a way that will allow us to do so without dropping beauty, art, religion, love, feeling, the good, and so on into the abyss of the irrational or nonrational.

It will perhaps be surprising to some that I think Kierkegaard understood that point quite well. Because he understood that we can only understand the relation of reason to its supplement from within reason, he used pseudonyms and irony in his philosophical texts (at the same time that he was writing quite straightforward religious sermons). He wanted to pay appropriate due to reason without falling into the trap of making it independent of faith. As I understand Kierkegaard's best-known treatise on faith, *Fear and Trembling*, Abraham is faced with a paradox when he is asked to sacrifice his son Isaac. He must obey God, who commands him to kill his son, but he knows that it is unholy to kill another person. Revelation contradicts ethical obligation. It is not uncommon to understand this paradox as a

---

34. See Hans-Georg Gadamer, *Truth and Method*, 2nd rev. ed., trans. Joel Weinsheimer and Donald G. Marshall (New York: Continuum, 1993), for an important exposition of both the history of this mistake and an alternative to it.

contradiction between reason and revelation: revelation and reason are incommensurable and revelation trumps reason.

Instead, I think that the paradox of Abraham is not that revelation must contradict or trump reason, but that Abraham cannot make himself understood to foundationalist philosophers and those of Kierkegaard's countrymen who think they have gone beyond Descartes' methodological doubt to G. W. F. Hegel's rational certainty.[35] Abraham cannot speak, says Johannes de Silentio (Kierkegaard's pseudonymous author),[36] yet he does speak. What Abraham says however is "absurd," meaning that it cannot be heard by the foundationalist philosopher, not that it has no meaning. I take it that Kierkegaard is relying on the root meaning of the word *absurd*: "what cannot be said, what is voiceless," so also, "what cannot be heard."

The ab-surdity[37] to which the story of Abraham points is the voicelessness of what lies outside the strict economy of Cartesian doubt and certainty. As a result, the ab-surdity that Silentio discovers is only meaningless or irrational if we insist that meaning and rationality are products of only "the system," of only Cartesian rationality. To be sure, what is outside the system is paradoxical—in other words, strange and marvelous, rather than self-contradictory (again, I take Kierkegaard to be relying on the root meaning of the word "paradox": what is other than our expectations[38])—but it is not unreasonable or contrary to reason, except from the point of view of a reason that has

---

35. G. W. F. Hegel was an important German philosopher who lived at the end of the eighteenth century and the beginning of the nineteenth. Hegel is an idealist, arguing that history is the unfolding of what is most real and that the unfolding had completed itself at the end of the eighteenth century. To understand that history and the process of its unfolding is to know, in principle, all of reality.

36. Cited in Søren Kierkegaard, *Fear and Trembling: Repetition*, ed. and trans. Howard V. Hong and Edna H. Hong (Princeton: Princeton University Press, 1983), 115–20. Notice that the name Johannes de Silentio—"John of Silence"—suggests that it is really the author rather than Abraham who is unable to speak.

37. I hyphenate the word to remind us that I am using it in the special sense just explained.

38. *Oxford English Dictionary*, s.v. "paradox," and Henry George Liddell, Robert Scott, and Henry Stuart Jones, eds., *A Greek-English Lexicon*, 6th ed. (Oxford: Clarendon, 1968), s.v. "παραδοξία."

been artificially and narrowly defined. As I understand Kierkegaard, Abraham cannot be understood *if, and only if,* one rejects the origin of his knowledge (his religious experience), which modern philosophers (in other words, philosophers from Descartes through at least Hegel) and those who accept their views do reject.

To use Aristotle's word again, what is outside reason is, in fact, the *archē* of reason, its origin. But it is an *archē* that we can hear only from within reason (since we take account of things always from within reason). Thus, we tend to hear it as if it were also within reason. It is as if we are listening to someone calling from outside the house but we assume that they are inside, or perhaps more accurately, it is like hearing someone quietly whisper something to us and believing that we are hearing ourselves think.

Within reason, its *archē* can be said and, in fact, is always said. Reason can and does give an account of itself. The account is always ironic, however, in a way that I will try to explain. There is no straightforward, non-question-begging, rational account of reason. One can be deaf to reason's supplemental *archē*. One can refuse it recognition. One can refuse to hear what is said by means of, rather than merely within, reason. For the foundation or origin of reason does not show itself unambiguously, clearly and distinctly, in other words, theoretically. It cannot give itself clearly and distinctly, or it would be one more of the things *within* the realm of reason, rather than its supplement. But that something cannot be said clearly and distinctly does not mean that it cannot be said well, or that it cannot be heard, or that it cannot be understood without difficulty.

The profundity of the origin of reason is not necessarily the profundity of complexity and obscurity. The twentieth-century German philosopher Martin Heidegger (who himself sometimes, but not always, confused profundity with complexity) writes in *The Principle of Reason* of "the second tonality" of the principle of sufficient reason. This tonality does not deny that everything has an explanation but alerts us to the fact of the *archē*, of what can always be heard from beyond reason as well as always ignored.[39] Kierkegaard helps us see the necessity of such an *archē* by showing the impossibility of giving a merely theoretical explanation of Abraham, along with the impossibility of simply writing Abraham off as a madman, as one who acts without (in other words, outside of) reason. Narratives and deconstructions of texts can help us catch a glimpse of the *archē*, the unavoidable, but always indirectly seen "supplement" of reason. So can carefully listening to the "tone" of propositions in otherwise logical discourse, hearing what those propositions also say. But nothing can *guarantee* that we will hear what comes to us from the *archē*, from what reason must call its supplement but is really its origin. One must learn to read and hear with Kierkegaardian irony, which is not to say one thing and to mean another or to speak as if there were truth, "knowing" that there is not,[40] but to know that one always says more than is immediately apparent, and to take account of that "more than." To read and hear ironically is, thus, always to say something about one's extrarational foundations, but often and, finally, only implicitly.

Since we must assume that we speak ironically whenever we speak reasonably, we must also be suspicious of taking up irony as a posture. In the first place, if Kierkegaard, Heidegger, the Medievals, and important other thinkers—such as Nephi, the son of Lehi—are right, then ordinary language, even the "clear and distinct" and often not-so-ordinary language of rational philosophy is already ironic.[41] I need not add anything to it for it to be ironic. In the second place, only the character of the speaker can give a guarantee that what he or she says

39. Martin Heidegger, *The Principle of Reason*, trans. Reginald Lilly (Bloomington: IN, 1993), 39–40.

40. Thus, the irony of which I speak is not the irony of Nietzsche or Richard Rorty in which no one way of speaking of things is closer to the truth than any other, if indeed there *is* any truth besides that which one creates. The irony of which I speak assumes that the truth exceeds what one says about it, requiring one to say it again and otherwise, not that there is no truth to be said.

41. Nephi tells us of the importance of plain language but quotes extensively from Isaiah. (See 2 Nephi 25:4 and 26:53.) His idea of plain language is not the same as ours, and he makes the point ironically, though seemingly unconscious of his irony.

is said with the proper irony, and no speaker can guarantee his or her own character except by being of good character.

Thus, the answer to the question of how we are to understand the *archē* of reason from within reason is related to that of Plato: we understand the origin of reason as we understand the sun, not by looking at it directly with philosophical and theoretical eyes, but by the light it sheds on the things in the world, by the fact that we can see at all, by the fact that reason is possible. We see reasonably, in other words, we see by the light of the origin of reason, without ever seeing that origin directly.[42] Nevertheless, the *archē*, like the sun, is never far from us; it is everywhere to be seen and never to be pointed out directly even though when we point at anything we point by means of it.

But why is that *archē* to be thought in terms of faith rather than, as for Marxists, in terms of material history or, as for feminists, in terms of the history of oppression? That question is the hardest one I brook, but I think I can say something about it. I can at least make what I think is a reasonable suggestion.

The first, quick answer is deceptively simple: for something to be the ground for a knowledge claim, I must trust it and be faithful to it. Truth requires that I be true and faithful to that of which I speak or give an account. But, as I said, the simplicity of this answer is deceptive. Hidden in it are a host of questions and philosophical problems, such as what it means to be faithful to an experience.

With an eye toward beginning to say something about the profundity of that simplicity, let me explore one way of talking about the relation of reason to its supplemental, archaic origin. It takes very little to notice that reason and explanation often involve our obligation to others. One can, of course, point out that not all reason begins with obligation. It is not difficult to think of cases of reasoning that have not been initiated by an obligation. That response, however, can

---

42. Wrathall has reminded me that Plato says the philosopher does eventually see the sun straight on (*Republic* 516b). That is true, but the allegory of the cave does not have the philosopher see the sun in this world, and I part company with Plato at exactly the point where he proposes another world in which to see it.

perhaps be overcome by arguing that other uses of reason are parasitic on reason as a response to obligation. Or it may be overcome by arguing that the word *obligation* must be understood more broadly. The last is, I believe, the correct explanation. In any case, for now, grant the thesis that reason begins in obligation to another. That is, by the way, a thesis that I take from Levinas.[43] Why reason except to explain? Why explain if there is no one to whom we owe an explanation? In a solipsistic universe, reason and explanation make no sense (at least because language makes no sense). The solipsist who argues for his solipsism contradicts that solipsism in making his argument. The solipsist either contradicts himself by issuing self-refuting propositions or by one aspect of himself contradicting some other aspect of himself in a ridiculous and pointless merely internal exercise.

If it is true that reason begins in obligation, then what is outside of reason, making it possible, is essentially not a thing or principle, but another person. The principle of noncontradiction is necessary to all reasoning, but its necessity comes not from itself but from the demand that I give an acceptable explanation to another.[44] In Levinas's terms, the principles of reason have their origin in the apologetic character of reason, which is the very basis for my existence as a unique individual.[45] He says, "[The singularity of my existence] is at the very level of its reason; it is apology, that is, personal discourse, from me to the

---

43. See, for example, *Totality and Infinity*, 201.

44. It is important to realize that this demand is not necessarily either explicit or conscious. The point is not that a person says, "I demand this of you," but that the person's existence before me requires me to do and say things, regardless of what the person says. The demands of a person's existence before us may even contradict his or her spoken demands, as they often do when our young children demand things of us—things that we know we ought not to give them, things which their being-before-us not only does not demand, but demands that we refuse.

45. Besides the quotation that follows, see *Totality and Infinity*, 252–53; see also 40, 219, 240–46, 284, 293, and 301.

others."[46] With an argument that I can only allude to here, Levinas argues that the other person is, ultimately, God.[47]

Although she does not deal directly with Levinas, the contemporary philosopher Marlène Zarader helps us understand Levinas's recourse to God by pointing out that in the Jewish tradition (she points explicitly to the medieval commentator on the Torah, Nachmanides), language, and therefore reason, is, in its essence, a response to God.[48] The Bible understands language to be a matter of experience, the experience of hearing a call and responding. When God speaks, he does not reveal himself in the hurricane or the fire, but in a voice that addresses us.[49] Zarader takes prophetic speech to be paradigmatic of all speech and says: "The prophet speaks to the people and can be

---

46. *Totality and Infinity*, 253. It is important to remember that for Levinas *apology* is a term of art. It has the meaning of its Greek roots: "explanation to" rather than "excuse." Note that I have spoken of the origin that is outside of any chain of reasons. Levinas speaks of the idea that overflows the one who thinks it (e.g., *Totality and Infinity*, 20–21). These are two ways of making the same point.

47. See, for example, *Totality and Infinity*, 77–79. Whether Levinas speaks of God is a complicated matter. As Westphal points out, Levinas says, "It is our relations with men . . . that give to theological concepts the sole signification they admit of. . . . Everything that cannot be reduced to an interhuman relation represents not the superior form but the forever primitive form of religion" (*Totality and Infinity*, 79; cited in Westphal, 27). Some will note, however, that Levinas also speaks of the necessity of atheism (*Totality and Infinity*, 77). Quite surprisingly, however, he does so in the same place where he says that atheism is necessary to a relation to God. His point is that a true relation with God requires that we separate ourselves from the god of superstitious worship. See also Paul Ricoeur on this theme: "Reason, Atheism, and Faith," in Alistair MacIntyre and Paul Ricoeur, *The Religious Significance of Atheism* (New York: Columbia University Press, 1969), 58–98. (Ricoeur was a French philosopher of the last half of the twentieth century who also taught in the United States.) Although I have doubts about the clarity of the dichotomy which Ricoeur makes between proper worship and superstition, I think it is clear that Levinas does believe that what we could call his "fundamental ethics," the relation to others that grounds reason, points us toward God. It is also important to note that Levinas's notion of atheism is a notion of something prior to any affirmation or negation of the divine. (See *Totality and Infinity*, 56.) Indeed, as Brant Bishop points out to me, his account of "atheism" is very similar to D&C 93's discussion of agency.

48. Marlène Zarader, *La dette impensée. Heidegger et l'héritage hébraïque* (Paris: Editions du Seuil, 1990), 62; *The Unthought Debt: Heidegger and the Hebraic Heritage*, trans. Bettina Bergo (Stanford, CA: Stanford University Press, 2006), 49–50.

49. Recall 1 Kings 19:11–13.

understood by them because his speaking remains ordained by a call that preceded it."[50]

To Levinas's argument that obligation to God and fidelity to him is the _archē_ of reason, I would add at least one thing, also at least partly a matter of faith. But adding this additional point will return at least some of what I suggested could be taken away when I suggested that nonobligational reason may be parasitic on obligational reason. In addition, what I say will question whether God is the only origin, or supplement, of reason.

I am interested in what has sometimes been called Heidegger's paganism, a description of his work used to denote the fact that Heidegger does not consider the world simply as something created _ex nihilo_, but as something that has its own existence and, therefore, its own power to appear to us and to demand our attention, a power that cannot be completely attributed to God's creative act. For Heidegger the power of the world to reveal itself not only cannot be reduced to Divine fiat, it also cannot be reduced either to our subjective wills or to the objects of rational research.[51] The world itself has the power to ground our conclusions.

---

50. Zarader, _La dette impensée._ The discussion that my paragraph précises is centered on pages 61–64. English translation, 48–51. In criticizing Heidegger, Zarader argues that, as the Bible has been read in the Jewish tradition, it offers an alternative to our usual understanding of language and philosophy—an alternative that has many things in common with the alternative we find in Heidegger's work but which does not insist on only the Greek origins of that alternative and that escapes some of the problems that Heidegger's thinking encounters.

51. One reason that the world and its power to reveal itself cannot be reduced to the objects of rational research is that the object of rational or scientific research is not the thing that we encounter. (See note 14.) Instead, the object of scientific research is a conceptual relative of that thing, a relative created by adumbrating a set of conditions and assumptions that define the ways in which we will take up and examine the thing in question. In other words, the scientific object is not the thing itself, but an object created by the methods of science and the background assumptions of those methods. As a result, strictly speaking, the object of research is a product of the subject, not an independent thing that demands our attention. This does not, as many may worry, imply that Heidegger is arguing that scientific conclusions are merely subjective. Quite the contrary. His point is that the very possibility of doing science requires that we deal with things as objects and that objects are, by definition, one end of an intentional ray that has a subject at the other end and a particular context that makes it possible as the object that

Levinas's understanding of matters is more in line with traditional theology and its supposition of the creation of the world from nothing.[52] The consequence of such an understanding is that the world itself and things in the world do not have their own existence, so they do not have their own power to show themselves to us, to reveal something. If the world is created *ex nihilo*, then revelation comes from God *in toto* and, ultimately, he is the only supplement of reason. But Latter-day Saint belief rejects the notion of *ex nihilo* creation and, so, implicitly includes the idea that the things of the world have power of their own to reveal themselves. Though all things are dependent on God for their existence in the organized world as what they are and, so, all things point to his existence (Alma 30:44), each thing also has an aspect of independent existence and, so, the power to show itself (D&C 93:30). The appearing of the world is not reducible to will, neither to that of the Divine nor to that of human beings. Heidegger's so-called pagan understanding of the world as existing, in some sense, in itself, is more useful to Latter-day Saint thinkers than is Levinas's, though the latter does much to help us understand reason as response.

Heidegger also speaks of our relation to and understanding of the world in terms of two registers or orders of thinking.[53] Though

---

it is (in the case of science, its methods and background assumptions). For more on this point, see Martin Heidegger, "The Age of the World Picture," in *The Question Concerning Technology and Other Essays*, trans. William Lovitt (New York: Harper Colophon, 1977), 115–54. See also E. A. Burtt, *The Metaphysical Foundations of Modern Physical Science* (Atlantic Highlands, NJ: Humanities, 1980, rpt. 1932), especially pp. 298–99.

52. It is important to point out that Levinas explicitly gives another meaning to the term *ex nihilo* than that we find in the theological tradition. He says that creation *ex nihilo* means that the created being is completely different from and separate from the Creator, that he or she is not reducible to a part or affect of the Creator. (See *Totality and Infinity*, 63.) Given this understanding there is a sense in which a Latter-day Saint could subscribe to the idea of creation *ex nihilo*, though that notion would be an idiosyncratic one. But since in Levinas, things of the world do not have their own existence, I take it that he subscribes not only to this weaker idea of creation *ex nihilo*, but also to the stronger form of the theological tradition. As a result, I use the term *ex nihilo* with its standard meaning even when talking about Levinas.

53. See Martin Heidegger, *What Is Called Thinking* (New York: Harper & Row, 1968), for one of the central locations of this discussion. See also Heidegger, *The Principle of Reason*, 39–40.

Heidegger uses the word *reason* for only one of those registers, I think that is a mistake; there is no reason not to speak of each as reason. One of the registers of thought is what we usually think of when we think of reason, a thinking determined by logic. That is a register that we cannot do without. If thinking is to be at all useful, it must include logic.

Nevertheless, the logical register of thought requires another, the register of faithfulness, memory, and recognition. In other words, logic requires the relation to a supplement that makes it possible and meaningful. Without the relation to a supplement, the first register remains free-floating and, so, pointless. But unlike Levinas, Heidegger believes that it is as possible to be faithful to the things in the world that come to us, to be called by the things we encounter and to hearken to that call, as it is to be called by another person and to hearken to her.[54] For Heidegger, faithfulness to the world is as possible as is faithfulness to another person, and I believe that Heidegger has much for Latter-day Saints to think about in this regard.

Reason in the fundamental sense is the welcoming, remembering, recognizing response to a call from someone or something. Fundamental reason is a response that makes possible reason in the second, narrower sense.[55] As Otto Pöggeler points out, for Heidegger the essence of thought is not questioning, though the thinker must question. The essence of thought is not questioning because questioning relies on already finding oneself called by something and submitting oneself to it.[56] One cannot question unless one is already in a world

---

54. Nevertheless, relation to the other person remains fundamental, for it is in relationships with others that we learn language. Others, in particular God, give us the tools we need to respond to be faithful to the things we encounter in the world.

55. Of course, to designate one fundamental or primary and the other secondary or narrower is not to demean the second. The first is the relation to the *archē* that makes the second possible, but the first without the second is incomplete.

56. Otto Pöggeler, *Der Denkweg Martin Heideggers* (Pfullingen: Neske, 1963), 268–80; *Martin Heidegger's Path of Thinking*, trans. Daniel Magurshak and Sigmund Barber (Atlantic Highlands, NJ: Humanities Press International, 1987), 233. See also Jacques Derrida's discussion of this in *De l'Esprit. Heidegger et la question* (Paris: Galilee, 1987); *Of Spirit: Heidegger and the Question*, trans. Geoffrey Bennington and Rachel Bowlby

that reveals itself and makes demands. In other words, the essence of thinking—of reason—is response, and very like the response of religious faith, even when it is a response to something other than God.[57]

As Zarader explains, the idea that reason is a matter of response is not new. In fact, in discussions of how knowledge is understood in the Bible it is almost a commonplace that Hebrew thought takes knowledge to be a matter of hearing, acquaintance, and obedience, and Greek thought (which gave us philosophy and, so, the primary way in which we think about thinking and reason) takes it to be a matter of sight, possession, and control. Too simply put (but perhaps good enough for our purposes here), for the biblical prophet, to know the truth is to be called and to obey that which calls one. For the Greek philosopher, to know the truth is to see something and to grasp what one sees.[58] We ask someone "Did you get it? Did you grasp it?" But as David Banon says, for biblical writers, the basic structure of knowledge is not that of "'possession,' but that of 'fidelity.'"[59] Heidegger's view has much in common with the biblical view, in spite of the fact that he not only seems to have been unaware of that fact but took pains

(Chicago: University of Chicago, 1981). Both Pöggeler and Derrida refer specifically to Martin Heidegger, *Unterwegs zur Sprache* (Pfullingen: Neske, 1961), 174; "On the Nature of Language," *On the Way to Language*, trans. Peter D. Hertz (New York: Harper & Row, 1971), 68–69. (I am grateful to Marlène Zarader for pointing out this shared reference. See *Dette impensée*, 223 n. 36; English translation, 217 n. 37.)

57. Zarader gives an excellent overview of Heidegger's understanding of thought. See *Dette impensée*, especially pp. 92–100 and 112–23; *Unthought Debt*, 80–85, 100–112.

58. Fuller discussions of this notion are available in any number of places. For a detailed linguistic discussion of the Old Testament understanding and its relation to the Greek and New Testament understandings, see Gerhard Kittel, ed., *Theological Dictionary of the New Testament*, trans. G. W. Bromily (Grand Rapids, MI: Eerdmans, 1964–74), s.v. γινώσκω, γνῶσις, ἐπιγινώσκω, ἐπίγνωσις, καταγιώσκω, ἀκατάγνωστος, προγινώσκω, πρόγνωσις, συγγνώμη, γνώμη, γνωρίζω, γνωστός (Rudolf Bultmann). For broader discussions, see Thorlief Boman, *Hebrew Thought Compared with Greek* (New York: W. W. Norton, 1970); my "Greek and Hebrew Thinking," *Tools for Scripture Study* (Provo, UT: FARMS, 1999), 135–53, which relies heavily on Bowman; or David Banon, *La Lecture infinie: Les voies de l'interprétation midrachique* (Paris: Seuil, 1987).

59. Banon, *Lecture infinie*, 173. As does Banon, many discussions of this difference note that in Genesis 4:1, "And Adam knew Eve his wife," the use of the Hebrew word for knowledge (*ya'da*; ידע) as a term for sexual relations is not a euphemism. From an Old Testament point of view, knowledge is a matter of intimacy rather than possession.

to insist that faith and "thinking" (his term for philosophy from this broader perspective) were separate matters.[60]

Given the similarity between Heidegger's understanding of knowledge and the biblical understanding, it may see strange when Levinas worries that Heidegger's paganism opens the door to idolatry. Nevertheless, it is well that he should worry. In the first place, idolatry succeeds best when it imitates the truth.[61] In the second place, Heidegger's biography shows why we should worry.[62] But the door that opens to idolatry also opens to God. Because false worship is an imitation of true worship, what leads to one can also lead to the other.[63] Though Levinas is unwilling to allow the irony of Heidegger's understanding of

60. Zarader, *Dette impensee*, convincingly demonstrates both the similarity of Heidegger's thought to biblical thought and his denial of that similarity. Of course the traditional interpretation of the Old Testament would have it, as Levinas does, that knowledge as it is understood in the Old Testament comes ultimately from the demands of God and would not leave room for the demands of things. It remains a fact, however, that Heidegger's understanding of knowledge and the Bible's have a great deal in common, and I suspect that Latter-day Saints will generally have no trouble with the idea that things have some kind of existence beside the existence that God gives them, though no thing exists completely independent of God.

61. Jean-Luc Marion's *L'idol et la distance* (Paris: Grasset, 1977) says a great deal about why this is the case. Marion is a contemporary French philosopher.

62. In a part of his life that remains wrapped in difficulty as well as confusion, Heidegger joined the Nazi party in the early 1930s. He supported the Nazi take-over of the universities in the speech he gave at his installation as rector of the University of Freiburg im Breisgau, although the Nazis later refused to acknowledge his support or his status as a Nazi rector.

Heidegger's relation to Naziism is unfortunate—at best it is ambiguous; at worst it is collaboration with and denial of evil. There are a good many books on the issue, from those that smack of yellow journalism, on one hand, to the queasily apologetic, on the other. For those looking for a readable discussion of Heidegger's thought that includes a discussion of his involvement with Naziism, see either George Steiner, *Martin Heidegger: With a New Introduction* (Chicago: University of Chicago Press, 1989) or Richard F. H. Polt, *Heidegger: An Introduction* (Ithaca: Cornell University Press, 1999).

63. This has always been the case. See the aforementioned piece by Ricoeur, "Atheism." See also Marion's discussion of the relation between worship and idolatry in both *L'idol et la distance* and *God Without Being*, trans. Thomas A. Carlson (Chicago: University of Chicago, 1991). Although I do not believe in the absolutely transcendent god whom Marion discusses, much of his discussion, particularly that of the difference between an idol and an icon, is illuminating. It can help us think about our own God-talk even if, in the end, we find Marion's analysis insufficient.

the world, we ought to welcome it. Even knowing the dangers that Heidegger's understanding courts (and nothing of central importance can avoid danger), we ought to welcome Heidegger's "pagan" understanding of the world as a world that gives itself to us and demands our response, our reason.

There are several reasons why the risk involved is ultimately worth running. The first is that to call Heidegger a pagan, as Levinas does, is really only to say that he accepts the world itself as a thing of value and does not assume that its only value comes either from our interaction with it or from the fact that it was created by God. In other words, he is a pagan because he implicitly rejects the idea of *ex nihilo* creation. Latter-day Saints should not find that particularly troubling. The second, more substantial reason for accepting this risk is that faith requires it. Without risk, there is no faith. Of course that is not to say that we ought to seek out risks or that the riskier a faith claim the more likely it is to be true. It is only to say that risk-free knowledge is not the kind of knowledge we can have of these matters.

Thus, using Heidegger's thought as a corrective to Levinas's, I am willing to say that not only are other persons—ultimately the divine Person—the *archē* or supplement that makes reason possible, but so is the appearing of the world.[64] Contrary to the philosophical as well as the theological tradition, the *archē* is not singular. The unity of the *archē* is in us, in our lives, acts and everyday understanding, rather than in our wills and theoretical speculations, for the latter are but a manifestation or representation of the former. That is why, on a daily basis as well as ultimately, practice must take precedence over theology and speculation. The ultimate unity and, therefore, the ultimate rationality of our lives is to be found in our acts (including what we say and think) rather than only in our reflections and theories. The impetus and unity of our lives is practical rather than merely cognitive.

---

64. Though I now would side with Heidegger's position more strongly than I did, for more on this "conflict" between Levinas and Heidegger see my, "The Uncanny Interruption of Ethics: Gift, Interruption, or . . . ," *The Graduate Faculty Philosophy Journal* 20/2 and 21/1 (1998): 233–47.

Thus, my understanding of the relation of faith and reason is simple: We find ourselves in the world, surrounded by things and people, both of which lay claim on us, call us, making demands that we respond, that we account for ourselves, that we act. Of course we know from latter-day revelation that we initially found ourselves before God, to whom we responded. He is, after all, our Creator, even if that creation was not *ex nihilo*. He called us into existence and continues to call us: "Hear O Israel."[65] But once we were in relation with him, we also found ourselves in the presence of others and of things, both of whom call to us, demanding our response by posing problems and questions, whether explicitly or not. If we take those calls seriously, being sufficiently faithful to those making demands on us, whether God, people, or things, that we make an adequate response to their calls, we act rationally. In its multiplicity, the call is sufficient as an origin of reason. It is basic; it cannot be reduced to one of my beliefs. It stands outside of beliefs as their origin, their supplement, initiating chains of reasons.

Because we exist, we account for ourselves before God, in relation to others, and in the world. We cannot avoid giving those accounts; we cannot avoid reason. Reason begins in an act of faith (trust and fidelity), faithful response to those beings who surround and precede us, whose very existence calls to us, making demands on us that interrupt our being: first God, then persons, then things. Even defiance, such as that of Satan, first begins in a response to a call. Even defiance, in spite of itself, first entails faithfulness and, therefore, contradicts itself.

But not only does reason require faith—faith also requires reason. Although their relation is asymmetrical, with more area covered by

---

65. This call to Israel is frequent in the Old Testament, sufficiently frequent that we may think of it as the essence of the Lord's demand of Israel. For example, see Deuteronomy 5:1, 6:3–4, 9:1, and 20:3; Psalms 50:7 and 81:8; Isaiah 44:1 and 48:1; Jeremiah 2:4, 10:1, and 42:15; Ezekiel 18:25; Hosea 4:1 and 5:1; Amos 3:1 and 5:1; Micah 3:1 and 3:9. It is also the way in which the Savior introduces the first great commandment in Mark 12:29, quoting not only the commandment to love God, but the command to hear. Neither Judaism nor Christianity can conceive of religion without doing so in terms of response to God's call.

faith than reason, either without the other is lame or blind or both. Faith makes space for us to talk, to reason with God, with each other, and with the world, By creating the space for reason, faith makes it possible for us to live responsibly, responsively. That space for response created by faith and carried out with reason, the room to talk, is the room into which Truman Madsen invited so many of us to enter, an invitation for which I thank him.

CHAPTER THREE

A MORMON VIEW OF THEOLOGY: REVELATION AND REASON

The contemporary Catholic theologian David Tracy points out that the difference between philosophy of religion and theology is that the latter requires "some notion of revelation as well as divinely en-gifted reception of that revelation called 'faith'—a knowledge born of revelation,"[1] while the former does not. One can examine religious be-liefs philosophically, including a belief in revelation or a claim to faith, without assuming the reality of either revelation or faith. However, the consequence of assuming divine revelation and knowledge based on that revelation is that "theology can neither ignore nor be sublated by philosophy."[2] It cannot be sublated by philosophy because by beginning with revelation and knowledge produced by that revelation, it contains an element that philosophy cannot take into itself. Revelation takes us further than can reason by itself. Presumably, theology cannot ignore philosophy because philosophy is that discipline by which we examine knowledge. However, that it cannot ignore philosophy does not mean that theology can be reduced to philosophizing about a particular sub-ject matter. In his article Tracy addresses Latter-day Saints, asking how *we* understand the relation between philosophy and theology.

The easy answer is that, as he suggests, the situation in Mormon-ism is similar to that in Catholicism: theology cannot ignore philoso-phy but is not subsumed by it, and the theology of Latter-day Saints

1. David Tracy, "A Catholic View of Philosophy: Revelation and Reason," in *Mormonism in Dialogue with Contemporary Christian Theologies*, ed. David L. Paulsen (Macon, GA: Mercer University, 2007), 449.
2. Tracy, "A Catholic View," 449.

most often tends toward one of two forms, rationalism or fideism, neither of which can be neatly separated from the other. Like Tracy, Mormons would agree that theology must be grounded in revelation. However, that agreement is complicated by the fact that Tracy separates revelation and religion, a separation that most Mormons cannot make and that may be contradicted by Tracy's turn to hermeneutics, to a philosophy that takes interpretation to be the basic relation of human beings to the world. Though Tracy does not explicitly tell us what he means by "religion," he seems to mean something like "the practices and institutions of a particular religious tradition, often carried out in response to revelation." On that basis, I doubt that many Latter-day Saints would allow the distinction of revelation from religion since revelation is assumed to be part of our religion's practices and institutions and since many of our practices and institutions were specifically given by revelation. To understand how best to understand the relation between philosophy and revelation, I will argue that philosophy and theology must understand religion and belief as part of a way of life. Since that way of life includes revelation, revelation cannot be neatly tweezed apart from it.

Latter-day Saints are primitivists: we believe that the original Christian church was restored in 1830 through the Prophet Joseph Smith. The restoration began in a literal revelation to Smith: Just as Jesus-God made himself manifest in first-century Palestine, God and Jesus Christ appeared to Joseph Smith and spoke to him, and they appeared as physical beings. Later, angels—physically embodied angels with whom one could shake hands—appeared to him and others, speaking with them, relaying divine counsel, and ordaining them to the priesthood by putting their angelic hands on the mortal heads of Joseph Smith and Oliver Cowdery. The primary revelation of early Christianity, the appearance of God as man, repeats itself at the founding of Mormonism. As a result, the events that led to and included the founding of the Church of Jesus Christ of Latter-day Saints are called, by Mormons, "The Restoration."

Mormon primitivism means that Smith's encounter with transcendence was not an encounter with a metaphysically transcendent world, but with a world that most Mormons assume is ontologically like our own.[3] Though few Mormons claim to have had a similar experience (I have met none), the possibility of that kind of revelation—direct, unmediated, physical encounter—remains permanently open.[4] Jesus Christ is present not only in the "word (proclamation) and sacrament (those disclosive signs which render present what they signify)."[5] It is also always possible that Jesus will be present *in physical person*. Indeed, we generally assume that kind of revelation did not cease with Smith, but continued with some succeeding prophets as well as other people.

Mormons also recognize forms of revelation that are much more like what other Christians speak of. We assume that revelation most often comes as inspiration and impression, "the whisperings of the Spirit,"[6] rather than as voice, vision, or visitation. Nevertheless, for Latter-day Saints, revelation is assumed to be a common as well as a fundamental religious experience, and it is an experience that has at its base the possibility of an unmediated encounter with God, an encounter that is ontologically comparable to that of the first Christians.

The Book of Mormon is explicit about the importance of revelation:

> And when ye shall receive these things, I would exhort you that ye would ask God, the Eternal Father, in the name of Christ, if these things are not true; and if ye shall ask with a sincere heart, with real intent, having faith in Christ, he will manifest the truth of it unto you, by the power of the Holy

---

3. However, see my "Divine Embodiment and Transcendence: Propaedeutic Thoughts and Questions," *Element: A Journal of LDS Thought* 1/1 (2005): 1–14, for a discussion of some of the ways in which the divine world and our world differ and some theological questions those differences raise.

4. One of many examples: "Revelation may come through dreams or visions, the visitation of angels, or, on occasion such as with Moses, by face-to-face communication with the Lord." Hugh B. Brown, in Conference Report, October 1961, 96.

5. Tracy, "Catholic View," 457.

6. *Teachings of Gordon B. Hinckley* (Salt Lake City: Deseret Book, 1997), 364.

Ghost. And by the power of the Holy Ghost ye may know the truth of all things. (Moroni 10:4–5)

This passage has become more and more doctrinally important among Mormons—it is, for example, an important element in the proselytizing program of the church—and I think we find it implicitly behind Terryl Givens's argument that the Mormon understanding of revelation is unique in that it is "dialogic." According to Givens, revelation allows Mormons to appeal to God for answers to questions and problems, without the restraints of a closed canon. The result of that revelation is often knowledge with a propositional content given directly to particular individuals by God rather than, *but not excluding*, revelation as the experience of divine grace, the content of scripture, or the self-disclosure of God.[7] As mentioned, revelation need not come in the form of propositions literally heard or understood, but one form of revelation, perhaps the form most often referred to when Latter-day Saints speak of revelation, has a propositional content, though not necessarily a propositional form. Little scholarly work has been done on what the term *revelation* means to Mormons, but there is sufficient discussion of it in non-scholarly contexts to give us a reasonable idea: it includes an unmediated response from God in a form that can often be given a propositional exposition. This understanding of revelation as fundamentally propositional goes a long way toward explaining the dominant Mormon understanding of theology as rational or systematic. It is natural to assume that if revelation is propositional, then, at least in principle, those propositions can be organized into a systematic whole.

Nevertheless, Mormons today, intellectuals or otherwise, do not use the word *theology* in a consistent way. From the beginning of the church to the present, Latter-day Saints have often assumed that

---

7. Terryl L. Givens, "The Book of Mormon and Dialogic Revelation," *Journal of Book of Mormon Studies* 10/2 (2001): 16–27. See also the relevant portions of Givens, *By the Hand of Mormon* (Oxford: Oxford University Press, 2002). I think it remains a question whether Givens is right that the LDS understanding of revelation as dialogic differs significantly from the experiences of personal revelation by other Christians, such as evangelicals.

theology means "rational or systematic theology." (By "systematic" I mean a theology in which the doctrines are assumed to be interrelated and capable of structured exposition rather than a theology that is divided into the traditional branches of Christology, pneumatology, etc.) The nineteenth-century work, *The Lectures on Faith*,[8] arranged in a catechetical format and, for a while, included in the Latter-day Saint canon, is an excellent example of a work that makes this assumption. We find another example in the controversial writings of Orson Pratt, also in the nineteenth century. John A. Widtsoe's *A Rational Theology*,[9] first used as a manual in weekly classes for the church's lay priesthood and later in adult classes of the church's Mutual Improvement Association, is yet another.[10] We see contemporary examples in Bruce R. McConkie's *Mormon Doctrine*[11] (more of an encyclopedia than a theology, and self-described as a compendium, but nevertheless an attempt at systematic exposition) and Blake Ostler's series *Exploring Mormon Thought*.[12] Thus, when in 1995 Chieko Okazaki equated the word *theology* with "theorizing about the gospel,"[13] I doubt that anyone found that usage unusual.

Our widespread understanding of theology as rational theology seems to spring from our interpretation of claims we find in scripture, such as "The glory of God is intelligence" (Doctrine and Covenants

---

8. Traditionally *The Lectures on Faith* have been attributed to Joseph Smith. However, there is disagreement over its authorship. See Noel B. Reynolds, "The Authorship Debate Concerning *Lectures on Faith*: Exhumation and Reburial" in *The Disciple as Witness: Essays on Latter-day Saint History and Doctrine in Honor of Richard Lloyd Anderson*, ed. Stephen D. Ricks, Donald W. Parry, and Andrew W. Hedges (Provo, UT: FARMS, 2000), 355–82. I suspect *Lectures* was removed from the canon because its teaching about the Holy Ghost do not cohere with early twentieth-century proclamations by the church's First Presidency.

9. John A. Widtsoe, *A Rational Theology; as Taught by the Church of Jesus Christ of Latter-day Saints* (Salt Lake City: Printed by Deseret News, 1915).

10. The Mutual Improvement Association was an organization for young men and women.

11. Bruce R. McConkie, *Mormon Doctrine,* 1st ed. (Salt Lake City: Bookcraft, 1958); 2nd ed. (1966).

12. Blake Ostler, *Exploring Mormon Thought* (Salt Lake City: Kofford Books, 2001, 2005, 2008).

13. Chieko Okazaki, *Aloha!* (Salt Lake City: Deseret Book, 1995), 54.

93:6). Widtsoe characterized the Mormon understanding of theology
as rational theology this way:

> Whether knowledge be obtained by any or all of the methods
> indicated [namely, the senses, inward feeling, transmitted
> knowledge], it should be carefully examined in the light of
> reason. . . . A man should therefore use his reasoning faculty
> in all matters involving truth, and especially as concerning
> his religion.[14]

Brigham Young called theology his favorite study, comparing it to
law, "physic," and astronomy.[15] An impetus for identifying theology
with rational theology can be found in a Mormon belief that truth
is ultimately "one great whole,"[16] a whole that has, for historical and
broad cultural reasons, been assumed to be systematically rational.
Surely the fact that, for Mormons, revelation is often, if not exclusively,
propositional is largely responsible for the general understanding of
theology as systematic: reflection on revelation is a matter of making
the propositions of revelation rationally coherent.

However, from early in church history–and still today—the word
theology has also been used more loosely, as a synonym for belief or
teaching. George Q. Cannon, of the Council of Twelve, spoke of his
children's favorite study as theology.[17] Marion D. Hanks, speaking
to Brigham Young University students in 1960, described theology
as "religious doctrine and knowledge."[18] And in 2002 Neal A. Maxwell, another member of the Twelve, speaking in the church's General

---

14. Widtsoe, *A Rational Theology*, 4th ed. (Salt Lake City: Deseret Book, 1937), 8.

15. Brigham Young, in *Journal of Discourses*, 6:315.

16. See, for example, *The Teachings of Howard W. Hunter*, ed. Clyde J. Williams (Salt
Lake City: Deseret Book, 1997), 182.

17. Cannon, "Suffering of the Latter-day Saints—Importance of Educating Children—
Importance of Teaching Correct Principles—Need to Donate to Building Schools—Law
of Tithing Still Required," in *Collected Discourses*, ed. Brian H. Stuy, 5 vols. (Burbank,
CA: B. H. S. Publishing, 1987–1992), 2:39.

18. Marion D. Hanks, "Steps to Learning," 4 May 1960, *BYU Speeches of the Year,
1959–60* (Provo, UT: Brigham Young University, 1960), 2.

Conference, equated "the restored gospel" with theology.[19] My anecdotal experience is that Mormons seldom distinguish between these two different meanings: sometimes *theology* means "what we believe" or something like that, and sometimes *theology* includes explaining what we believe by giving it a rational structure. Often it is not obvious which of those is intended.

This broadness in the meaning of the word *theology* is at least partly the result of the fact that there has not yet been anything like an official Mormon theology. If *theology* means "beliefs," then there is a widely accepted theology, though there is considerable variability in even that. However, if *theology* means formal reflection about religious beliefs and practices, then Mormonism does not even have a widely accepted theology, much less an official one, though it has and has had several practitioners.

In spite of the prevalence of equating the terms *theology* and *beliefs* in Mormonism, when I use the term *theology* in this book, I will not use it that way. Though I intend to continue to use the word broadly, whatever else *theology* is, I assume that it includes a reflective, explanatory component. It is more than "what most Mormons believe." When *theology* is used in the way I propose, we can accurately say that few Mormons have done it in an academic way.[20] We could describe those who come closest today, such as David Paulsen and Ostler, as doing either the philosophy of religion or theology, though

---

19. Neal A. Maxwell, "Encircled in the Arms of His Love," *Ensign*, November 2002, 16.

20. There is interest in the philosophy of religion among LDS intellectuals. Paulsen's classes at BYU are always full and Ostler's books sell well. There is an e-mail discussion group, LDS-Phil, dedicated to discussions of Mormonism and philosophy, which, for obvious reasons, often discusses topics in the philosophy of religion. Clark Goble has a Web site devoted to his philosophical reflections on that topic: www.libertypages.com/clark ("Mormon Metaphysics," 11 July 2006 posting, accessed 1 August 2006 and 3 March 2009). One can find nonacademic discussions of the philosophy of religion fairly regularly on LDS blogs such as the group blog, Times and Seasons (timesandseasons.org for 1 August 2006). But I think few, if any, of these would call what they do theology, and this constitutes a small group within Mormonism as a whole, even within educated or intellectual Mormons.

I believe that one hears their work referred to most often as "philosophy of religion." There are notable exceptions, but Mormons have not done much theology, and since about the beginning of the twentieth century, we generally avoid calling what we do theology.

One obvious reason for the relative absence of theology among Mormons is that the church is still young. A tradition that is not yet two hundred years old has not had time to develop the kind of theological discussions that one finds in much older Christian traditions, such as Catholicism. Furthermore, though deciding cause and effect here is difficult (assuming it is relevant), the absence of theological work in the Church of Jesus Christ today is also probably related to the fact that fideism seems to have grown in popularity among contemporary church leaders. For example, speaking of church history and the origins of Mormonism, Maxwell said, "Reason, the Greek philosophical tradition, dominated, then supplanted, reliance on revelation," but with the restoration, "Revelation . . . replaced the long and inordinate reliance on reason."[21] Though this more fideistic approach has become increasingly obvious during the last half of the twentieth century, it is not a completely original development.[22] Among other precursors, we find Joseph Smith saying things like, "Without a revelation, I am not going to give them the knowledge of the God of heaven"[23] and, speaking of the rest of Christianity, "[they] are bound apart by cast-iron creeds, and fastened to set stakes by chain-cables, without revelation."[24] Revelation trumps reason.

---

21. Maxwell, "From the Beginning," *Ensign,* November 1993, 18. Taking a somewhat ameliorated position, Dallin H. Oaks has said, "The source of the ancient conflict between (1) reason or intellect and (2) faith or revelation is the professor's rejection of revelation, not the prophet's rejection of reason." Oaks, *The Lord's Way* (Salt Lake City: Deseret Book, 1991), 50.

22. One would have to do a more thorough study of the documents to decide, in fact, whether this movement from more focus on rational theology to more focus on fideism is as pronounced as I take it to be. I have not made that study, so I rely on my intuition that it is.

23. *Discourses of the Prophet Joseph Smith,* comp. Alma P. Burton (Salt Lake City: Deseret Book, 1977), 37.

24. *History of the Church,* 5:215.

Let me briefly offer three additional reasons for the dearth of theology among Latter-day Saints: the belief in continuing revelation, the nature of scripture, and the fact that, like many Jews, Mormons understand their religion primarily in terms of practices and attitudes rather than in terms of beliefs.[25] Of these, of course, perhaps only the first is unique to Mormons. The other two reasons can also be found in other religions. Indeed, Tracy argues (and I agree) that the nature of scripture requires us to rethink theology,[26] and he also sees the importance of practice, arguing explicitly that theory and a way of life ought to join themselves, and recognizing that "such a remarkable union seems clearly present in Mormon philosophies."[27]

Continuing revelation makes theology more challenging—if *theology* means "rational theology"—because, as Spencer J. Condie says, "Change is an inevitable consequence of continuous revelation."[28] Two iconic events in Mormon history, the 1890 prohibition of polygamy and the 1978 declaration that all worthy male members of the church were to be given the priesthood, remind Latter-day Saints of the fact that a belief in living prophets who give continuing revelation means that, not only is our canon not closed, but what has been an authoritative teaching can become radically nonauthoritative, even when the original authority was direct revelation from God. Our religion requires that we always recognize the possibility that we will have to give up doctrines and practices that we thought central and authoritative.

The first of the two iconic practices, the practice of polygamy, was supported by a well-developed theology, a theology based on official teachings, scriptural and prophetic, that made polygamy a religious requirement for some.[29] In the second case, though there was

---

25. See chapters 4 and 5 in this volume for expanded discussions of these three claims.
26. Tracy, "Catholic View," 452, 457.
27. Tracy, "Catholic View," 462.
28. Spencer J. Condie, *In Perfect Balance* (Salt Lake City: Bookcraft, 1993), 106.
29. Perhaps the experience of having a thorough theological justification for the necessity of polygamy only to have polygamy abandoned is also at the root of less and less theology in the twentieth century and afterward—not in absolute numbers, but in

neither authoritative revelation nor explanation for why Blacks were not ordained, there was a great deal of speculation, speculation that many Mormons took as quasi-authoritative. The belief that there was a doctrinal basis for the exclusion of Blacks from the priesthood was so strong in the church that, even among those Mormons who, prior to 1978, refused to give revealed status to the practice, few thought that the practice would be discontinued in the foreseeable future. Many Mormons assumed that the practice could be explained in terms of authoritative church teachings, even if no one seemed able to say what that explanation was. However, in spite of their authoritative place within church belief and theology, revelations from prophets over-turned both practices and their associated beliefs and explanations. (In the first case, the overturning took a while to complete; in the second, the effect was essentially instantaneous.) In neither case did the church give a theological explanation of the change—in my eyes, evidence that the prophets in question did not see their revelations as responses to questions, but as responses to a divine call. One can ask "Why?" of an answer to a question, but it does not make sense to ask that of the re-sponse to a call. The answer to "Why are you responding that way?" is quite different than the answer to "Why do you believe that?"

Though not impossible, it is difficult for any rational theology to contain the proposition, "Important authoritative propositions in this theology could be authoritatively denied at any moment, requiring the complete re-rationalization of the propositions that remain." As a result, some modes of rational theology have been difficult for Mor-mons, but we have seldom recognized other kinds of theology, except theology as a set of beliefs. Those are the only two options most Mor-mons have considered.

As I pointed out earlier, the second reason that we find little academic rational theology among Latter-day Saints, the nature of

relation to the membership of the church: there are substantially fewer people doing aca-demic theology as a percentage of church membership than there were in the nineteenth century prior to polygamy.

scripture, is not unique to us. My point about the effects of the nature of scripture on theology of any kind is similar to one that Tracy has made: We often speak of and use scripture as if it were a set of propositions that are poorly expressed or, at best, "merely" poetic. We then try to discover the propositional content (doctrine) that we assume is lurking behind or implicit in those poorly expressed or poetic expressions and to disentangle the relations of those propositions. But that approach misunderstands scripture. Instead of a poetic expression of implicit propositional truths, it is an inspired resource that allows us to question ourselves and our world through reading and reflection. Scripture requires our interpretive, mediated response to its questions: the appropriation of scripture—in Mormon terminology, likening it to ourselves—more than its rational exegesis (cf. 1 Nephi 19:23).[30] Of course, the appropriation proper to scriptural understanding remains inherently theological—reflection on belief—albeit not narrowly rational.[31]

Few Latter-day Saint thinkers, conscious of themselves as doing theology, have taken up the task of this appropriation, but why? Part of an answer is, I think, the belief in continuing revelation combined with the cultural assumption that scripture is to be understood as collected prophetic declarations that set forth a particular, unique set of propositions, though those propositions are often only implicit. (That is, of course, not an assumption found only among Mormons.) Whatever the reason, though we find relatively little systematic theology among Latter-day Saints, a theology of appropriation fits well with our insistence on continuing revelation. Indeed, though it is not usually done in a rigorous way, appropriation of scripture is ubiquitous among Latter-day Saints. I assume that a more rigorous theology of appropriation would be a hermeneutic theology—and that it would bring together our reliance on scripture and our belief in continuing revelation.[32]

---

30. See chapter 7 in this volume for a fuller discussion of *likening*.
31. Cf. David Tracy, *The Analogical Imagination* (New York: Crossroad, 1981), 104.
32. I assume that what many Latter-day Saints do when they read and talk about scripture is such an appropriative theology, though a naive one.

Of the three reasons, however, (continuing revelation, the nature of scripture, and the fact that religion is primarily a matter of practice rather than propositional belief) the latter seems to be the most important. To say that Mormons focus primarily on practices is, of course, not to say that beliefs are irrelevant to Latter-day Saint religion. Rather, it is to say that they are what they are and have their importance only in terms of the practices of which they are part. To use language taken from Martin Heidegger, it is to say that beliefs have their importance only as they are part of a way of being, and for Latter-day Saints that way of being is defined by the call of God.[33] Latter-day Saints are more concerned with whether they have paid their tithing, visited an ill fellow congregant, done their home or visiting teaching,[34] and performed vicarious ordinances in the temple than they are with how to explain the grace of God or the Word of Wisdom.[35] (Of course, that one thing is more important than another does not mean that the second is *un*important.) Perhaps the most important reason that Latter-day Saints have done little toward giving an intellectual clarification of revelation is that our experience of religion is fundamentally practical and, so, does not lend itself readily to systematic theological reflection. The faith-knowledge engifted by revelation, perhaps most obviously seen in the faith-knowledge of scripture, is practical rather than theoretical knowledge, so one theology that can deal appropriately with that knowledge would be a hermeneutical theology, a theology of listening for the word of God and saying what one hears and how one hears it.[36] Naturally, this hermeneutic would

---

33. For more discussion of this point, see chapter 5 in this volume. For more on Martin Heidegger, see chapter 2, note 62.

34. Home and visiting teaching are church programs in which members of the church are assigned to visit each other each month in pairs—men for home teaching; women for visiting teaching—to encourage and to watch over the members of the congregation.

35. The Word of Wisdom is a revelation forbidding the use of coffee, tea, and alcoholic drinks, and urging moderation in eating meat (see Doctrine and Covenants 89).

36. For an excellent philosophical article on what a hermeneutic theology might look like, see Paul Ricoeur, "Toward a Narrative Theology: Its Necessity, Its Resources, Its Difficulties," in *Figuring the Sacred: Religion, Narrative, and Imagination*, ed. Mark I. Wallace, trans. David Pellauer (Minneapolis: Fortress Press, 1995), 249–61.

be more than a hermeneutic of texts. It would especially be a hermeneutic of relations, practices, and events. Indeed, there is an important sense in which, without calling it "theology," Latter-day Saints have practiced hermeneutic theology since shortly after the founding of the church. They have been intensely interested in and written much about church history, understanding Mormon history—the things we have done and experienced—as the key to understanding what it means to be a Mormon; understanding the interpretation of Latter-day Saint history as disciplined reflection on what it means to be a Latter-day Saint, in other words as quasitheological, even if only implicitly. Perhaps this explains why the *Encyclopedia of Mormonism*,[37] though it contains articles on traditional theological questions such as God's foreknowledge, devotes proportionally much more space to articles on church history. It also explains why Latter-day Saint academics and students, as well as church members outside the academy, often have an avid interest in Mormon history, even though they are not themselves historians. The fact that the Mormon History Association has thousands of members while the Society for Mormon Philosophy and Theology has, at most, hundreds, says something about where Mormons find theology. Finally, understanding Mormons as doing hermeneutical theology by doing history explains why the dispute over how history should be done—a dispute that was resolved only by the participants changing topics and, so, a dispute that remains implicit in much Mormon discussion of our history—was so strong.[38]

Some Mormons, including Mark Wrathall and myself, have made the hermeneutical approach more explicit, using philosophical rather than historical hermeneutics to think about their faith. Though thinkers like Heidegger, the twentieth-century German, Hans-Georg Gadamer (a student of Heidegger), and the twentieth-century French philosopher, Paul Ricoeur (who taught in the United States for some time)

37. *Encyclopedia of Mormonism*, ed. Daniel H. Ludlow, 4 vols. (New York: Macmillan, 1992).

38. See, for example, the essays in George D. Smith, ed., *Faithful History: Essays in Writing Mormon History* (Salt Lake City: Signature Books, 1992).

are not among the philosophers to whom most Mormons are likely to refer, that seems to be changing. Of course, hermeneutical theology is not the only Mormon alternative to rational theology and its offspring. Though less well known than the work in the philosophy of religion done by Paulsen and Ostler, there are a number of contemporary Mormon thinkers who are exploring alternatives. Kathleen Flake has taken the Mormon interest in history and used it to think about Mormon faith through narrative theology, a cousin if not a sibling of hermeneutical theology.[39] Some Mormon thinkers, like Brian Birch and Keith Lane, use D. Z. Phillips's Wittgensteinian understanding of theology as a basis for their reflections. One Latter-day Saint thinker, Adam Miller, takes his theological cue from the work of Alain Badiou. All of these alternative approaches, even Miller's, assume as fundamental that practice, belief, and reflection on practice and belief are temporal and situated. In that sense they too are hermeneutic.

Thus, the answer to the question, "How do Mormons understand the relation between philosophy and theology," turns out to be complicated. Traditionally, we have taken theology to be strongly rationalistic, though there has also been an important and growing fideistic strain in Latter-day Saint thought, a strain that may be a reaction against rationalist theology more than a positive assertion about the nature of reason and faith. But, because the practical rather than theoretical understanding of religion is fundamental to Mormonism, perhaps the most important Mormon theological work to date has been the work of Mormon historians. Though people like Paulsen and Ostler continue to labor for theological understanding in a more systematic fashion, it appears that the theological work traditionally done by attention to history is beginning to be supplemented by theologies of scriptural appropriation, narrative, Wittgensteinian analysis,

---

39. Flake, "Translating Time: Joseph Smith's Translation of the King James Bible," unpublished manuscript delivered at "God, Humanity, and Revelation: Perspectives from Mormon Philosophy and History," New Haven, Yale University, 24 March 2003. Notice that *history* takes the place in the title of the conference where one would expect to find *theology*.

and hermeneutics, theologies that do not take the implicitly objective view taken by rational theology, and theologies for which continuing revelation plays a more central role than it does in rational theology. Mormon theology is beginning to take part in the larger theological discussion, moving more in the direction of multiple theologies and, particularly, theologies that, as Tracy so well put it, "accord priority to 'possibility' over 'actuality,'" "take history and historicity with full seriousness," and recognize truth as manifestation, disclosure, or disclosure-concealment.[40]

---

40. Tracy, "Catholic View," 460.

CHAPTER FOUR

MYTH AND RELIGION:
THEOLOGY AS A HERMENEUTIC OF
RELIGIOUS EXPERIENCE

L angdon Gilkey[1] (1919–2004) was a prominent Protestant theolo-gian. Interned in a Japanese camp during World War II—he was teaching English in China when war broke out—Gilkey's thinking was heavily influenced by that internment and by his studies with Reinhold Niebuhr, one of two or three of the most important Protestant theo-logians of the twentieth century. Gilkey once said, "I believe in God because to me history precisely does not represent . . . progress."[2] But he recognized that he lived in an age when, though there were crises to which religion was relevant, such as the civil rights movement in the United States, many could not see how it was. One can understand much of his work as an attempt to show how the language of religion is relevant to the secular society in which we live.

Gilkey tells us that theology has moved from the question of the nature of religious language to the more radical question of the possi-bility of meaningful religious language. The question is not just, "How is religious language relevant today?" but "How can religious language even be meaningful?" He suggests that if religious language is no lon-ger a possible mode of meaningful discourse, it is because religious

---

1. Though Gary Dorrien is the author of the piece to which this was a response, Dorrien writes about Langdon Gilkey's theology. As shorthand, therefore, I will refer to Gilkey, assuming that Dorrien's portrayal of Gilkey's position is correct. Dorrien's piece is "Langdon Gilkey's Myth-Creative Liberal Theology: Synthesizing Tillich, Niebuhr, Schleiermacher, Ricoeur, Eliade, and Whitehead," in *Mormonism in Dialogue with Contemporary Christian Theologies*, ed. David L. Paulsen (Macon, GA: Mercer University Press, 2007), 385–410.

2. Quoted in Adam Bernstein, "Langdon Gilkey Dies: Theologian, Author, Educa-tor," *Washington Post*, 22 November 2004, page B06.

language is no longer related to experience and life. The undeniable and irreversible triumph of secularism in the modern world has meant the loss of religious meaning. In response to that loss, Gilkey proposes to disclose "the meaning of religious language . . . by developing a hermeneutical phenomenology of experience,"[3] and he argues, quite reasonably, that in rejecting the importance and meaningfulness of the conceptual/symbolic order that religion offers, secularism is unable to recognize or explain the order that makes secularism itself possible.[4] Secularism cannot understand its own possibility, so Gilkey proposes to give an interpretation of human experience that shows how religion offers strategies for understanding and coping that we need but do not have in the merely secular world.

Explaining Gilkey's thought, Gary Dorrien says the secular mind "invariably resorts to mythical language in expressing its 'anti-mythical' world view,"[5] but it remains tone-deaf to the mythical character of its own language. Examples from secular myth are "the image of the critical, scientific 'man of reason'"[6] and the assumption that "the realization of freedom is always a moral good."[7] With the triumph of secularism, the theologian's job cannot be to cast out secularism. Rather, says Gilkey, the theologian must give a better interpretation of myth for secular consciousness. He or she must reawaken secular consciousness to the mythic rather than argue against secularism per se. Thus, Gilkey's general strategy is to reinterpret Christian understanding in light of the myth of secularism, but at the same time to show the inadequacy of the latter. Secularism, for example, cannot deal adequately with the inevitability of change. That requires reference

---

3. Dorrien, "Myth-Creative Liberal Theology," 389.

4. Gilkey collapses the terms *myth* and *symbolic* or *conceptual order*. Though I think there are not only useful but important distinctions to be made between the two, to make the connection to Gilkey, I follow him here, using the term *myth* to refer to both myth and symbolic/conceptual order. It is important to note that, as used in these kinds of discussions, *myth* does not mean "false story." Instead, it means "an organizing story."

5. Dorrien, "Myth-Creative Liberal Theology," 397.

6. Dorrien, "Myth-Creative Liberal Theology," 94.

7. Dorrien, "Myth-Creative Liberal Theology," 397.

to ultimacy, something missing in the secular myth but available in Christianity.

Following thinkers like Mircea Eliade and Paul Ricoeur, Gilkey argues that myth shapes human existence by giving us a structure on which we hang our understanding of society and the world: "The purpose of myth is to organize the total 'world' of one's desire, environment, and social situation into a reflective form that makes sense of the world."[8] Theology is a response to myth: "The purpose of theology is to explore reflectively the meaning and validity of mythical discourse"[9] in order to "disclose the latent sacral elements of experience."[10]

Consider Gilkey's claim that both myth and theology are reflective. In a broad sense, as a response to the human condition, of course myth is reflective. However, if by "reflection" we mean "taking up something as an object of conceptual or intellectual inquiry" (and, presumably, that is the way theology is reflective), then given Gilkey's understanding of myth, it cannot be reflective in the same way that theology is. To say that both are reflective is to equivocate. As a framework that makes understanding possible, the symbolic realm of myth and ritual is broader than that of philosophical and theological reflection. Given Gilkey's view, as a conceptual framework, myth makes intellectual realms possible and, so, makes intellectual reflection on myth complicated. We can never have the whole myth before us as we reflect on it, unless it is not the framework that we use for understanding that upon which we reflect.[11] Thus, if myth is an organizing framework for understanding, it cannot also be the uncomplicated

---

8. Dorrien, "Myth-Creative Liberal Theology," 399. Here is a place where I believe that the distinction between myth and the symbolic order would be useful. The latter is the structure that organizes our concepts. Myth is the narrative in which we find that structure displayed.

9. Dorrien, "Myth-Creative Liberal Theology," 399.

10. Dorrien, "Myth-Creative Liberal Theology," 391.

11. This point is important to a criticism I make later in the paper. There is another objection, one that is related to my concern about myth and conceptual or symbolic ordering: If myth is not a conceptual ordering (it could be either a symbolic ordering or, more likely, a kind of narrative), then it is not the kind of thing that is concerned with reflection. Reflection involves at least conceptual analysis and myth is not conceptual.

object of reflection except on the basis of some other myth or through a work of immanent critique. Gilkey's criticism of secularism is a form of such immanent critique, showing that secularism depends on the very thing it rejects. Presumably theology can also perform such a critique within a particular religion, but that is not how Gilkey deals with religion.

Given Gilkey's position, there can be no standpoint from which to analyze myth that does not depend on myth, but his assumption that myth is reflective tempts him to go beyond immanent critique. Gilkey says:

> What makes modern theology distinctive in religious history is the fact that modern theologians know that their myths are myths. Theology no longer claims to be able to make indicative statements about matters of fact. It is only as broken myth that Christianity's mythical inheritance can be appropriated.[12]

Given Gilkey's understanding of myth, this claim about theology must depend on some conceptual structure. Which one? Is this a claim made possible by a position within religious myth or by a position within the myth of secularism? The fact that religious myth is said to be broken is evidence that the claim has its basis in secularism. Since Gilkey sees secularism as having completely triumphed over religion that is not surprising. If the world is, indeed, irredeemably secular, then one can do theology and talk about religious myth only from a secular framework and one must, as Gilkey proposes to do, give a new interpretation of religious myth for secular consciousness.

To do so, however, is to undo the mythic function of religion, to rob it of its status as a way of understanding the world. Consider the biblical story of creation as an example. It is common to understand religious creation accounts as reflections on the origin of the cosmos, answers to the question "Why?" that are in some sense parallel to the scientific question "Why?" That is a mistake. There may be cases in

---

12. Dorrien, "Myth-Creative Liberal Theology," 399.

which myth functions as a kind of primitive science, but the biblical story of creation is not one of them.[13] Of course, secularists are not the only ones to assume that the Bible story of creation is a case of primitive science. Some religious people also make that assumption, especially those who consider themselves literalists. Ironically, when people argue for creation science or for what is usually called a literal reading of the Bible, they are agreeing with the secular understanding of things.[14] They use conceptual structures taken from secularism, such as the necessity that explanations have a scientific form, to try to understand the Bible. Some give up or metaphorize the Bible when faced with the project of making the Bible and science answer the same questions, but some keep the Bible and insist that its account can be brought within the secular myth, though of course they would not say that is what they are doing. But both those who metaphorize and those who would make the Bible scientific do essentially the same thing: they begin from a secular understanding of the Bible. Thus, Gilkey shares the view of those we often refer to as "biblical literalists." Both assume that secularism gives us the basic structure of understanding and that all accounts must be hung on that structure. They disagree about what conclusions that leads one to, but they agree that the secular myth is the one that must be used for understanding.

When the Bible tells us how the world was created, however, it does so with interests, goals, and basic assumptions so different from those of science that we ought to be suspicious of claims that both are answers to the same question, "How did the world come to be?" Such claims equivocate, for the question does not mean the same thing in a biblical context that it means in a scientific one. The great temptation

13. Those unfamiliar with this view should see, for example, André LaCocque and Paul Ricoeur, *Thinking Biblically* (Chicago: University of Chicago Press, 1998), and Northrop Frye, *The Great Code: The Bible and Literature* (New York: Harcourt Brace Jovanovich, 1982).
14. I quarrel with the description of "fundamentalist" readings of the Bible as literal readings. Such readings are exactly *not* literal—by the letter—readings; they are secularized readings, though in disguise. For more on this, see my "Scripture as Incarnation," chapter 8 in this volume.

is to assume that mythic accounts of creation are cases of primitive science. Perhaps some are. Surely we do not want to claim that all myth has the same goals. But it is far from obvious that all creation myths are primitive science. In fact, in the case of the Bible, those who take it to be a scientific or quasiscientific account have the considerable burden of proof. The interest of the biblical origin stories is much more on things like how the human condition came to be what it is, how evil came into the world, and why the covenant applies to each person than it is in the physical processes involved in creation. It is not clear that the biblical stories of origin has any interest in the latter at all.

The result of this difference between the biblical story of origin and the scientific story is that comparisons of the two, comparisons we find made by those who wish to argue for creationism, on the one hand, or those who wish to treat the biblical story as, at best, metaphor and poetry, on the other, are problematic.[15] It is not a simple matter to ask which of them is true. In fact, it is generally an impossible matter. If I assume that the conceptual schema for deciding truth is the scientific, secular one, then I assume that the questions and purposes of science are the relevant ones. Having done so, if I compare the claim that God created the heavens and the earth to a secular claim about the origin of the earth and then ask which is true, I will conclude that the secular account is true. On the other hand, if I assume that the relevant schema is that of the scriptural story with its questions and purposes, then when I compare the two claims about creation, I will conclude that the scriptural account is true.

But to say that the scriptural account is true is not to say that the scriptural account is a good scientific account. It is not to assume that the two accounts are the same kinds of explanation and, therefore, that the scriptural account is better than the scientific one. Rather, it is to say that the scientific account doesn't deal with the questions of

---

15. For perhaps the best discussion of this issue available, see Peter Winch, *Trying to Make Sense* (New York: Blackwell, 1987), 132–39.

the biblical text in a fashion adequate to the project of the narrative in Genesis, assuming that the scientific account deals with them at all. Both accounts claim to tell us how things are, so they both make truth claims; I am not arguing for a naive relativism. To the degree that the differing accounts make truth claims about the same things, they are comparable. It makes no sense to speak of a different kind of truth in one than in the other (as some, though not Gilkey, are tempted to do), unless by doing so one is covertly denying the truth of one or the other, perhaps by metaphorizing it. However, at least for biblical religions, it is far from obvious that myth and science make claims about the same things. Therefore, it is far from obvious that we can compare the truths of the scientific and the biblical accounts in order to decide which is superior, though Gilkey gives secularism the ability to decide truth and requires that religious truth find a way to fit within the secular schema.

Gilkey is willing to cede secularism the authority it demands and, so, to accept it as the story that determines truth. Thus, he says that although "myth refers to both the finite and the transcendent . . . its references to the finite must be understood to have no normative meaning as historical or scientific information."[16] This can only make sense if he assumes that religious myth makes claims about matters of fact that are the same as the fact-claims of modern science. Though that assumption is common, it is incoherent. Gilkey recognizes the problem of assuming that myth is a primitive form of science, but he falls prey to the temptation when he accepts the secular assumption that the mythic claims of secularism are the ones by which we will understand all claims to truth, in other words, all facts.

Secularism tries to insist that there is no myth at all. Gilkey shows that to be self-contradictory. In other words, he shows that, in spite of what seems to be the case and in spite of the claims of secularism and its domination of our thought, it has not completely triumphed over religion because it shares religion's reference to a background myth.

---

16. Dorrien, "Myth-Creative Liberal Theology," 398.

Why, then, grant the myth of secularism in thinking about religion? Doing so robs religion of its claims to truth and, so, of its power to have real effects. It makes religion only metaphorical. If only secularism can yield facts, then religion is an untrue though sometimes useful fable. Such a position takes the word *myth* to mean exactly what Gilkey denies that it means: merely a fable. Thus, the question is whether Gilkey has not given up too much, continuing Bultmann's demythologizing project without intending to. If his critique of secularism's rejection of myth is valid, as I believe it is, then the revelation of secularism's broken, self-contradictory character opens a space in which religious myth can be considered, not from the secular point of view, but from out of itself. Within a secular consciousness that considers itself whole, Christianity can be appropriated only as broken myth. That is at the heart of Gilkey's thought. But the break in secularism to which Gilkey points opens a space for considering religious myth differently.[17]

One way to do so is to show, as Gilkey has tried to do, how the sacred manifests itself in and through the finite. The problem is how to deal with a phenomenology of religious experience in a way that will yield valid claims about divine transcendence. Though Gilkey has passed over that issue, at least two contemporary philosophers come to mind who have dealt with it extensively, Jean-Luc Marion and Michel Henry, the latter a late-twentieth-century French Catholic thinker, the former a contemporary one. To illustrate what attention to the issue might allow, let me briefly describe Marion's work as well as the criticism of it.[18] Then let me suggest an alternative that I believe takes up the insights of Marion's project and avoids the criticisms.

---

17. This possibility is one that might be undertaken in a deconstructive theology, something that Gilkey has, understandably, been unable to do.

18. Marion has made his case in work after work, from *L'idol et la distance* (Paris: Grasset, 1977); *The Idol and Distance*, trans. Christina Gschwandtner and others (New York: Fordham University Press, 2001) to *Du surcroît* (Paris: PUF, 2001); *In Excess*, trans. Robyn Horner and Vincent Berraud (New York: Fordham University Press, 2004). For an excellent version of the argument, see his "The Saturated Phenomenon" in Janicaud and others, *Theological Turn,* 176–216. Marion's primary work on transcendence is *Being*

The German thinker Immanuel Kant (1724–1804) is one of the most important thinkers of Western philosophy. He argued that, because reason is limited in what it can do, we cannot know about anything transcendent. As part of making that argument, Kant gave us a rich and carefully argued account of how our experiences of phenomena are possible. Edmund Husserl, another German, who lived in the last half of the nineteenth century and the first half of the twentieth, also gave a rich and carefully argued account of phenomena. Husserl's analysis was based on the observation that consciousness is always intentional—directed at something—and that the understanding of phenomena would require an analysis of this directed consciousness rather than a pure consciousness existing independent of the world.

For both Kant and Husserl, a phenomenon must be understood within a horizon and according to an I. In other words, there are bounds within which the phenomena appear and they always appear to someone. My desk is here in my office when no person is, but it is not appearing, "showing itself," unless there is someone to whom it appears. All phenomena are, therefore, conditioned by the horizon within which they appear and the person to whom they appear. The impossibility of an unconditioned phenomenon, the impossibility of a pure experience of transcendence, results from this fact about phenomena.

The problem, as Kant's first critique argues, is that to the degree that we deal only with conditioned phenomena we do not deal with what is transcendent. That is, in a nutshell, Kant's argument: we cannot deal with what is transcendent because to do so we would have to experience an unconditioned phenomenon, and that is impossible. Marion's response is to argue that an unconditioned phenomenon is

Given: Toward a Phenomenology of Givenness, trans. Jeffrey L. Kosky (Stanford: Stanford University Press, 2002). Someone with little background in phenomenology would do well to begin with a secondary source, such as Christina M. Gschwandtner, *Reading Jean-Luc Marion: Exceeding Metaphysics* (Bloomington: Indiana University Press, 2007).

possible.[19] His strategy is to argue for "saturated phenomena" (phenomena of which we have an intuition but that are not constituted by the horizon and the ego) rather than the "impoverished phenomena" of Kant and Husserl—impoverished because they are constituted by their horizon and subject, with little or nothing given by intuition.[20] Marion points out that his suggestion of this possibility is not as wild as it may seem at first glance. After all, we find something like this in Kant's aesthetic, in which the aesthetic idea is an intuition for which no adequate concept can be formed. The fact that there is no adequate concept of the aesthetic idea means that it is not constituted.

In Kant's aesthetic, the concept is impoverished (limited) not the intuition (raw experience) for the intuition gives more than we can conceptualize. Kant says this excessiveness of intuition is *inexposable*; Marion uses, instead, the word *invisible*. The invisible phenomenon is "invisible, not by lack of light, but by excess of light."[21] The saturated phenomenon is invisible to the categories of understanding because it exceeds them. We don't have to think that excess in terms of enormity. All that is necessary is that it be impossible to apply a successive (in other words, additive) synthesis (of the elements of our intuition) to the phenomenon in order to gather those elements together as a conceptual whole. The invisible is excessive of understanding because no successive synthesis is possible.

Marion argues, however, that in spite of the impossibility of performing a successive synthesis and, thereby, coming to a knowledge of the whole, it is possible to have an *instantaneous* synthesis of the saturated phenomenon. Amazement and bedazzlement are examples of such instantaneous syntheses. We look toward something when we are amazed or bedazzled, but it exceeds our understanding. What I

---

19. Marion makes this argument in various ways in the body of his work, but for our purposes, I will refer to the short essay mentioned earlier, "The Saturated Phenomenon." It is perhaps the best abbreviated version of his argument.

20. In philosophy, the word *intuition* refers to immediate knowledge of any kind. Perhaps the most common example is sense perception: under normal conditions, I know that I feel something cold immediately on touching it.

21. Marion, "Saturated Phenomenon," 197.

see in the vision of the saturated phenomenon is not darkness, but something so bright that it blurs my vision, something I cannot see clearly: "Because the saturated phenomenon, due to the excess of intuition in it, cannot be borne by any gaze that would measure up to it 'objectively,' it is perceived 'subjectively' by the gaze only in the negative mode of an impossible perception, the mode of bedazzlement."[22]

For Marion, we do not find amazement and bedazzlement only in the exceptional case. With Martin Heidegger, Marion believes that such experiences are the fundamental modes of our experience with the world and, so, determinative of phenomena. We can—indeed, must—"cover over" our amazement at and bedazzlement with things in order to get on in the world. I live most of my life as "one" lives life,[23] seeing what others see and speaking of those things as they do. I do not see each thing in its uniqueness. Instead, I see each thing as a member of a class of things. This thing on which my fingers are tapping is a keyboard, like many other keyboards, not a thing unique in itself. The person who brings me my dinner at a restaurant is a server. Even if he tells me his name I do not treat him as someone absolutely unique. Rather, we interact as customer and server interact, according to moral and social codes that dictate what each is to do. We live by general rules for behavior with regard to things and persons rather than taking each thing or person up as a new and unique entity.

Heidegger calls this way of living *inauthenticity*, literally "non-individuality" (*Uneigentlichkeit*) because in ordinary life I cannot treat each entity I encounter as new and unique. To try to do so would be madness, for it would be completely disordered. When we behave authentically, we cover over the world's uniqueness; we each behave in the same way—according to social and moral norms. This covering

22. Marion, "Saturated Phenomenon," 201. Note that the words *objectively* and *subjectively* are between quotation marks in the quotation because bedazzlement is exactly not something constituted by the subject; in other words, not an object of a subject. Thus, the language of subjectivity and objectivity is inadequate.

23. Cf. Heidegger's discussion of "the they" in *Being and Time*, trans. John McQuarrie and Edward Robinson (New York: Harper & Row, 1962), §§26–27.

over is a way of proceeding that is not mine, that I have been given by my history, culture, and context, and it is necessary to my existence as a person among other persons. Inauthentic behavior is not necessarily wrong and is often absolutely right.[24] Nevertheless, the covering over of ordinary life and experience is possible only on the basis of a "prior" encounter with things in which amazement and bedazzlement are essential. Marion's way of saying this is to say that because the saturated phenomenon is always "disfigured" by the horizon(s) in which it appears and the knowing subject who apprehends it, it is not recognized as what it is. Nevertheless, even this disfiguring (in other words, inauthentic apprehension) is a manifestation of the thing itself.

Marion argues that because the experience of the saturated phenomenon is an experience of what I do not and cannot constitute, of what is excessive of understanding, it is an experience of my finitude and impotence. It is an experience in which I find myself constituted rather than constituting because I no longer have a dominant point of view over that which is intuited. Instead the intuition overwhelms me: "The *I* loses its anteriority and finds itself, so to speak, deprived (*destitué*) of the duties of constitution, and is thus itself constituted: it becomes *me* rather than *I*."[25] In the experience of the saturated phenomenon—of transcendence—I become a witness rather than a subject. Pointedly, Marion calls this event, in which I become a witness of what overpowers me, "revelation."[26]

For Marion's critics, this is where the problem arises. According to Marion, since the intuition of a saturated phenomenon is an intuition in which the I is constituted as me, that intuition is a pure

---

24. See Heidegger, *Being and Time*, trans. McQuarrie and Robinson, §27. Note that he says: "*The 'one' is an existential and belongs as a primordial phenomenon to the positive constitution of Dasein*" (p. 121; emphasis in original, translation modified).

25. Marion, "Saturated Phenomenon," 211.

26. It is important to note that revelation is not the only kind of saturated phenomenon and that revelation is not only the revelation of the Divine. Historical events are also saturated phenomena and revelation includes the picture as spectacle (the "idol") and the particular face that bedazzles me (the "icon"), as well as the intuition of a gaze that envisages me and loves me (theophany). Marion, "Saturated Phenomenon," 214–15.

intuition of transcendence, one unmediated by concepts and without structure.[27] But a pure intuition is, arguably, impossible. The idea of a pure intuition is the idea of an intuition with no content whatsoever because there is neither horizon within which it can gain meaning relative to other things nor ego to which it can be meaningful; it is the idea of an experience to which no thought at all is attached, not just the experience of the overflow or excess of one's concepts but an experience in which all concepts are absent. As thought-provoking as Marion's analysis is, the argument is that it goes too far. Quoting Marion, Dominique Janicaud asks, "What remains phenomenological in a reduction that, 'properly speaking, *is* not,' and refers back to a 'point of reference [that is] all the more original and unconditioned as it is more restricted'?"[28] Janicaud's answer is pointed: nothing. A phenomenon requires that which makes it a phenomenon. It requires the I. A pure phenomenon is unintelligible.[29]

But Marion's case is not as difficult as Janicaud's criticism makes it seem. In "The Event, the Phenomenon, and the Revealed,"[30] Marion addresses the question directly, arguing that the pure phenomenon is an analytic concept derived by a phenomenological reduction of the event in which something is given to intuition. In point of fact, the given never occurs apart from a *given-to*, a *me*. Marion says, "One can take the risk of saying that the given . . . projects itself onto the given-to (consciousness, if one prefers) as onto a screen; . . . immediately provoking a double

---

27. For examples of criticisms that focus on this point, see the piece by Janicaud in *Theological Turn* and his later work, *La phénoménologie éclatée* (Paris: L'Eclat, 1998). See also Marlène Zarader's "Phenomenology and Transcendence," 106–19, as well as Beatrice Han's "Transcendence and the Hermeneutic Circle: Some Thoughts on Marion and Heidegger," 120–44, both in James E. Faulconer, ed., *Transcendence in Philosophy and Religion* (Bloomington: Indiana University Press, 2003).

28. Janicaud, *Theological Turn*, 62.

29. Zarader's piece in *Transcendence in Philosophy and Religion*, 106–19, makes this point very clearly.

30. Marion, "The Event, the Phenomenon, and the Revealed," in Faulconer, ed., *Transcendence in Philosophy and Religion*, 97–105.

visibility,"[31] namely the visibility of the phenomenon giving itself and the visibility of the me receiving it. But we cannot analyze this event of given-and-given-to using its two terms, *given* and *given-to*. That division allows us to speak of the given, a pure intuition of transcendence, apart from the given-to.

Nevertheless, even if Janicaud's criticism holds—that there is no pure intuition of transcendence—that does not mean, as Kant and Husserl argue, that every reference to transcendence remains trapped within the world of subject and object, remains constituted and, so, does not at all refer to transcendence. To deny that there are unconditioned phenomena is not to assert that there is never anything of the unconditioned in phenomena. Intuition does not disappear. We experience the overflow of our concepts, the excess of intuition. As mentioned, without reducing transcendence to a phenomenon and without arguing for pure intuition, Heidegger has already shown that transcendence is revealed in immanence. For example, he argues that the work of art reveals transcendence in immanence, revealing more than itself.

Of course, Heidegger is hardly the only philosopher to have dealt with this problem or to have argued that we experience transcendence in immanence. The problem is how to talk about those experiences, for, at first glance, we seem unable to speak without speaking merely immanently and categorically. Our concepts are concepts of the phenomenal. How, then, can we use them to speak of what transcends the phenomenal, of overflow and excess, the unconditioned aspect of experience? This problem is an ancient one. Pseudo-Dionysius responds with negative theology. Plotinus speaks of the *trace*, a term that has been picked up and used in contemporary work, such as that of Emmanuel Levinas and Jacques Derrida. Heidegger uses a variety of terms, among them words clustered around the word *Riß*: *rift*, *tear*, and as a root in words meaning "sketch," "design," "outline,"

31. Marion, "The Event, the Phenomenon, and the Revealed," in Faulconer, ed., *Transcendence in Philosophy and Religion*, 101–2.

"boundary."[32] Those in literature, such as Roland Barthes, speak of *subversion*, a term that Marlène Zarader borrows. Finding a way to allow the subversion, interruption, supplementation, or tracing of the unconditioned to show itself in what we say is the "solution" to the problem of whether Marion is ultimately right or wrong.[33] Though there are interesting and important differences between these thinkers of interruption and subversion, one can make the general observation that all such talk points to the fact that we always find ourselves in a world that we constitute and, at the same time, we find that something unconstituted disturbs the horizon (context) and the I (consciousness), which implicitly claim to account completely for things and the world.

Heidegger's discussion of the work of art and his frequent references to poetry are one way to understand such speaking: art and language cannot be reduced to their categorical content, and phenomenological analysis shows that. Marion has also used phenomenological analyses of the work of art to talk about our experience and communication of transcendence.[34] However, given that the experience of transcendence is not necessarily the experience of divine transcendence, being able to talk about transcendence is not enough. The work of art reveals what we might call the transcendence of things, but that is not necessarily the same as divine transcendence. In what do we find divine transcendence?

Like many, perhaps even all religions, biblical religions call us to live in a certain way.[35] They may do so conceptually, but they need not.

32. See, for example, Heidegger, "The Origin of the Work of Art," 188.

33. This solution has much to do with the difficulty we find in reading such thinkers as Levinas and Derrida, though it is not the only explanation.

34. See, for example, Marion, *La croisée du visible* (Paris: PUF, 1996); *The Crossing of the Visible*, trans. James K. A. Smith (Stanford, CA: Stanford University Press, 2004). Also, Marion, *Du surcroît* (Paris: PUF, 2001); Marion, *In Excess: Studies of Saturated Phenomena*, trans. Robyn Horner and Vincent Berraud (New York: Fordham, 2003).

35. There is considerable discussion of biblical religion as response and call. See, for example, Ricoeur, "Experience and Language in Religious Discourse," in *Theological Turn*, 127–46; and especially Marlène Zarader, *La dette impensée, Heidegger et l'héritage hébraïque* (Paris: Seuil, 1990), 56–69; Zarader, *The Unthought Debt: Heidegger and the*

They can also do so by means of scripture and ritual and, especially, in their practices. As Kierkegaard points out, "The Christian thesis goes not: *intelligere ut credam* [Think in order to believe], nor *credere ut intelligam* [Believe in order to think]. No it goes: Act according to the commands and orders of Christ; do the Father's will—and you will become a believing-one."[36] On this view, the religious experience of transcendence is to be found in acts more than in concepts, whether those concepts are mythic or rational. Just as works of art testify of the disruption of the ordinary world by transcendence, the acts, rituals, and scriptures of the religious testify of the disruption by divine transcendence. They testify of a call from beyond themselves and their horizon that the religious are bound to hear and obey.[37] Because it accepts the secularization's triumph over religious language, Gilkey's understanding of religion seems to leave no room for such a call, for being called or chosen rather than choosing. But if there is no room for the call, then there seems to be no room either for testimony and witness.

The theologian is the person who responds to religious testimony reflectively. The materials for that reflection are the revelations of divine transcendence in religious immanence, namely acts, rituals, and scriptures. And the method of that reflection must be hermeneutic. As Ricoeur says, in the presence of revelation and the absence of universal religious phenomena we are left "to run the gauntlet of a hermeneutic and more precisely of a *textual* or *scriptural* hermeneutic."[38] Unlike Ricoeur, I include religious ritual and practice among the things to be examined hermeneutically, but I do not think my inclusion changes

Hebraic Heritage, trans. Bettina Bergo (Stanford, CA: Stanford University Press, 2006). Zarader's discussion is replete with references both to biblical texts and to other authors.

36. *Søren Kierkegaard's Journals and Papers*, ed. and trans. Howard V. Hong and Edna H. Hong (Bloomington: Indiana University Press, 1975), 3:363. I am grateful to Keith Lane for this reference.

37. Of course, false and misleading or misunderstood testimony is always possible. That religious experience testifies of the divine is no proof of the divine. Neither does it follow that all testimony is of equal worth.

38. Ricoeur, "Experience and Language in Religious Discourse," in *Theological Turn*, 130.

Ricoeur's point much. A hermeneutic of these texts and practices can awaken us again to the witness they offer, the witness of a divine call.[39] Thus, faced with the "triumph" of secularism, the theologian can stand in the break opened in secularism by Gilkey's critique and read the rituals, practices, and scriptures of his or her religion reflectively, testifying hermeneutically of the divine transcendence witnessed in those texts, of the disruption of secular reality that they demonstrate. Testimony makes it possible for the secularist to hear something of the call to which the religious respond.

An understanding of theology as a hermeneutic of texts and practices is particularly appropriate in biblical religions, religions in which response and call rather than doctrine and dogma are fundamental. A theology that offers a hermeneutic analysis of the scriptural call that initiates religious practices, and of the practices themselves, not only analyzes the texts and practices to which it attends—its analysis also testifies of the call of the Divine heard in those texts and practices. Hermeneutic theology is, therefore, among the acts appropriate to religious life. It is testimony. The testimony of the hermeneutic theologian is a second-order testimony, for it testifies of the bedazzlement of the divine transcendence that reveals itself in religious life. Theological testimony can be meaningful in a secular world, as Gilkey's critique of secularism shows. Hermeneutic theology cannot serve as the proof for God's existence that some may demand. Neither will it make biblical religion fit comfortably into a secular understanding of the world nor make it obvious to the secularist that religious language is meaningful. We do not escape the difficulty of being religious (and Kierkegaard is right that we should not). Nevertheless, a hermeneutic theology can speak in the space of secularism's self-contradiction. Testimony and attestation of religious experience, of the experience of

---

39. Paul Moyaert's "The Sense of Symbols as the Core of Religion: A Philosophical Approach to a Theological Debate," in *Transcendence in Philosophy and Religion*, 53–69, is an excellent example of such a hermeneutic. In that essay the Catholic understanding of the sacrament of the Eucharist is the object of his analysis. Moyaert's argument is important to chapter 1 as well as to chapter 8 in this volume.

divine transcendence, calls both to those who are presently religious, helping them hear the divine call again, and to those who are not religious, seeking to open their ears to the call of the divine. Like quotidian life, secularism washes everything in gray. Like art, hermeneutic theology can remove some of that gray, perhaps allowing light to shine through once again.

CHAPTER FIVE

WHY A MORMON WON'T DRINK COFFEE BUT MIGHT HAVE A COKE: THE ATHEOLOGICAL CHARACTER OF THE CHURCH OF JESUS CHRIST OF LATTER-DAY SAINTS

It is a matter of curiosity to many and an annoyance to a few that it is sometimes difficult to get definitive answers from members of the Church of Jesus Christ of Latter-day Saints to what seem like straightforward questions—questions of the form "Why do you believe or do *x*?"[1] Latter-day Saints subscribe to a few basic doctrines, most of which they share with other Christians (such as that Jesus is divine) and some of which differentiate them (such as the teaching that Joseph Smith was a prophet of God). They also accept general moral teachings, the kinds of things believed by both the religious and the nonreligious. Apart from those, seldom can one say without preface or explanation what Latter-day Saints believe.

I will argue that this apparently curious situation is a result of the fact that, like many, probably most, other religious people (including many Hindus and Jews), Latter-day Saints are atheological.[2] In other words, they are without an official or even semi-official philosophy that explains and gives rational support to their beliefs and teachings. To make that argument, I will argue that what we say about being Latter-day Saints is an expression of what it means to be Latter-day Saints,

---

1. Occasionally that annoyance becomes a charge of duplicity or of an esoteric doctrine. Though I think the charge is seldom justifiable, I understand its origin and have some understanding of why some people make it.

2. I agree with Rémi Brague, who says "The project of a rational elucidation of divinity . . . is specific to Christianity." Brague, *The Law of God: The Philosophical History of an Idea* (Chicago: University of Chicago Press, 2007), 6.

but being Latter-day Saints is irreducible to a set of propositions.[3] As I use the word *theology* here, it begins with belief and uses the methods of rational philosophy to give support to that belief: I mean dogmatic, systematic, or rational theology. I recognize that, especially to someone who is not a member of the Church of Jesus Christ, it may seem a bit outdated to criticize rational theology since there are also other kinds of theology such as narrative, liberation, liturgical, and feminist theologies. Nevertheless, since rational theology is what most Latter-day Saints first think of when they think of theology, since dogmatic (in other words, church-sanctioned) theologies are rational, and since I think at least some of what I say of rational or systematic theology may also apply to other theologies, I think it reasonable to focus on rational theology.

In describing the Church of Jesus Christ as atheological I intend to explain why the church neither has an official theology, explicit or implicit, nor encourages theological speculation. My explanation will be that the absence of theology reflects the Latter-day Saint understanding of religion as a set of practices, beliefs, and attitudes and that such an understanding is fundamental to Latter-day Saint religion.

Of course, the absence of theology is also characteristic of many noncreedal denominations (and of many theologians). And, of course, some Latter-day Saint leaders and thinkers have devoted considerable energy to formulating theologies of various kinds. Nevertheless, none of those efforts have come to fruition (none has been accepted as official by the church, and none has articulated a theology exclusively accepted or adopted by authorities or members), and I think none will.

To argue that the Latter-day Saint religion is atheological I will look at what seems to be accepted, established practices among

---

3. For purposes of my argument, I distinguish, roughly, between a provisional account (one that is adequate for its purposes, but provisional) and an adequate account (an account that can be submitted to the critical demands of reason without remainder). I deny Latter-day Saint theologies that claim (usually implicitly rather than explicitly) to be adequate rather than provisional, though that may be to deny the exception rather than the rule.

Latter-day Saints, and I will use the Word of Wisdom as my basic example. I think it will give us a foothold on which to rest a discussion of the place of theology in Mormon belief and practice. In February of 1833, Joseph Smith received a revelation that said, among other things: "Strong drinks are not for the belly. . . . And again, hot drinks are not for the body or belly" (Doctrine and Covenants 89:5–9). His brother and Assistant President of the church, Hyrum Smith, later clarified that "hot drinks" meant coffee and tea.[4]

Latter-day Saints often speak of the Word of Wisdom as a health law, and there is evidence for that way of understanding it. Nevertheless, there is no official explanation of its prohibitions and there is anything but a universal practice, especially regarding, for example, the consumption of caffeine. There is little consistency among Latter-day Saint practices regarding caffeinated drinks and no more consistency regarding the explanations of those practices. Consider that many Latter-day Saints abstain from all caffeinated drinks, presumably believing that it is the caffeine in coffee that makes it forbidden; and thus that other drinks with caffeine are also forbidden. However, only a few of those who abstain from caffeinated drinks in general will drink decaffeinated coffee, though consistency would dictate that decaffeinated coffee is not prohibited. The permutations are many: most who would drink neither a decaffeinated coffee nor caffeinated sodas might eat a chocolate bar, though its caffeine levels are on a par with those in decaffeinated coffee. Few would drink tea who do not feel obliged to abstain from sodas with caffeine. And so on. Just as it is possible to draw a line representing some equation through any set of points on a two-dimensional plane, it is perhaps possible to find some rule that will explain these variations in orthodox Mormon practice. But it will not be easy to do so, and it is doubtful that the resulting rule will be useable.

---

4. Joseph Lynn Lyon, "Coffee," in *Encyclopedia of Mormonism*, 1:289. Latter-day Saints have not always taken the Word of Wisdom to be binding on them as a commandment. Indeed, the revelation was originally given "not by commandment or constraint" (D&C 89:2). Now, however, it has become a requirement for members in good standing.

The difficulties we encounter in explaining the ways in which Latter-day Saints practice the Word of Wisdom are illustrative of the difficulties we encounter with other Latter-day Saint beliefs and practices. There are few explanations of such things on which all Latter-day Saints in good standing agree.[5] As mentioned, there are basic beliefs, doctrines, and practices about which there is widespread and even universal agreement. Among these is the central doctrine that Jesus is the Messiah—that his life, suffering, death, and resurrection were literal. Other teachings include that Joseph Smith was the prophet through whom Jesus worked the restoration of his ancient gospel, that the Book of Mormon is a historical record of an ancient people, and that all human beings must be baptized. It is difficult, to the point of being inconceivable, to imagine the Church of Jesus Christ abandoning these. Nevertheless, though it is clear that such foundational beliefs and teachings exist, there is no official list of them.

Though it is easy to say that there must be foundational beliefs and it is easy to point to beliefs that appear to be among them, if we look closely at any particular belief, it isn't difficult to imagine changes in that belief that could come through the prophet and result in quite different practices and beliefs. Beyond whatever foundational beliefs Latter-day Saints hold, there are many other beliefs that are generally though not universally held, such as belief in the doctrine of eternal progression;[6] and there is considerable disagreement among those who do hold such beliefs as to what they mean or imply. Further,

---

5. I say "few" to be safe. I can think of none.

6. The belief is that we continue to progress after this life until, eventually, we are deified. Early Latter-day Saints were more clear about what deification means than are contemporary members of the church. For those mid- to late-nineteenth-century Latter-day Saints who considered the topic, it was clear that deification meant becoming like God the Father and creating worlds of one's own. Many Latter-day Saints continue to believe that, but there is also a number for whom the concept of deification is more ambiguous (see, for example, David Van Biema, S. C. Gwynne, and Richard N. Ostling, "Kingdom Come," *Time*, 4 August 1997, 56) or more in line with standard Christian doctrines of *theosis*. And, though they are a small minority, there are Latter-day Saints in good standing who do not at all believe in progression to deification.

whether we are talking about foundational or other beliefs, there is little thought about how to make those beliefs and practices a rational whole and even less agreement about whether to do so.

Thus, relatively few of what are often described as the beliefs and teachings of the Church of Jesus Christ are required of its members, and even fewer beliefs have a generally agreed-upon rational explanation or description. Yet most Latter-day Saints are not bothered by the absence of official theology—and the leadership of the church seems not to be looking to fill in that absence.

Joseph Smith's anticreedal feelings may be the origin of the continuing Latter-day Saint suspicion of theology. He said, "The Latter-day Saints have no creed, but are ready to believe all true principles that exist, as they are made manifest from time to time,"[7] and "the truth of the system, and power of God" had been "bound apart by cast-iron creeds, and fastened to set stakes by chain-cables, without revelation."[8] Though creed and theology are not the same, it is easy to see that someone opposed to the first might also be opposed to the second.

The absence of official explanations and rational descriptions of beliefs and practices, and of differing and inconsistent explanations and descriptions within the membership of the church, is what I will try to "explain." I will offer three possible responses to the question of Latter-day Saint atheology (only one of which is unique to Latter-day Saints). My responses will focus on prophets, practice, and scripture.[9]

---

7. *History of the Church*, 5:215. In spite of this antipathy toward creeds, as Daniel Graham has pointed out, not only do we have something very like a creed in the Articles of Faith, we find something even more like one in D&C 20:17–28.

8. *History of the Church*, 6:75.

9. I recognize that theologians and philosophers of religion are likely to find nothing new in what I say and to know of more nuanced and informed discussions of these matters in other places. Given my lack of training in either area, that is not surprising. Nevertheless, I believe that what I say here gives reasonable explanations for the absence of theology among Latter-day Saints. It is at least a place from which one could begin talking about that absence.

Prophets

My first response to the question of why Latter-day Saints are fundamentally atheological is that of my hairstylist, Geoffrey Huntington, who has not only the interest in philosophy common to those of his profession, but also some academic training in philosophy. When I asked him why we believe and do what we do, his answer was, "Because the prophet said so." At first glance, this may seem to be a remark about obedience. But I think that Huntington's response is not so much about obedience as it is about continuing revelation: if we take the idea of continuing revelation seriously, then anything we believe or do happens "under erasure," and that is especially true of any explanation of what we believe or do. As individuals, we may find a theology helpful to our understanding, but no explanation or system of ideas will be adequate to tell us what it means to be a Latter-day Saint. For a Latter-day Saint, a theology is always in danger of becoming meaningless because it can always be undone by new revelation.

My point is a logical one: To believe in continuing revelation, to believe that God can do what he did when he commanded Abraham to go to Moriah, when he challenged Peter's understanding of clean and unclean, when he ordained and then ended the practice of plural marriage, and when he told President Kimball that we should begin ordaining all worthy male members of the church is to believe that any account of our beliefs is, logically, in danger of being undone by new revelation. But we can go beyond the logical point: To believe in continuing revelation is more than to believe, as most Christians do, that no human-made theology will be adequate to God's divine theology, and, therefore, require revision. It is to believe, though often only implicitly, that that-which-is may not be static, so *there may be no final, atemporal rational understanding of the totality of things*, no ultimate rational theology toward which our human theologies could strive but never reach.[10]

_____

10. The absence of a final, atemporal account of everything is frightening only if we assume that divine knowledge requires such an understanding. However, unlike the

The word *theology* comes from the Greek words *theos* ("God") and *logos* ("reason" or "account"). Plato uses it in the *Republic*, where it means the account of divine things.[11] Nevertheless, except for scripture and what the prophet reveals, there is no authoritative *logos* of the *theos* for Latter-day Saints, and given that the prophet can and does continue to reveal things, there is no *logos* of what he reveals except the record of those revelations, scripture that remains an open canon.[12] For Latter-day Saints, the *logos* is both in principle and in practice always changing. Continuing revelation precludes an account of revelation as a whole. Thus, finally our only recourse is to the current revelations of the prophet since, speaking for God, he can explain, qualify, alter, or revoke any particular belief or practice at any moment, or he can institute a new one, and he can do those things with no concern for how to make his pronouncement rationally coherent with previous pronouncements or practices.

The Word of Wisdom illustrates this possibility of change that may have a historical explanation but has no systematically rational one. Its text says that it is given "not by commandment or constraint" (D&C 89:1). But in the early twentieth century, it became a commandment, and it is now expected that members of the church will abide by at least its most obvious parts. I know of no theological explanation of the Word of Wisdom that explains this shift in the status of the Word of Wisdom, from advice to commandment.

---

classical God, if God is within the universe rather than outside it (as Joseph's revelation of God's embodiment strongly suggests—see D&C 130:22), and if he interacts with others like ourselves who have agency, then though he must know—be intimately acquainted with—all the things there are, he does not need to have the kind of omniscience that the classical God has; a knowledge of all past, present, and future facts (assuming that the phrase "future facts" has any meaning at all). As long as God knows all that there is and has the power to adjust his own behavior to the behaviors of others in such a way that he will not be overcome by them in some way, then he has both all-knowledge and all-power, without having the kind of knowledge that we attribute to a Platonic or Aristotelian god.

    11. *Republic*, book 2.

    12. I think the openness of the canon, and the resulting need for keeping a record of what the prophets have said, helps explain the unusual interest in history among Latter-day Saints.

Polygamy illustrates the difficulty of systematic theology even better. Instituted by Joseph Smith, the practice of polygamy was revoked by Wilford Woodruff, the fourth prophet. Church intellectuals, some of them also prominent ecclesiastical leaders, had produced any number of theologies in which polygamy figured prominently and even centrally,[13] but with Woodruff's manifesto,[14] those theologies became incoherent, as Bruce R. McConkie so pointedly illustrated, having firmly held a theological belief that the priesthood would not be extended to black men in mortality and then, almost immediately after the revelation, recanting that belief, seemingly without embarrassment.[15]

Of course, Latter-day Saints offer explanations for such changes in practice, and many of those explanations are quasi-theological. But there is no more reason to think that those explanations are definitive than there was to think that the explanations given before the cessation of the practice were definitive. Latter-day Saint theological explanations are provisional and, in principle, personal (even when widely shared). Thus, one reason that Latter-day Saints are generally atheological is that theology serves little purpose in the way that doctrines and practices are decided. As Latter-day Saints understand continuing revelation, it always trumps theology.

Let me end my first argument with a syllogism that will perhaps serve as a summary:

1. Theology assumes the existence of an immutable set of beliefs that, in principle, shows to be rational and coherent.
2. Continuing revelation reserves the right to radically restructure Latter-day Saint beliefs.

---

13. For a representative claim, see Joseph F. Smith's statement that plural wives are necessary for a fullness of glory and joy in the celestial kingdom in *Journal of Discourses* 20:28–31, especially p. 30.

14. See Official Declaration 1 in the Doctrine and Covenants for the announcement of the prohibition of polygamy.

15. See, for example, Bruce R. McConkie, "All Are Alike unto God," CES Religious Educators Symposium, 18 August 1978.

3. So, an adequate theology and continuing revelation are at odds with one another.
4. Thus, since Latter-day Saints insist on continuing revelation, they cannot have an adequate theology.

Practice

We can also explain the absence of a theology in the Church of Jesus Christ by arguing that practice rather than belief is central to Latter-day Saint religion. It is not uncommon to understand religion as essentially a belief content: to be a Latter-day Saint is to believe that *x*, *y*, and *z* are true. If that is the case, then the content of those beliefs can be expressed in rational terms and related to each other by reason. In other words, they can be loosed from their connection to ritual, ordinance, history, etc., and then examined without losing any meaning in the process. On this assumption, a fully developed and relatively complete theology is in principle possible.

In spite of the commonness of thinking of religion as belief, particularly in Protestantism, I doubt that many would find that understanding of religion philosophically satisfactory. There are at least two problems with it. First, it doesn't accurately describe religious belief. As Paul Moyaert says, "One could not say . . . that someone is a good scientist if he does not know the basic principles of science, whereas a person who is unable to accurately explain the basic tenets of his or her religion can still be an exemplary and pious believer."[16] The proverbial farmer in Santaquin need not be able to give a proper theological account of his or her beliefs to be a good member of the church. Indeed, that farmer need not even have a coherent set of beliefs nor must all of his or her beliefs be coherent with the beliefs of most other Latter-day Saints. A person can be a good Mormon, whether a stake president or a Primary teacher, without having a good theology or much of a theology at all.

---

16. Paul Moyaert, "The Sense of Symbols as the Core of Religion: A Philosophical Approach to a Theological Debate," in *Transcendence in Philosophy and Religion*, ed. James E. Faulconer (Indianapolis: Indiana University Press, 2003), 54–55.

The gospel is a divine activity, the saving activity of God. It is not the belief content associated with that activity, even though the activity of the gospel necessarily has belief content. To be a believer is to accept the gospel: it is to believe that God can save, but not merely to believe (since mere belief would not be religious belief). To be a believer is to respond to God's saving activity with repentance and in rebirth and with tokens that testify of God's saving power. One can do that and, at the same time, have some, perhaps many, false beliefs. But if the exemplary pious person can have false beliefs about his or her religion,[17] then belief cannot define what it means to be religious. The locus of religion is practice rather than belief, though particular beliefs are often inseparable from practices. The practice of baptism cannot be the practice that it is without the beliefs that accompany it.

Further, Latter-day Saints understand much religious practice in terms of covenant and priesthood, as in Exodus 19:5–6: "Now therefore, if ye will obey my voice indeed, and keep my covenant, then ye shall be a peculiar treasure unto me above all people: for all the earth is mine: And ye shall be unto me a kingdom of priests, and an holy nation." Perhaps referring to that passage, Latter-day Saint revelation says:

> In the ordinances [of the priesthood], the power of godliness is manifest. And without the ordinances thereof, and the authority of the priesthood, the power of godliness is not manifest unto men in the flesh; for without this no man can see the face of God, even the Father, and live. Now this Moses plainly taught to the children of Israel in the wilderness. (D&C 84:19–24)

To be a Latter-day Saint is not merely to be a member of a particular community, sometimes identifiable by common beliefs or by particular habits or speech patterns or ways of organizing socially.

---

17. Defending an older man who had been accused of preaching false doctrine, Joseph Smith said, "It dont prove that a man is not a good man, because he errs in doctrine," *The Words of Joseph Smith: The Contemporary Accounts of the Nauvoo Discourses of the Prophet Joseph Smith*, ed. Andrew F. Ehat and Lyndon W. Cook (Orem, UT: Grandin, 1994), 184, original spelling retained.

Fundamentally to be a Latter-day Saint is to be one of the children of God and to serve him in formal practices, including ordinances.[18]

It is arguable that even if there were a rational account of Latter-day Saint beliefs in their relation to each other, it would not be—*and could not be, not even in principle*—an adequate account of Latter-day Saint formal practices, and thus it neither would nor could be an adequate account of Latter-day Saint religion.[19] This is because arguably there is no adequate account of practices in general, and thus, no adequate account of Latter-day Saint formal practices. To show that there can be no adequate account of practices one would have to show that practices exceed the possibility of giving a fully adequate account of them. One could do that by showing that it is impossible to apply a successive synthesis[20] to the phenomenon of practice in general, that it is impossible to take up and link its parts into a conceptual whole—even though a synthesis (an instantaneous rather than successive synthesis, and so knowledge though not conceptual knowledge) is possible. I take Jean-Luc Marion's arguments in "The Saturated Phenomenon" and in "The Event, the Phenomenon, and the Revealed,"[21] among other works, to straightforwardly imply[22] that there can be no successive synthesis of

18. Scholars speak of these as "cultic practices." However, given the abuse that the word *cult* has taken and the misunderstandings it may engender among some readers, I prefer to speak of the formal practices of a religion. I do not think that all formal practices are ordinances. The Word of Wisdom is a formal practice that is not an ordinance. I mention ordinances particularly because they are unambiguously formal practices.

19. It is important to remember that "adequate account" means "an account that can be submitted to the critical demands of reason without remainder."

20. Kant uses the term *synthesis* to mean what, following Jean-Luc Marion ("The Saturated Phenomenon," in Dominique Janicaud and others, *Phenomenology and the "Theological Turn": The French Debate* [New York: Fordham University Press, 2000], 199), I am calling a "successive synthesis": "But if this manifold [of space and time] is to be known, the spontaneity of our thought requires that it be gone through in a certain way, taken up, and connected. This act I name synthesis," Immanuel Kant, *Critique of Pure Reason*, trans. Norman K. Smith (New York: St. Martin's Press, 1929), A77.

21. Marion, "The Event, the Phenomenon, and the Revealed," in Faulconer, *Transcendence in Philosophy and Religion*, 87–105. For an overview of Marion's thinking, see the earlier discussion in chapter 4 in this volume.

22. In the first of these, Marion argues that there are phenomena, which he refers to as "saturated," for which there can be no successive synthesis. In the second, he argues,

practice. If so, then practice is excessive of conceptual understanding because no successive synthesis is possible, though such a synthesis is requisite for conceptual understanding.[23] Religious knowledge and understanding are possible, but to the degree that religious knowledge is the knowledge inherent in practices, it need not be able to give a conceptual account of itself. It need be neither conceptual nor propositional. Marion's argument excludes the possibility of an adequate, rational account of practice in general, though it leaves open the possibility of provisional accounts that are not harbingers of some as-yet-to-come adequate account.

However, rational theologies are not just unneeded, they are dangerous. I have no quarrel with someone who seeks a rational understanding of his or her Mormon faith—*if* that seeking doesn't involve the false assumption that such an understanding is necessary to genuine, meaningful participation in Latter-day Saint religion. Nevertheless, I wonder about those, like myself, who have the need for such seeking. My wonder is Nietzschean: "What motivates that search?" My suspicion is that we implicitly make the professor's assumption that understanding requires reasoning, concepts, and propositions. The atheological character of Latter-day Saint religion questions that implicit assumption, putting revelation, ordinance, scripture, history, and practice at the heart of religious understanding rather than reason and conception. That is not to say that rational understanding has no place in religion. Humans are rational beings, so religion must also address their rationality. But rationality, particularly in its narrow sense, is not the be-all and end-all of human being.

Several twentieth-century and contemporary thinkers have explicitly questioned the assumption that all understanding requires concepts.[24] The contemporary French philosopher and historian,

---

among other things, that events are saturated phenomena. It requires almost nothing to expand that argument so that it applies also to practices.

23. See Marion, "Saturated Phenomenon," 176–216.

24. See, for example, Michael Polanyi's *The Tact Dimension* (Garden City, NY: Doubleday, 1966) as well as Hubert Dreyfus, "Understanding," in *Being-in-the-World*

Rémi Brague, argues that the demand for rational explanation is a result of movements in the early stages of European history, movements that take place within the novel Greek idea that one could conceive the physical world as something in itself and present before human beings for investigation: "It was there [in Greece] and there alone, that that 'distanced' position would appear, that 'Archimedean point' from which human beings, 'conscious of being a subject (*subjektbewußt*),' would be able to submit nature to objective research."[25] Though the idea that the world is an object apart from us, lying before us for our conceptual investigation, seems intuitively obvious to us, Brague argues that it was new, created by the Greeks, and that there are both consequences to accepting that idea and alternatives to it.[26] Seeing the world as something in itself, something to be investigated as an object, eventually leads to an understanding of wisdom as the exercise of a power (that of critical investigation and theorizing) over an object. The idea of an adequate model of the world by means of which one can investigate and dominate that world symbolically is necessary to every rational, in other words, conceptual, description of the world. The idea of a world-model is at the heart of all science in the widest sense of that term—as it ought to be. This means, however, that, regardless of the motives and intentions of individual theologians, by presuming that there is, in principle, an adequate rational—in other words scientific—understanding of God and his relation to the world and human beings, we presume also that he can be understood as part of

Commentary on Heidegger's 'Being and Time,' Division I (Cambridge: MIT, 2001), 184–214.

25. *The Wisdom of the World: The Human Experience of the Universe in Western Thought*, trans. Tersa L. Fagan (Chicago: University of Chicago Press, 2003), 14. Translation modified.

26. The assumption that there is some final and adequate divine rational theology toward which human rational theologies strive is a consequence of assuming that God has the relation of a subject to a world that lies outside and apart from him. The assumption is that the world is known by God objectively—as an object—rather than as something in which he participates. (See note 10.)

a world-model or he cannot be understood at all.[27] The problem is not science. It is the assumption that all true understanding is ultimately scientific understanding.

Brague argues that intellectual, conceptual description of the world-model turns out to be, in principle, inseparable from intellectual domination, and I think his argument is cogent, though there is not room here to reproduce it. But if he is right, then when the rational theologian gives an account of that model, he or she implicitly presumes that the theologian can intellectually dominate the religion of which he or she speaks. If to be religious means to be mastered by something, to be awed by it, then neither religion nor that to which religion is a response can be something over which one has mastery. The conflict between religion and rational theology is the conflict between the willingness to submit and the desire to master. Sometimes that will to mastery shows itself in attempts to master others, as in a man who thinks that his priesthood has given him some power over his wife and children. Sometimes, however, it shows itself in subtler ways, as when a person insists on his own autonomy, cloaking the will to mastery in the guise of intellectual maturity.

In scripture and prophetic teaching, the question is not "What can I know?" and, so, "What can I master?" but "How should I be?" and "What should master me?" In them, knowledge means being related to others and the world, in experience and acquaintance, in the right way. But, since we believe that our relation to God defines what it means to be related to others and to the world in the right way, it follows that knowledge is ultimately a religious matter, a matter of one's relation with God. For the inheritors of the Hebrew tradition, knowledge is inseparable from experience and practice. To have those experiences and to engage in those practices is to know God, and to speak of that experience and to practice is to testify of one's relation to God.

---

27. One need not assume the classical understanding that God is outside of what-is in order to doubt that he can be understood as part of a world-model. It is enough that he is a person to make that assumption dubious. Christianity, Judaism, and Islam all claim that he is a person.

It is not to give a list of beliefs.[28] The danger of theology, any theology, is the temptation to valorize the intellect and its understanding, and to allow mere belief to displace Christian practice and testimony. Thus I think that we can understand the Latter-day Saint avoidance of theology as an insistence on practice, an effort to avoid the temptation of the intellect in its relation to God.

I offer this syllogism to summarize my second argument:

1. Religion is essentially a matter of practice rather than belief; for Latter-day Saints, among the essential practices are ordinances.
2. Theology cannot capture the practices of religion (because practices per se cannot be captured philosophically and rationally; something about them is always missed).
3. So, theology is either irrelevant, sometimes comforting, or useful in apologetics, but by focusing on belief rather than practice, it poses a danger to religion.

Scripture

My third explanation of the atheological character of Latter-day Saint religion is related to my second. As I understand scriptural texts and therefore also revelation, they are not rational, conceptual texts and cannot be turned into that without changing them drastically.[29] If we read the scriptures looking for a rational justification of something, including the teachings of scripture, then we read them at cross-purposes to their intentions. We can read them for conceptual understanding, in

28. Ricoeur reminds us that testimony is "an assurance always bound to acts" rather than beliefs. *Figuring the Sacred: Religion, Narrative, and Imagination*, ed. Mark I. Wallace, trans. David Pellauer (Minneapolis: Fortress, 1995), 117.

29. Ricoeur has discussions of the issue in several places; for example, it appears in general terms in *Time and Narrative*, trans. Kathleen McLaughlin and David Pellauer, 3 vols. (Chicago: Chicago University Press, 1984, 1985, 1988); and it is more clearly religious in his essays on the Bible, written with LaCocque (André LaCocque and Paul Ricoeur, *Thinking Biblically*, trans. David Pellauer [Chicago: Chicago University Press, 1998]), and in his essay in *Phenomenology and the "Theological" Turn*. Alain Badiou has argued that at least some scriptural texts, specifically Paul's letters, are antiphilosophical (and, so, antitheological) as well as antirhetorical. Alain Badiou, *Saint Paul, La fondation de l'universalism* (Paris: PUF, 1997).

other words, as quasi-philosophical texts, but when we do, we do not read them as scripture.

I believe that the message of scripture can be summed up in Deuteronomy 6:4–7: "Hear O Israel: The Lord our God is one Lord: And thou shalt love the Lord thy God with all thine heart, and with all thy soul, and with all thy might. And these words, which I command thee this day, shall be in thine heart." The scriptures, revelations, and ordinances call us to hear, to hearken—not to understand, at least not if the word *understand* is taken to mean "understand conceptually."[30] Of course, scripture does not preclude understanding. Neither do scripture, ordinance, and revelation forbid our conceptual understanding. But, for the most part conceptual understanding is irrelevant to their purposes.[31] Like the prophets, the scriptures call to us, asking us to listen, bearing witness of who we are and who we ought to be, bearing witness of our separation from God and his ability to overcome that separation. The scriptures seldom explain to us. Instead, they testify and ask us also to testify with our lives. To be religious is to hearken to that testimony and to respond.

The command to hearken implies that I have not yet heard, so if I take that command seriously, then I must continue to wonder whether I have heard as I should: at the heart of the religious experience of reading scripture is the experience of being questioned, of being brought up short by something rather than explaining it.[32] Philosophical/theological questions like "Why does God allow evil?" can be interesting and they have their place, both in apologetics and in

---

30. Notice that the first section of the Doctrine and Covenants, written in 1831 as a preface to the book as a whole, begins with the word "hearken": "Hearken, O ye people of my church, saith the voice of him who dwells on high and whose eyes are upon all men; yea, verily I say: Hearken ye people from afar; and ye that are upon the islands of the sea, listen together."

31. To point out something in scripture that we cannot make rational sense of may only be to point out that it does not serve the same purposes as do texts meant to give rational understanding.

32. Of course, scripture reading is not the only religious experience where we find ourselves brought up short. It occurs in other ordinances, in the temple, in Sunday meetings, in living with each other.

strengthening faith.[33] Nevertheless, they also may interfere with understanding scripture as divine call, in this case the call to avoid doing evil and to ameliorate its effects in the world. Philosophical and theological reflection seeks for intellectual understanding and, thus, they run the risk of turning the scriptures into resources for conceptualizing. But the scriptures do not ask for our intellectual understanding; they ask for our repentance.

As a result, I believe that, whatever the arguments for or against theology, for many religious people, including the Latter-day Saints, ultimately the only possible *logos* of the *theos* is that which occurs in response to revelation and scripture. That *logos* is produced in welcome and response, in repentance and rebirth, and in testimonies of that repentance and rebirth, rather than in sets of beliefs or intellectual distancing and questioning.

Thus, a final summarizing syllogism:

1. We encounter the essence of religious faith in scripture and prophetic revelation, but that essence is not a set of propositional beliefs, it is a testimony and a questioning that calls us to new life through repentance.
2. Theology aims to understand propositional beliefs and their ordered relations.
3. Therefore, theology does not deal with what is essential to religious faith.

What Will Become of Me?

Given these points about prophets, practices, and scripture, what will become of me? If I have successfully explained why Latter-day Saint religion is essentially atheological, I have also raised questions for people like myself who have an inclination toward theology. Given the difficulties to which I have pointed, one can reasonably ask what kinds of provisional accounts are possible.

---

33. For an excellent example of a religious and philosophical response to this question, see Ricoeur, "Evil, A Challenge to Philosophy and Theology," in *Figuring the Sacred,* 249–61.

First note that reasons why the Church of Jesus Christ of Latter-day Saints has neither a dogmatic theology nor an informal theology—and is unlikely to—are not reasons for avoiding theology. That it is not necessary does not mean that it is something to be avoided. Nor does my argument imply that Mormons ought never to do systematic theology. Nevertheless, I believe my arguments suggest that some kinds of theology are more useful for Latter-day Saints than are others.

The parallel between religious knowledge and ethico-political knowledge suggests that Aristotle provides a clue for one way to do theology, one way that allows the door to remain open and more easily avoids the danger of theology. Presumably there are also others.[34] Aristotle distinguishes between the kinds of things we know epistemically and the kinds of things we know in ethics and politics and, at least in the early part of *Nicomachean Ethics*, he argues that the latter are not reducible to the former. Scripture treats religious matters as Aristotle treats ethical matters, as things known *in* experience with them and, so, as things that Aristotle argues are not knowable epistemically. In Marion's terms, scripture deals with matters known in an instantaneous synthesis, rather than as the objects of an epistemic intention requiring a successive synthesis. So when philosophy makes religion its object, it may find a model in the way that Aristotle deals with ethics and politics, rather than in his metaphysics: *phronēsis* rather than conceptual intellection would be our goal.

---

34. For example, "radical orthodoxy" may offer another alternative. See John Milbank, Catherine Pickstock, and Graham Ward, *Radical Orthodoxy: A New Theology* (London: Routledge, 1999). The work of Marion, to which I referred earlier, may also. Both ask about transcendence, the latter by arguing that it makes itself known in phenomena, the former by arguing that it makes itself known in Platonic participation. Though there is considerable overlap between these two views, they are not the same. Of the two, I prefer Marion's approach because it does not require creation *ex nihilo* (though I am sure he accepts that orthodox Roman Catholic teaching), and I think his approach is compatible with what I will describe.

Several contemporary philosophers, such as Hans-Georg Gadamer and Paul Ricoeur, follow up on Aristotle's insight and provide possibilities for a theology on that model. These philosophers argue that human understanding is fundamentally hermeneutic. It is fundamentally a matter of interpreting our place in the world in relation to others and to our history. Rational, conceptual knowledge is an outgrowth from and abstraction of hermeneutic understanding. But because it is interpretive rather than rational, a hermeneutic theology would necessarily be provisional, escaping one danger of rational theology.

Historical narrative shows the advantage of a hermeneutic approach. Historical narratives are essential to Christianity because Christianity is revealed in those narratives. Without Jesus in history—God incarnate in the world—Christianity itself evaporates. Latter-day Saints recognize this by insisting not only on the historicity of the Bible, but also on the historicity of Joseph Smith's first vision and the historicity of the Book of Mormon. History shows us the sense in which God's plan inextricably requires working through history, through the choosing, scattering, and gathering of his people.

This insistence on historicity goes against a common understanding of truth. We commonly assume that a narrative can be an important illustration of a truth, but not its essential revelation. That is because truth is commonly assumed to have a universality that can be illustrated by the particularity of a historical narrative but cannot be equal to that particularity. On this view, truth—as universal—necessarily remains above, beyond, or other than, the particularity of history. Thus, since theological truth, like its sister philosophical truth, requires universality, it follows that theological truth is fundamentally incompatible with scriptural truth, with truth that reveals itself in the particularity of history[35]—unless scriptural truth is reduced to allegory or illustration, ways that philosophers have often

---

35. It is important to note that by "history" I do not mean "historiography." For an explication of this difference and my understanding of how it applies to scripture, see chapter 8 in this volume.

dealt with scripture. Particularity is a scandal to conceptual thought, but Judeo-Christian religion (at least) never gets away from the particular, whether the particularity of its narratives, the particularity of its associations and habits, the particularity of its formal practices, or the particularity of the incarnation of Jesus and his life at one moment of time rather than another, in a physical, particular body.[36] There is a fundamental incompatibility between the particularity of religion and the aim for universality that we find in any philosophical discipline like theology.[37] The incompatibility is not insurmountable, but it must be addressed.

Hermeneutics shows a way out of this problem: it does not require that we reduce the truth of religion to metaphor or example. If it thinks hermeneutically, philosophy can think the particularity of historical phenomena, like religion, religious experience, and scripture, and avoid the scandal of particularity by not being scandalized. Hermeneutics is one of perhaps several ways that we could do provisional theology more adequately.

In the end, however, any theology worth its salt, whether hermeneutic or not, must remember that testimony is central to both religious speech and religious ritual. Both testify of that which exceeds one's conceptual grasp but is nevertheless known. Theology can use the tools of philosophy to reflect on the claims and practices of religion, but if it is true to the object of its reflection, it will conduct its reflection in a way that continues to testify. To the degree that a theology does not testify, it divorces itself from that which it purports to explain, and I think that systematic theology is more likely to make this divorce than are some of the alternatives.

---

36. Latter-day Saint belief puts particularity at the core of what-is by insisting that even God is embodied: *nothing* breaks free from particularity, so the conceptual is always an abstraction in the root sense of that term, "something that pulls away."

37. As Nietzsche says: "A historical phenomenon, known clearly and completely and resolved into a phenomenon of knowledge, is, for him who has perceived it, dead." *Untimely Meditations*, ed. Daniel Breazeale, trans. R. J. Hollingdale (Cambridge: Cambridge University Press, 1997), 67. Christianity in general and Mormonism in particular are living historical phenomena.

To conclude by returning to the example of the Word of Wisdom: There is no rational account of the Word of Wisdom; no systematic theology will explain it adequately, neither its origin nor its practice. I might offer a provisional, rational explanation of why and how I observe that commandment, and my explanation could serve an apologetic or heuristic purpose, but that is the most that it could do. For example, I could say that, though the Word of Wisdom is not an ordinance, it is a formal practice of Latter-day Saints, a sign and reminder of my membership in the church. Since the scriptural text that establishes the Word of Wisdom says nothing about caffeine nor has the prophet made a declaration against caffeine, I can have a Coke if I wish, though coffee is forbidden. But the prophet could declare caffeine forbidden tomorrow. Even if he does not, I have no grounds for believing that my explanation of the commandment and my observation of it does any more than give me a way, for now, of understanding my own practice, a practice whose primary function is to testify of my being in the church, of my relation to God, to the church, and to fellow Latter-day Saints.

If I wish to explain the Word of Wisdom theologically, no way of doing theology is excluded, but some may be more useful than others. In particular, historical, narrative, and other hermeneutical theologies stand out as possibilities. But whatever theology I take up, like that which it seeks to explain, my theology must testify of Christ. The testimony inhering in revelation, Latter-day Saint practices and ordinances, and scripture must be part of any explanations of those revelations, practices, or scriptures or it will be untrue to them.

CHAPTER SIX

RETHINKING THEOLOGY:
THE SHADOW OF THE APOCALYPSE

According to the Gospels, one of the most frequently repeated of Jesus's messages during his earthly ministry was "The kingdom of God [or heaven] is at hand."[1] Indeed, early in his ministry Jesus describes preaching the kingdom of God, the reign of God, as his very message.[2] He does not announce that the kingdom *will* come near, but that it has already done so. As odd as it may sound to our ears, in the New Testament to preach the gospel is to preach the present nearness of the kingdom of God.

But the Lord does not only announce the nearness of his kingdom in the New Testament. He also announces it, indeed insists on it, in the Doctrine and Covenants, which opens with a call to all the world to hear his voice and a warning of destruction for those who do not (D&C 1:1, 4, 11–13). The second coming, the Apocalypse, begins with the restoration and it is figured in the lives of all who hearken to its call: "the Lord is nigh" (D&C 1:12; see also verses 35–36). To hear the gospel preached is to experience the nearness, both temporally and spatially, of the kingdom. It is to have an experience figured by the Apocalypse, the revelation of God's kingdom; the revelation of the kingdom of God to a person is figured by, is a type of, the revelation of

---

1. See, for example, Mark 1:15 and Matthew 10:7. The verb translated "is nigh" means, literally, "has come near": ἐγγίζω: to draw near in space or time. Walter Bauer, Frederick William Danker, W. F. Arndt, and F. W. Gingrich. *A Greek-English Dictionary of the New Testament and Other Early Christian Literature*, 3rd ed. (Chicago: University of Chicago Press, 2000).

2. Luke 4:43: "I must preach the kingdom of God to other cities also: for therefore am I sent."

his kingdom that will happen at the last day.[3] Thus, the revelation of the reign of God is not only something far away in time, something to be awaited, but something here and now. It happens in our lives when we become part of the kingdom of God. When that happens, the reign of God—his rule over us—has begun, a fact we signify when we agree to take his name on us (Moroni 4:3). In such an experience the Apocalypse does not so much refer to the end of the world, though it also refers to that, as it refers to the moment when the nearness of the kingdom of God is revealed to the believer and the believer's life is oriented by that kingdom rather than by the world. To hear the gospel preached is to experience a type or shadow of the Apocalypse, to "stand before the judgment seat of Christ" (Romans 14:10), not as a criminal, but as one freed. So the Apocalypse as the revelation of God's kingdom is not something to be feared, but to be hoped for, longed for.

The Book of Mormon uses the terms *type* and *shadow* as equivalents (Mosiah 13:10). We sometimes speak of figures and mean the same thing. Types, shadows, and figures are the things in the world by means of which we see the things of God. The various meanings of *type* (including a small block with a raised, reversed letter on it for printing; a kind; an exemplar, and a symbol) result from the fact that they share the same etymological origin: in Greek a *typos* is the mark of a blow or a stamp, an imprint.[4] If we see the world through religious eyes, we see the imprint of God's work in everything, as Paul sees Christ in Adam (Romans 5:14). And some things particularly bear that imprint. When I see my relation to my children as something to be shaped by the relation I have to my Father in Heaven, I see my fatherly work as a type of the work of the Father, as if what I do is a shadow cast by his work, as something figured or formed by him and what he does. So, when I understand what it means to be a father, I have a better understanding of who the Father is and what he does.

---

3. I rely here on the fact that the Greek word ἀποκαλύπτω, the root of *apocalypse*, means "to uncover, to disclose, or to reveal." Bauer and others, *A Greek-English Dictionary*, s.v. ἀποκαλύπτω.

4. Bauer and others, *A Greek-English Dictionary*, s.v. τύπος.

I see him through the things in the world because those things are "stamped," or figured by him. I know of no Book of Mormon term for what shows itself in the type or shadow, but the technical term is *antitype*, though I prefer the less common noun, *prefigure*.[5] When Christ's second coming, the prefigure, is fully revealed, the old world will end, the new reign of God will begin, and no one will be able to resist (Mosiah 27:31). The individual's encounter with the risen Lord is a figure of that second coming, for in each event the old world ends and a new world begins. Like Christ himself, whose beauty is not apparent, so that people do not see his desirability (Isaiah 53:2), the prefigure of his second coming remains invisible to most because they cannot see its figuration in the world. It remains invisible to all who have not encountered the Lord, whose experience of the world is not a figure, type, or shadow of his coming. Without the orientation to time and the world that is provided by entry into the kingdom one cannot see the things of the kingdom. Thus, seeing and hearing the announcement of Christ's coming and the nearness of his kingdom does not require that we acknowledge this, that, or another fact, but that we experience the world as God's kingdom. The experience of the nearness of the Apocalypse does not produce an answer to a question, but a response to a call. Of course, to have that experience will result in facts that one acknowledges, but the orientation and the experience which it engenders is fundamental rather than the facts.

Having read to his people from Isaiah's prophecy of Israel's eventual redemption, Jacob says:

> O then, my beloved brethren, come unto the Lord, the Holy One. . . . And whoso knocketh, to him will he open; and the wise, and the learned, and they that are rich, who are

---

5. In Greek, *antitypos* means "that which corresponds to something else" (Bauer and others, *A Greek-English Dictionary*, s.v. ἀντίτυπος). The type is the shape impressed in the soft wax. The antitype is that which has struck the wax, forming the impression. Cf. 1 Peter 3:21: "which [referring to the salvation of Noah's family in the ark] was a prefigure [*antitypos*] of baptism."

puffed up because of their learning, and their wisdom, and their riches—yea, they are they whom he despiseth; and save they shall cast these things away, and consider themselves fools before God, and come down in the depths of humility, he will not open unto them. But the things of the wise and the prudent shall be hid from them forever—yea, that happiness which is prepared for the saints. (2 Nephi 9:41–43)

Those who trust what their riches, learning, or worldly wisdom allow them to see will not be able to see the happiness prepared for the Saints. The results of the gospel are hidden from, invisible to, the merely learned; without the figured, typological experience of conversion we cannot see the truth of the gospel. Jacob's insight has been, I believe, shared by other thinkers. It is, for example, a variation of Augustine's admonition, "Believe that you may understand,"[6] which became Anselm's motto, "faith seeking understanding."[7] These thinkers agree that the understanding that the Christian seeks can only be achieved if he or she first has faith; without faith understanding will be blind.

As I understand the implications of Jacob's teaching for theology, they include that as long as theology remains merely a matter of learning we can see neither the gospel nor its teaching. The doctrine that the Messiah has come into the world and died so that all might come to him—meaning that we repent, are baptized, receive the Holy Ghost, and endure to the end (3 Nephi 27:13–16)—remains invisible

---

6. *Tractates on the Gospel of John* 29.6. Augustine was an adult convert to Christianity and lived in the fourth and fifth centuries AD. He became bishop of Hippo (in North Africa), and was highly influential in using philosophical ideas, particularly those of Plato, to understand Christianity. His most famous work is *Confessions*, perhaps the first autobiography, though he did not think of it as one.

7. As Anselm explains in the preface to *Proslogion*, that motto was the original title of his *Monologion*. Anselm was an eleventh-century Catholic theologian and thinker who was made archbishop of Canterbury in 1093, though he spent a good deal of his time as archbishop in exile because of church-king conflicts that foreshadowed those to come during the reign of Henry VIII.

if the gospel is merely a matter of learning.[8] However, as long as the Good News and God's kingdom are invisible in a Christian theology, it cannot really be talk about God. What we say may concern itself with his effects in this world or with our ideas and understanding of him. It may be about our doctrines, our understanding of his revelation: such a theology may say a good deal about those who espouse it. Theology may be about many things, but it is not about him if it does not reveal him, and it does not reveal him if it does not announce the nearness of his kingdom. In light of what Jacob tells us, theology must go beyond mere learning to allow the things of God to be opened or revealed to us. Our theology must be a figure of the Apocalypse, a theology that reveals God himself, even if only as a figure, rather than revealing only our understanding of him.

Chapter 4 addressed the question of how Latter-day Saint theology is possible. There I argued that the absence of official rational explanations or descriptions of beliefs and practices, and the presence of differing and inconsistent explanations for and descriptions of belief within the membership of the church, suggests that we have little if any official systematic, rational, or dogmatic theology. (I use those three terms, *systematic theology*, *rational theology*, and *dogmatic theology*, as synonyms.[9]) We are "a-theological"—which means that we are without a church-sanctioned, church-approved, or even

---

8. In scripture *the* doctrine is the preaching of the gospel described by Christ in 3 Nephi. The word *doctrines*, in the plural, is used exclusively to refer to false teachings. Louis Midgley, review of *Doctrinal Commentary on the Book of Mormon: Volume I, First and Second Nephi; Volume II, Jacob through Mosiah*, by Joseph Fielding McConkie and Robert L. Millet, *Review of Books on the Book of Mormon* 1/1 (1989): 92–113, especially p. 100. It seems that scripture generally understands doctrine to be the preaching of the gospel rather than a collection of beliefs.

9. As used in theology, *dogmatic* means "pertaining to doctrines/teachings," not "asserting . . . opinions in an authoritative, imperious, or arrogant manner." (*Oxford English Dictionary*, s.v. "dogmatic.") Though dogmatic and systematic theologies are not the same, the difference between them, namely the sanction of a church for the first but not the second, is irrelevant here, so I ignore it.

church-encouraged systematic theology—and that is as it should be because systematic theology is dangerous.[10]

I made my argument using three sub-arguments:

(1) *Continuing revelation is primary to Mormonism.* Since Latter-day Saints insist on continuing revelation, they cannot have a dogmatic theology that is any more than provisional and heuristic, for a theology claiming to be more than that could always be trumped by new revelation. Dogmatic theology, however, tempts us to think we have found something more since, as a rational system, it gives the appearance of being complete.

(2) *Practice or response is more important than belief, particularly explicated belief.* By focusing on belief rather than on practice, dogmatic theology poses a danger to true religion (see James 1:27), threatening to invert the relative importance of thought or belief, on the one hand, and practice, the acts of life in covenant relation, on the other, as it eventually did in the early church.[11]

(3) *Scripture is more important than rational explanation.* In addition to continuing revelation, the locus of explanation for Latter-day Saint belief is scripture. However, unlike rational/dogmatic theology as it is usually construed, but like prophetic revelation, scripture is testimony that questions us, thereby calling us to new life in Christ rather than to a set of rationally-ordered belief propositions to which we are asked to assent. In other words, dogmatic theology does not deal directly with the substance of religious faith: life *in* Christ rather than beliefs *about* Christ.

10. See chapter 5 in this volume.
11. In "Ritual as Theology and as Communication" (*Dialogue* 33/2 [2000]: 117–28), John L. Sorenson makes a case that for Latter-day Saints the ritual—a practice—is our most common theology. Needless to say, I find Sorenson's paper persuasive.

If my arguments are right, then systematic theology is dangerous, and it is not surprising that we find little official sanction for it in the church.

Of course, for Latter-day Saints, talk about God that reveals God—the best sense of the word *theology*—is, first of all, the revelations given through the prophets. We dare to say that God continues to reveal himself authoritatively to human beings through another human being. Unless one insists that all theology be systematically rational, and I know of no one who does, it makes sense to call prophetic revelation theology. Indeed, revelation is *the* Latter-day Saint theology. However, I believe that those Saints who have done theology in the nonrevelatory sense have, for the most part, done it systematically and rationally.[12] In the nineteenth and early twentieth century Orson Pratt and John A. Widtsoe come to mind, both in works that few today would find philosophically or scientifically acceptable.[13] Some, such as BYU's David Paulsen and the independent scholar Blake Ostler, do it today with interesting and well-respected results.

These kinds of thinkers see no difficulty in holding to two propositions, "Theology is the continuously revealed word of God" and "Theology is rational, dogmatic, or systematic theology." I do not know what either Paulsen or Ostler believes regarding the second of these claims,[14] though I assume that they accept the first as one meaning for the word *theology*. Regardless of their positions, however, based on more than thirty-five years of talking with other Latter-day Saints about theological questions, I believe that most of us who do theology or some informal version of it assume that God's knowledge is a systematic whole, and that he reveals parts of that whole

12. I ignore the fact that I think church history has been, for many Latter-day Saints, the place where our theology has been expressed. (See chapter 3 in this volume.) I do so because few, if any, church historians or other Saints have seen history as at the same time theological.

13. Some of Pratt's work is particularly flawed, but to my mind both Widtsoe and Pratt accept Newtonian science as if it were unquestionable, making each untenable.

14. Either of them, for example, could believe that systematic theology is merely one of several kinds of theology rather than either the fundamental or the only kind.

over time, gradually revealing more and more if it. If so, then those who think that way assume that, using the part of the whole that has been revealed so far, they can tentatively speculate as to the systematic whole that stands behind the part. However, as reasonable as that may seem, I think it is mistaken.

For one thing, to claim that our speculations are concerned with an eternal, rational system of truths that God reveals to us over time assumes that knowledge is fundamentally and essentially systematic and rational. In other words, it assumes that all knowledge is either self-evident,[15] incorrigible,[16] or a result of direct sense perception—or it can be rationally and systematically derived from those three kinds of knowledge. But much of twentieth-century philosophy, with work ranging from that of Martin Heidegger, to American pragmatism, to Alvin Plantinga, Nicholas Wolterstorff, and others in the analytic tradition of philosophy, has made that assumption about the character of knowledge dubious, each in different ways. It is questionable whether it makes sense to believe that there is an eternally existing set of systematically related fundamental truths expressed at least in part in our accurate understanding of things. Indeed, I believe that most who have dealt with the question carefully have concluded that the notion is rationally incoherent. But it does not follow from that rejection of an eternal, static realm of truth that is metaphysically prior to or beyond this world that there is neither truth, nor that there is no eternal truth. Indeed, the revealed truth that God is embodied and, so, within the cosmos in some way rather than metaphysically apart from it, suggests that the realm of truth is not metaphysically prior to the cosmos within which human beings find themselves. Instead the truth is part of the cosmos, perhaps as its happening. We can reject the Enlightenment formulation of truth (a formulation that continues to use the traditional God as its model even if it sometimes rejects

---

15. For example, axioms.

16. For example, my genuinely held beliefs about what I am currently, explicitly thinking.

his existence) without rejecting truth itself. However, the assumptions of modern rationalism and the Enlightenment have become so much part of our common sense that we may sometimes have to struggle to rethink them.

Thus, some forms of systematic theology that we find among Latter-day Saints are philosophically problematic and, whether a particular kind of systematic theology is entangled in those problems or not, it is dangerous. But the possible problems of systematic theology mean neither that systematic theology per se is impossible nor that those who do it sin. We need apocalyptic theology, to be sure—at least as continuing revelation—but apocalyptic theology is not a *kind* like "dogmatic theology" or "liturgical theology." A *kind* is a group of related objects, and apocalyptic theology is not in the same group as dogmatic, liturgical, or other ways of doing theology, for it is not a method for doing theology. Dogmatic and other kinds of theology are defined by their objects and methods. They differ by having differing objects and methods, but they are alike in that they are defined by their objects and methods. In contrast, apocalyptic theology is defined by what it does rather than by objects and methods; it is defined by its revelation of the nearness of the kingdom of God.

So I would supplement my previous argument: though rational, dogmatic theology may be dangerous, it too can be apocalyptic. Indeed, systematic theology has an important place in apologetics as well as in critical theology, for it explains our beliefs to others and helps us understand the limits of our claims about God. I doubt that we could argue against a systematic theology, such as Orson Pratt's, without doing systematic theology in response, and I think that Pratt's theology is ultimately philosophically incoherent. Making that claim requires doing at least a minimal level of systematic theology. Perhaps, as I believe, other kinds of theology are less likely to fail to be apocalyptic, but no theology is, in itself, incompatible with apocalyptic theology, and no theology can, in itself, avoid the dangers of theology.

How, then, does a theology avoid the heresy[17] of being nonapocalyptic, of making the gospel something I choose rather than something God gives? Theologizing by those who are not prophets may put
the kingdom at a distance by making talk about the gospel merely talk
about our own learning, but how does theologizing by nonprophets
avoid doing that and, at the same time, take seriously the proximity of
the kingdom, inviting us to enter it?[18]

With Jacob as our guide, as a first step toward understanding
what apocalyptic theology is, we could say that it opens a moment of
understanding and conversion, a moment on the way toward membership in the kingdom of God. Thus, we could recast the discussion
in these terms: Philosophy thinks being-in-the-world.[19] Theology
thinks being-in-the-world directed toward God. If we recast the discussion further, using the terms of apocalyptic theology we can say
that philosophy thinks being-in-the-world while apocalyptic theology
thinks being-in-the-world as a figure of the Apocalypse. The danger is
that the addendum, *directed toward God*, will cease to be the compass
of our thinking. When it does, our being-in-the-world is no longer a
type and shadow of the Apocalypse. The nearness of God's reign no
longer defines as a whole the movement of our life with others and
among things.

---

17. I depend here on the meaning of the Greek root, *hairetikos*, "to grasp," "to take for
oneself," "to choose." Bauer and others, *A Greek-English Dictionary*, s.v. αἱρετικός. That
which is truly heretical is that which we make for ourselves, taking the things of God as
if they were our property, to do with as we please.

18. I am, of course, using the word *prophet* here in its narrow sense, namely to refer
to those called and set apart as prophets. In its wider sense, "someone who genuinely
speaks the word of God," the term *prophetic theology* would mean the same as *apocalyptic
theology*.

19. This phrase comes from the work of the twentieth-century German philosopher
Martin Heidegger. He argued that our fundamental encounter with the world is not one
of a consciousness faced with something outside of or opposed to it. Rather, we are beings
who find ourselves already in a world of things and others, with projects to accomplish.
Reason, abstraction, explicit consciousness—these arise as part of and in response to our
initial situation in the world. "Being-in-the-world" describes that initial situation. (For
more on Heidegger, see chapter 2, note 62 in this volume.)

Of course, theology occurs in the world. However we theologize, whether with dogmatic theology or some other kind (hermeneutic, feminist, liberation, liturgical . . .), the challenge is to do it without succumbing to the unavoidable risk that theology turns in on itself, becoming a merely academic, only mental exercise that claims to refer to God but in which he does not make himself known and within which he does not call us to his kingdom because it is an exercise referring to our own ideas. But the alternative to that mistake is not a thinking that is outside of or beyond the world in some way, the thought of that which is absolutely other than this world—and given the Latter-day Saint belief in God's immanence in existence, his indwelling in existence, we ought not even to desire such supposed purity of thought. The challenge is not to think another world or to think other than the world. It is not to create a Platonic metaphysics. The challenge is to think our being-in-the-world differently, to think it as directed toward God by his self-revelation in the world. In other words, apocalyptic theology aims to remake the world of its hearers and readers by allowing the kingdom to be revealed.[20] An apocalyptic theology is one in which the theologian can see the "happiness which is prepared for the saints" in this world (2 Nephi 9:43).

The contemporary French philosopher-theologian Jean-Luc Marion makes a distinction that we can use to think further about the difference between apocalyptic and nonapocalyptic theology because it mirrors the distinctions of scripture. Marion writes of the "idol" and the "icon."[21] Begin with an icon: an icon reveals something other than itself, something divine. Apocalyptic theology as I am describing it is iconic. It reveals the nearness of the kingdom, its coming, something I can anticipate but which is not present. In contrast, with an idol I claim to produce something that re-presents, that makes manifest, the Divine. The idol creates the appearing of the god rather than merely

---

20. "Allowing" is essential. We cannot force or guarantee that the revelation will occur. We can only strive to make it possible.

21. See, in particular, Jean-Luc Marion, *The Idol and Distance: Five Studies* (New York: Fordham University Press, 2001).

creating a locus in which that appearing may happen. In creating an idol I have the audacity to claim to make the Divine appear, even if only in an image, a representation.[22] If *theology* means only "our talk about God," then it is idolatrous, for in it I use my powers of language to create an image or representation of God, violating the second of the Ten Commandments (Exodus 20:4–5; Deuteronomy 5:8–9). I walk in my own way and after the image of my own god, "whose image is in the likeness of the world, and whose substance is that of an idol" (D&C 1:16). I reveal myself—*my* ideas, *my* world, *my* perspective on God—in what I say; I do "autology" rather than theology. By contrast, in an icon the Divine reveals itself through something made by human beings (cf. D&C 1:17). As Christian theologians know (and not only Latter-day Saint Christian theologians), absent revelation theology is idolatry. In my terms, unless a theology is apocalyptic, it is idolatrous.

Marion's terminology helps us see more clearly something about theology that we have already glimpsed—namely, that the difference between the two ways of doing theology is not methodological. The difference between them is how they exist in our world, not what properties they have. Just as is true for any religious object, any theology can be idolatrous, and any theology can be iconic. There is probably no theology that is, in itself, apocalyptic; there is probably no theology that is completely blind to "the things of the wise and the prudent" (2 Nephi 9:43). However, if the essential difference between idolatrous and apocalyptic theology is neither their objects nor their methods, then how can we describe the latter? If the difference between the two is primarily their existential how, what can we say of that how? What happens in a theology in which God reveals himself, an apocalyptic theology, that does not happen in one in which we merely examine our ideas of God, in an idolatrous theology? In

22. See Clifford Ando, "Idols and Their Critics," in *How Should We Talk About Religion: Perspectives, Contexts, Particularities*, ed. James Boyd White (Notre Dame, IN: University of Notre Dame Press, 2006), 33–54. Ando does an excellent job of explaining how pagans could understand the physical idol not only to represent their gods, but actually to be their gods.

apocalyptic theology, whatever we do, what is most important is not what we do or what we say, but what happens to us and our audiences. The passivity of experience is more important than the activity of reason and will (which does not make reason, will, or content unimportant). What happens, what we experience, is the coming of the kingdom. We find ourselves in the kingdom of God—at least at its periphery—rather than in the dark and dreary world. The practice of psychoanalytic psychiatry, whatever one thinks of the merits of that practice, provides a good analogy to apocalyptic theology.[23] The traditional psychoanalytic therapist encourages the patient to talk, asking questions to encourage more talk and to give direction to the patient's talk. Whatever cure finally comes is the result of the patient talking in response to the psychiatrist's questions. Trying to deal with the therapist's questions and aporias (puzzling difficulties), and trying to say something coherent in response, the patient comes to see the world newly. It is not that the questions led directly to the patient's insight. It is not that the content of the patient's responses was the cure. Rather, trying to formulate coherent responses to the questions and aporias brought the patient to the point of seeing things differently. A new world was revealed to the patient—*in* the patient if the therapy is successful—as he went through the therapy of being questioned. Using terminology I used earlier, we could say that the patient has been reoriented in the world.

We can think of doing apocalyptic theology as something like that. An apocalyptic theologian puts himself or herself in the position of the psychoanalytic patient.[24] An apocalyptic theology, therefore, confronts us with questions and aporias, whether it does so explicitly or not. The questions may arise in us without being explicitly proposed

---

23. I am indebted to an online discussion with Joe Spencer, and others, particularly Adam Miller, for this analogy.

24. It is probably no coincidence that the word *therapist* comes from a Greek word that means, not "healer," but "servant" or "companion in arms." In Homer the *therapon* is the person who fights with one against a common enemy. Henry George Liddell and Robert Scott, comps., *A Greek English Lexicon* (1843; repr., Oxford: Clarendon, 1996), s.v. θεράπων.

by the theologian. They may come from the philosophical tradition as things for us to ponder. They may happen as we read scripture and find ourselves accused, as did David, "Thou art the man" (2 Samuel 12:7). Of course the questions have content, as do our answers. Without a particular content, the questions are meaningless. But the questions and answers are not the point. The point is what happens to us in dealing with those aporias: trying to respond to them coherently, we find ourselves reinterpreted, resituated in the world. We find ourselves in a world revealed by the Spirit and directed toward a God who makes himself known. In the aporias I experience the second coming, the nearness of the kingdom. I hear a call that obliges me to respond, and I respond with acceptance.

I recognize that many will find this way of thinking about theology difficult. I suspect that the difficulty is rooted in our tendency to think of religion as a set of beliefs, a tendency inherited from the Christian tradition. On this view, religion is a set of beliefs and theology examines that set of beliefs in some way. Those who understand theology in that way do not understand talk of apocalyptic theology because they cannot see more than one basic kind of theology, and in the kind they see religion is defined by belief. Of course religion as we understand it entails beliefs. It is problematic to say, "I am a Mormon, but I do not believe what Mormons believe." Beliefs certainly matter. Nevertheless, believing what Mormons believe is not enough to make one a Mormon, so examining beliefs is not enough to understand Mormonism. We can imagine someone who believes everything that most Mormons believe but is, in spite of that, not a member of the church. Why? Because that person has not yet been baptized. Even in religions that do not—as do we Latter-day Saints—insist on the necessity of ordinances, religion cannot be reduced merely to belief.[25] Especially in a religion for which priesthood is essential and ordinances are required, beliefs are not sufficient to define religion.

---

25. See chapter 8, especially p. 192, n. 76 in this volume.

The Lord commands ancient Israel, "Ye shall be holy ["set apart," "consecrated"]: for I the Lord your God am holy" (Leviticus 19:2). Similarly, during his ministry in Israel, he commands, "Be ye therefore perfect [or "whole"], even as your Father which is in heaven is perfect" (Matthew 5:48), and he repeats that command when he comes to the Nephites (3 Nephi 12:48). To be in Israel, ancient or modern, is not only to hold a set of beliefs, but to make and keep covenants with God. It is to enter into a formal relation with him in which we imitate him. For Latter-day Saints, covenant rather than belief is the heart of religion. It is probably true that no covenants fail to entail beliefs, but the important point is that religious beliefs do not matter if they are not intimately bound up with covenants. Apocalyptic theology evinces that intimate connection to covenant. It is not enough to say what we think about God. It is not enough even to say what we know. If a theology is apocalyptic, it must go beyond learning to the gospel, to the *revelation* of Christ. It must be not only about beliefs; it must also be testimony. For Latter-day Saints, apocalyptic theology must go beyond learning and even testimony to being part of covenant life, for we cannot reveal God by re-presenting him in an idol of some sort, but he reveals himself in our covenant life.

That we cannot reveal God, make an image of him, represent him conceptually, takes us back to a point in Jacob's sermon: theology is not only a matter of going beyond learning through testimony and covenant, though it is that. It is also a matter of remaining a fool before God in knowledge. The fool is not empty-headed merely because there is some fact he does not yet know.[26] To be a fool is to be silly in the old sense of that word;[27] it is to be weak, to be deficient in judgment and sense. It is to be nothing (and King Benjamin reminds us that salvation requires that we recognize our nothingness; Mosiah 4:5, 8–9, 11).

---

26. *Oxford English Dictionary*, s.v. "fool," from the Latin *follem*, "bellows"—so "one full of air," "an empty-headed person."

27. *Oxford English Dictionary*, s.v. "silly." The older meaning was "deserving compassion, defenseless," "weak," or "rustic."

Of course the silliness, deficiency, and nothingness of the foolishness recommended by Jacob are before God rather than human beings. Foolishness and humility before God do not require that we say and know nothing in our relations with others. Being dumbstruck before God is one kind of deficiency, but so are many kinds of speech. Neither does foolishness before God require that we have no confidence in what we say. Indeed, divine foolishness may be the ground of our confidence before other human beings.[28] Nevertheless, the necessity of foolishness and humility before God means that if our theology is to be apocalyptic, it must demonstrate its foolishness before God in some way. One person may do so by an explicit, sincere statement acknowledging the not only tentative but foolish character of her speculation. Another person may do it in a style that reveals his humility.[29] Surely there are also other ways. In addition, I think that some theological methods are more conducive to demonstrating godly foolishness, including hermeneutic and narrative theologies, because they make questioning and being questioned rather than claiming the center of their methods.

Sometimes nothing is so helpful as an example, and in philosophy sometimes nothing is so rare. Let me try, therefore, to give an example of theological thinking that I hope will show one way that theology can be apocalyptic, showing our foolishness as thinkers before God as well as the nearness of his kingdom. My example will be the problem of theodicy, and my thinking about that problem will rely heavily on the work of the twentieth-century French thinker Paul Ricoeur.[30]

---

28. D&C 121:45 suggests as much.

29. I take this to be characteristic of David Paulsen's work: students love his classes, not as much because of what he teaches as because of what he is when he teaches. In my day, David Yarn was a popular philosophy teacher for the same reason.

30. See, for example, Paul Ricoeur, *Le mal* (Geneva: Labor et Fides, 1996). To a lesser degree, I also depend on the work of Philippe Nemo, *Job and The Excess of Evil* (Pittsburgh: Duquesne University Press, 1998). Ricoeur (1913–2005) taught not only in France, but also at the University of Chicago for fifteen years (1970–1985). He was one of the most important French thinkers of the twentieth century.

As classically formulated, the problem of theodicy is the seeming impossibility of believing four propositions at the same time, four propositions that most religious people believe:

1. God is all-loving.
2. God is all-powerful.
3. God is all-knowing.
4. Evil exists.

The argument is that if God is all-loving, all-powerful, and all-knowing, then the existence of evil is inexplicable, for such a God *could* create a world without evil—he has the power and the knowledge to do so—and he *would* create it, for his love would require that he do so. According to the argument, therefore, the existence of God is incompatible with the existence of evil. For many, the suppressed conclusion is that it is irrational to believe in God if one recognizes the existence of evil, as most people do.

Notice, first of all, that neither the prophets nor scripture has given us these propositions as they are understood philosophically. These are philosophical interpretations of scriptural and prophetic statements, and we must not assume without question that the translation of prophetic discourse into philosophical discourse is innocent, retaining the meaning of the former in the latter without changing it or introducing something not in scripture. Every translation of one language into another risks changing the meaning of the original, so we must be wary of changes that this translation might have made, changes which we do not notice.

Theologians have responded to the problem of theodicy in a variety of ways. For example, some have denied the reality of evil.[31] Others have argued that the problem is set up so that it demands that God

---

31. David Ray Griffin argues that all theologians prior to the twentieth century disputed the existence of evil: *God, Power, and Evil* (Philadelphia: Westminster, 2004). I suspect that if he is right, they did so as a consequence of assuming creation *ex nihilo*. If God created the world from absolutely nothing, then one can argue that either evil is not real or he created it. Latter-day Saints avoid that dilemma by not believing that the world was created *ex nihilo*.

do what is logically contradictory. That means that the problem itself is faulty. For example, one might argue that, by definition, embodied beings are necessarily passive as well as active, for they can be acted on: to be embodied is to be able to be affected. In technical terms, it is to be *pathetic* in the root sense of that word: to have things happen to one.[32] But to be pathetic is to suffer in the broad sense of the word: "to be affected."[33] If an argument from the nature of embodiment were successful, it would show that it is logically contradictory to create a world without creating suffering. Perhaps one could argue that if there is suffering in the broad sense, then it is impossible to avoid evil, suffering in the narrow sense, as well. If so, then it seems that the three characteristics describing God could continue to be held without contradicting the claim that evil exists. That is because the contradiction between God's character and the existence of evil is derived only if one supposes that God logically could create embodied beings that are not affected, and that supposition may involve contradiction.

Another tack is to take up the problem of theodicy in terms of the quantity of suffering: "Why didn't God create the world with less suffering in it than he did?" Most answers to this question accord with Leibniz's answer in some way: this is the best of all possible worlds; if there were more or less evil in the world, the world would be defective. The problem is that, by asserting that the way we find the world is, inexplicably, the way things must be, Leibniz's answer runs the risk of denying the evil of evil. If I say that the evil of the world is a necessity, then I no longer call it evil. At best, perhaps I express my lack of understanding; at worst, I acquiesce to or become complicit in its presence, implicitly assuming it to be a good in that it is necessary. The only answer of this sort that does not go in the direction of denying evil is one that goes in the direction of faith: though we cannot explain the degree of suffering we see in the world, we have to trust God as

---

32. The Greek word *pathos* from which our word "pathetic" is derived means "that which happens to a person." Liddell and Scott, *Greek-English Lexicon*, s.v. πάθος.

33. For our purposes, suffering is not best defined as "feeling pain" because feeling pain is a species of suffering, of being affected.

we confront that suffering. Of course, to say that I do and must trust God is not to answer the question, "Why isn't there less suffering in the world?" It is to deny that there is an answer for us. This may be the best of all possible worlds, but the claim that it is requires an incredible amount of optimism, an optimism explicable only on the basis of faith and, so, an optimism that begs the question.

There is yet another way of understanding the problem itself to be the problem: As usually set forth, the problem of theodicy assumes that God's power is essential to his being; the claim that God is omnipotent is crucial to the problem. That may sound reasonable at first, but it is questionable. Latter-day Saints are hardly alone in seeing in God, not power, but a kind of powerlessness, namely the holding back, allowing, suffering, persuasion, charity, gentleness, and absence of compulsion that is described so eloquently in Doctrine and Covenants 121:41–46 and that informs much of the scripture that we share with other Christians.[34] That seeming—but my mind only seeming—limitation of power appears to be correlate with God's power to save, perhaps the only power essential to his divinity. I take it that this way of understanding his power is among the reasons why the scriptures show us a very human God rather than an omnipotent one: After dinner, Abraham walks with God's messengers and perhaps with God himself, showing them the way to Sodom, and God bargains with Abraham over the fate of those who live there (Genesis 18). It is one thing to speak of God as all-powerful when we praise him and to mean what we say when we do. It is another to assume that our praise can be parsed directly into logical propositions that we can use to solve theological conundra such as the problem of theodicy. Whatever the case for dogmatic or rational theology, scriptural assertions of God's power are enriched and, therefore, complicated by instances in which his power is limited and, even more, by the importance he puts on his patience, persuasion, and love.

---

34. Modernism's definition of knowledge as power rather than relation (charity) puts modernism at odds with religion from the beginning. The solution is to rethink the intellectual and other advantages bequeathed us in modernism in terms of charity rather than in terms of power. See the discussion of knowledge as power in chapter 1 in this volume.

Still another way a Christian might respond to the problem of theodicy is to object to the question it asks. It would not be unreasonable for a Christian to argue that since even Christ suffered on the cross, with suffering incomparable to any of our own, we have no right to ask why we suffer. To do so is impertinent, perhaps impertinent to the point of blasphemy. To complain about my suffering when faced with the suffering of Jesus Christ is, implicitly, to deny the gravity and effect of his suffering. I have no right to ask why I suffer. Here is another way to put the same point: If Jesus Christ asked the question of God's justice while on the cross—"My God, my God, why hast thou forsaken me?" (Matthew 27:46; Mark 15:34)—we have no right to think that we can avoid the same question. And if he did not receive an answer in mortality, we have no reason to think that we can.

But thinking about the problem of evil need not be a complaint about my suffering. It could be a question about the suffering of others. As the name we have given to the problem suggests, our question is about God's justice as a whole, including his dealings with others. The question is not only a personal complaint, and the scriptures themselves show prophets from Abraham to Joseph Smith sometimes questioning God's justice. In fact, it is not unreasonable to construe their ability to question God's justice as a sign of their righteousness before God. Abraham's bargain with God over Sodom occurs immediately after the Lord has described him as someone who "will command his children . . . to do justice and judgment" (Genesis 18:19). Thus the Christian argument puts me in my place, but it does not dissipate the question of theodicy, for as a general question rather than a complaint, the question may be rooted in Christ-like compassion for our fellows rather than in a demand for a justification of my suffering.

My intuition as a philosophy teacher of Latter-day Saint students is that most Mormons who have tackled the problem have done so by reformulating the second proposition of its traditional formulation, namely that God is all-powerful. They do so by redefining what it means to be all-powerful in such a way that the paradox will disappear. That solution neatly dissolves the problem, but many Saints are uncomfortable with the limitation that the solution puts on God's power.

I have described a few of the ways of dealing with the problem of evil. There are any number of others, but I believe we see a pattern here. When we deal with the problem of theodicy, we often, perhaps always, find ourselves at an impasse that requires us either to give up, to reformulate the question, or to show how the problem is itself problematic; and even when we do seem to have dissolved the problem, it reappears soon afterward in some new form. But behind that impasse is a perhaps surprising assumption. If I look at the problem, its solutions, and its problems with a merely theological eye, I find in it the attempt to represent rationally a god who is God and also allows the evil we encounter. I create a god in my own image, a rational representation of God (an idol), and then I try to resolve—to dissolve—the problem of evil; I try to make it go away. I commit idolatry. Then I pretend that the enemy of God is either illusory or not really an enemy.

There is, however, another way to think about the problem, namely as a problem that makes things more difficult, a problem that will not go away. We may not be able to answer the philosophical problem. But the problem of evil will continue to call for our response—and dealing with the philosophical problem, whether with a solution or not, may be an obstacle to responding to the call. Though the problem of theodicy can be a legitimate topic of philosophical and theological thought, and philosophical and theological thought can be legitimate pursuits, even apocalyptic ones, seeing the problem of theodicy as one that makes thinking more difficult rather than as a problem to be dissolved tends toward apocalyptic theology.

Notice that the Christian talks about the problem of evil differently than does the philosopher. This difference is not just a matter of taste or style. It has everything to do with the difference between what each kind of discourse does. Sometimes we treat scripture and revelation as if they were simplified scientific explanations of things or poetic philosophizing, but I think that is a mistake, and sometimes a serious one. For it assumes that the rationality characteristic of science is the measure of all discourse. Though religious discourse may offer us explanations, its purpose is not explanatory, but soteriological: It is concerned, not with telling us how the world and the things in the world are (at least not in the way that science and philosophy do),[35] but with telling us about God's power to save and how we can be saved. Religious discourse calls for our repentance and good works rather than our rational reflection. It is not that the two are incompatible, but that religious discourse does something different than does the discourse of science and philosophy. Given its purposes, revelation ignores the problem of theodicy—which, since theodicy is a philosophical/theological problem rather than a religious one, is not the same as ignoring the problem we face in reconciling the evil we encounter with our faith in God.

That religion ignores the problem is deeply suggestive. Of course revelation is not blind to suffering.[36] Christian revelation often reminds us that we must be deeply concerned with suffering, especially with the suffering of others and with our own spiritual suffering. God wills neither and he offers answers to both. But Christian concern is with the proper, Christ-like response to that suffering, not with explaining its logical compatibility with God's existence. One can even imagine a Christian arguing that, as a speculative rather than a practical problem, the problem of theodicy distracts us from the existential problem.

Obviously I am sympathetic to the charge that the philosophical problem of evil and suffering is a distraction. However, since concern for the philosophical problem can be a concern for justice, it is not enough

---

35. And its explanations are not scientific, not even in a primitive way. For a discussion of the difference between religious thinking and scientific, see chapter 3 in this volume. For a discussion of how I understand scripture and, therefore, religious discourse, see chapter 8 in this volume.

36. Christ's healing miracles were not incidental to his mission. Indeed, in Jesus's first sermon he identifies himself as the one appointed "to heal the broken-hearted, to preach deliverance to the captives, and recovering of sight to the blind" (Luke 4:18; cf. Isaiah 61:1).

to ignore that problem as a distraction. My sympathy does not extend to agreement. Nevertheless, even if the problem of evil is not merely a distraction, it is also not a purely philosophical, theoretical problem. In the end, it *is* a problem for action, and philosophical speculation has little place among the actions required when we respond concretely to suffering and evil. At the second coming not only will every knee bow and every tongue confess, but also the lame and the halt will be cured.[37] Confession and cure show themselves in the type and shadow of our concrete responses to suffering rather than in rational speculation. They show themselves in the confession we make and the succor we offer in a world remade by our encounter with God.

Of course, it does not follow that careful thought is irrelevant or unnecessary, and by "careful thought" I am not just referring to the planning we must do to make our actions fruitful. Careful thought may include the rigorous analyses of rational philosophy. Philosophy does many things. It has many purposes, including the pleasure of philosophy, a good that does not require that I justify it by showing how it leads to some other good. But among its other purposes is that of showing us the limits of reason. When we think of philosophers who are concerned with the limits of reason, perhaps we most often first think of Immanuel Kant and the first critique. Kant says that knowing the limits of pure reason will remove obstacles that stand in the way of practical reason[38] and will make it possible to take morality and religion seriously.[39] But Kant was neither the first nor the last philosopher to think that we needed to consider the limits of reason. In fact, thinkers whose goal it is to make things difficult—Kierkegaard and Nietzsche come to mind—generally do so as a means of showing the limits of reason.

---

37. See Mosiah 3:5, where we see the first coming as a figure of the second. See also such passages as Jeremiah 30:17 and Alma 41:4.

38. Immanuel Kant, *Critique of Pure Reason*, trans. Norman K. Smith (New York: St. Martin's Press, 1929), Bxxv.

39. Kant, *Critique of Pure Reason*, Bxxx–xxxi.

In the fifth century, Pseudo-Dionysius gave us negative theology, not to demonstrate that we cannot have faith nor to attack religion, but to show us the limits of reason when reason tries to talk about God. He believed that by opposing negative theology to affirmative theology, a third way will show itself to us, the way of revelation.[40] Pseudo-Dionysius explicitly wanted to do apocalyptic theology and saw negative theology as a means for doing so. Others, such as Maimonides, have taken a similar approach. As I read Kierkegaard, though he does not do negative theology, he does show us the limits of reason by making it less philosophically clear how to understand what it means to be a Christian. For example, his claim in *Fear and Trembling* that Abraham can only be understood by means of the absurd is a claim that we *can* understand Abraham, but not philosophically.[41] Similarly, we can understand the problem of theodicy as demonstrating the limit of reason confronted by evil. We, therefore, can see the problem as an aid to foolishness, reminding us of God's greatness and our own nothingness.

However, to see the problem as demonstrating the limits of reason is not to reject reason. We can neither reject nor avoid it. We ought not to wish to do so. For reason not only helps us find solutions to problems, it sometimes sharpens the problem. I think the long history of the problem of theodicy is sufficient evidence that we are unlikely to find a solution that puts an end to that problem once and for all. The merely theological response is to take up the question of theodicy as a free-floating philosophical problem, but if we take it up, the most we can gain from it is the pleasure of philosophical thought. Few who are religious can deal with this issue only for its philosophical pleasure. The apocalyptic alternative is that the problem is a philosophical goad, a spur, an itch that will not go away, for it challenges our faith even when it points to the need for faith. Every call invites a response, and

---

40. For one of the best brief explanations of the thought of the fifth- and sixth-century thinker, Pseudo-Dionysius (also called simply "Denys"), see Jean-Luc Marion, *In Excess: Studies of Saturated Phenomena*, trans. Robyn Horner and Vincent Berraud (New York: Fordham University Press, 2002), 134–39, 145–48.

41. See chapter 1 in this volume.

in doing so it disturbs the status quo.[42] The problem of theodicy calls to us, challenging our faith and, by doing so, inviting us to respond. It invites us to see the world as still awaiting the second coming even if we live in a world that has been figured by the presence of Christ.

For some, faith fails in the face of that challenge by the problem of theodicy, but not for most. Most of us continue to believe even as we struggle with the problem. In fact, we struggle with the problem *because* we believe. We struggle only because we have faith. If we find the problem of theodicy to be a real problem rather than only an intellectual game, that is evidence that we have faith. Thus, by continuing to be a problem—by the fact that we seem unable to find any solution to the problem of theodicy that does not merely shift it some place else where it reappears in a new and slightly different guise—the problem of theodicy shows us the necessity of trust as well as the limits of reason. The problem of evil and suffering is intractable to our powers of reason. As believers we find ourselves foolish before it. Ultimately the only thing to which it is tractable is moral and faithful response: action.

Thus, the intractability of the problem of theodicy can be positive in Christian life rather than merely negative. First, it can continue to serve as a goad. That it is intractable can continue to remind us that evil and suffering are real and that they require our response. Second, the rational difficulty of the problem can provide an impetus for recognizing that faith is prior to reason.[43] To paraphrase something that Heidegger said of theology and that Kierkegaard could have said, the problem of theodicy may only render faith more difficult—that is, render it more certain that faithfulness cannot be gained through reason, but only through faith.[44] So, the problem of theodicy continues to be important to believers for two reasons: because it points to the ground

---

42. Jean-Louis Chrétien, *L'Appele et le Reponse* (Paris: Les Éditions de Minuet, 1992), 20.

43. Notice that I do not think faith is opposed to reason. I am not a fideist.

44. Heidegger, "Phenomenology and Theology," trans. James G. Hart and John C. Maraldo, in *Pathmarks*, ed. William McNeill (Cambridge: Cambridge University Press, 1998), 39–62, especially p. 46.

of our belief by showing a limit of reason, and because it reminds us that we must not neglect to respond to evil and suffering as Christian faith calls us to respond.[45] When the problem of theodicy does these things for us, we find ourselves not only awaiting but expecting the coming of Christ and seeing his nearness. When it does these things, it is apocalyptic.

In the end, therefore, the difficulty with merely philosophical or theological answers to the problem of theodicy is that every one of them looks for a way to integrate evil into our understanding of the world. To understand something is to understand how it fits with the other things that we understand, how they make sense together, as a whole. But it is evil to integrate evil into our understanding, to make sense of it and make it part of the wholeness of our existence. It is evil to do so precisely because evil *cannot* be made sense of, cannot be justified. It is evil to explain evil, to tame it, no longer to be horrified by it. If evil ceases to be horrible, but instead makes sense, then we cease to struggle with it. The shadow of the apocalypse is concrete struggle with evil, not abstract thought about it, which may well be relevant but is never enough. Our horror in response to transcendent evil is one with our eschatological hope for the good of the kingdom that is to come, and that hope makes no sense apart from the fight against evil. Only if the problem of theodicy is genuinely a problem—only if all solutions ultimately fail in this world without the Apocalypse, the Revelation of Jesus Christ—can we continue to know that evil is genuinely evil.

I hope it is not too much of a conceit to suggest that thinking philosophically about the problem of theodicy has a relation to the struggle for justice that is similar to the relation of prayer to that struggle: for the apocalyptic Christian theologian, the problem of theodicy is a kind of prayer.[46] To pray is to turn oneself toward God in response to his call.

---

45. Though this is not the place to explore the question, it may be that these two things are really one.

46. For a discussion of the phenomenology of prayer, see Jean-Louis Chrétien, "The Wounded Word," in *Phenomenology and the "Theological Turn": The French Debate* (New York: Fordham University Press, 2000), 147–75. Chrétien pays insufficient attention to

The believer who approaches the problem of theodicy also turns toward God, responding to the question of God's justice as to a question and a call: the question of his or her justice, the call to do good. At the same time, because that person's intellectual powers fail in responding to the call, the believer recognizes her own weakness, her own foolishness, a recognition requisite to prayer. And as every prayer ought, in responding to the problem of theodicy, the believer praises God's goodness, wisdom, power, and sovereignty, and prays for his kingdom to come—for the Apocalypse (Matthew 6:9–10, 13). Those are, after all, the divine attributes which give rise to the question that calls us to respond. Without those divine attributes, there is no problem of evil, only evil. Without the promise of the Apocalypse, there is no answer to the problem, only intellectual confusion and continued evil.

Finally, as is also true of prayer, to deal with the problem of theodicy is to be concerned for others beside oneself. Just as I always pray in community with others who pray, even when I pray only for myself—"our Father" rather than "my Father" in the Lord's Prayer (Matthew 6:9)—the problem of theodicy is a concern for others as well as myself. When thought apocalyptically, prayer and thinking come together in the problem of theodicy, and because it continues to remain a problem, the problem of theodicy can allow us to continue the prayerful thought of belief and a believing awareness of the nearness of the kingdom of God.

Theology is possible that, in responding to God's call, demonstrates our foolishness before God, praises God, and opens the possibility of seeing the world anew by seeing the nearness of God's kingdom (covenant life with others) both in time and space. Some theologies are better at doing that than others. As I have said, I believe that hermeneutic and narrative theologies—to which I would add liturgical, ritual, scriptural, and pastoral or practical theologies, as well perhaps as a theology modeled on what some Protestants call canonical theology

the fact that much prayer is petitionary and that the believer hopes that the requests of his petitions will be granted, but in spite of that his description of prayer is very helpful.

(without the forced assumption of scriptural inerrancy)[47]—are more likely to be apocalyptic.

However, ultimately the question of whether our theologies are, on the one hand, merely theology and, therefore, idolatrous or, on the other hand, apocalyptic is not a methodological question. It is a question of character and spirit—our own, our audience's. That is why, though some theologies may be more amenable to idolatry than others, none are immune to it. As human beings, we are not immune to it. Whether a theology is apocalyptic depends on what the theologian does and the experience of his or her audience, not on the content of what the theologian says nor on the method the theologian uses. Understanding the difference between theology *simpliciter* and apocalyptic theology brings us to understand that the danger of theology is ultimately the danger of human character: we may believe that the theological work we do is directed toward God—and be wrong; we may be right that it is, but our audience may fail to take it up as the apocalyptic theology that it is for us. The attempt to do apocalyptic theology can go wrong in many ways, all of them ways in which *we* are wrong.

It does not follow that we ought to avoid all theology. Rather, it follows that we ought not to do theology unaware of the danger of failure, of the danger that our theology may be a species of idolatry. Apocalyptic theology should be our goal, but idolatrous theology is its ever-present danger. If we do theology, whatever other reasons we have—and there are other good reasons—we must do it to announce "the Lord is nigh" (D&C 1:12) and to proclaim the revelations of the restoration (D&C 1:18), remaining weak, simple (D&C 1:23), and prayerful,[48] yet confident in the presence of God that figures our lives (D&C 121:45).

---

47. Canonical theology is a theology of the canon, of scripture. It seeks to understand the scriptures in their own terms rather than as documents to be deciphered as merely historical or so as to conform to some implied, preexisting theology. I would use, instead, the term *scriptural theology*.

48. Matthew 7:7: "Ask, and it shall be given you; seek, and ye shall find; knock, and it shall be opened unto you." This and its variations appear over and over again in scripture. In Alma 33, Alma particularly emphasizes the importance of prayer to faith, as does Amulek in Alma 34.

CHAPTER SEVEN

THE WRITINGS OF ZION

～

L et me hold in abeyance for a bit the question of what I mean by *the writings* in order to think a little about the word *Zion*. And let me begin that discussion by citing a few texts (perhaps promiscuously) and saying a few things about each of them that will, together, constitute a little story about Zion.

Begin with Doctrine and Covenants 82:14: "Zion must increase in beauty, and in holiness; . . . Zion must arise and put on her beautiful garments." For Zion, the beautiful and the holy are of a piece, so the way to holiness is the way of beauty: as we become beautiful, we also become holy, and vice versa. Indeed, the possible reversal of those—"as we become holy, we also become beautiful"—says a great deal about what *beauty* means.

In Exodus, the Lord tells Israel that the way of beauty is also that of language, of hearing: "If ye will hearken to my voice indeed, and keep my covenant, then ye shall be a special treasure unto me above all people: for all the earth is mine. And ye shall be unto me a kingdom of priests, and an holy nation" (Exodus 19:5–6; translation revised). Being Zion, the holy nation of God, being a kingdom of priests and priestesses, means hearing the voice of God. And what do we hear in that voice? Latter-day revelation answers the question:

[We hear] a voice of gladness! A voice of mercy from heaven; and a voice of truth out of the earth; glad tidings for the dead; a voice of gladness for the living and the dead; glad tidings of great joy. How beautiful upon the mountains are the feet of those that bring glad tidings of good things, and that say unto Zion: Behold, thy God reigneth! As the dews of Carmel, so shall the knowledge of God descend upon them! (D&C 128:19)

If we truly hear the gospel, our hearing is hearkening, and the voice to which we hearken is a voice of gladness, mercy, truth, glad tidings for the living and the dead, a voice of great joy. We hear the announcement of the coming reign of God. To hear that voice is to have the knowledge of God descend on us. To hearken to the word is to know God, and to know him is to be given and to receive gladness, truth, and joy.

When we hearken to God and know him gladly, truthfully, joyfully, we live in a new creation. Through Isaiah he says: "I have put my words in thy mouth . . . that I may plant the heavens and lay the foundations of the earth, and say unto Zion: Behold, thou art my people" (Isaiah 51:16; 2 Nephi 8:16). Giving us his words to speak is the means by which God creates a new world, one other than the world which we call "the world." His words are that by which he calls us to be his people, the people to inhabit that new world. But this new world is not something that we can merely await. We are commanded in several revelations of the Doctrine and Covenants: "Seek to bring forth and establish the cause of Zion" (D&C 6:6, 11:6, 12:6; cf. 14:6). Presumably, the work of interpretation, of understanding, is part of what bringing forth and establishing Zion requires.

Latter-day scripture also tells us in several places what Zion is when established. It is purity of heart: "Let Zion rejoice, for this is Zion—the pure in heart" (D&C 97:21). It is unity of heart and mind: "The Lord called his people Zion, because they were of one heart and one mind" (Moses 7:18). It is, therefore, also the vision of God and the coming of his kingdom: "Blessed are the pure in heart, for they shall see God" (Matthew 5:8; 3 Nephi 12:8). And: "Blessed are the poor who are pure in heart, whose hearts are broken, and whose spirits are contrite, for they shall see the kingdom of God coming in power and great glory unto their deliverance" (D&C 56:18). Purity of heart means unity of heart and mind. It means having a broken heart and a contrite spirit. And it results in seeing God's kingdom come in power and glory to deliver us from our poverty, both spiritual and physical—in this life.[1]

That purity and unity of broken heart and contrite spirit, delivering us from our impoverishment, means the fulfillment of the covenants of the Father with our fathers and with us. That purity and unity and richness in covenant is the beauty of Zion:

> Awake, and arise from the dust, O Jerusalem; yea, and put on thy beautiful garments, O daughter of Zion; and strengthen thy stakes and enlarge thy borders forever, that thou mayest no more be confounded, that the covenants of the Eternal Father which he hath made unto thee, O house of Israel, may be fulfilled. (Moroni 10:31; cf. Isaiah 52:1, 2 Nephi 8:24)

The story of Zion is the story of becoming beautiful.

Like any good Aristotelian story, it has a beginning, a middle, and an end. It begins with God speaking to us, moves to our hearing his words of gladness, truth, and joy, and ends in the new world of Zion, a world of unity, humility, and covenant as well as a world of power, glory, and deliverance. It ends with the holy reign of God in which all things are beautiful.

My thesis is that the revelatory writings of the church, especially, but not only the canonized scriptures, mean in such a way that they call us to join Zion, that they, in words of gladness, truth, and joy, call us to the beauty of unity and humility, of power, glory, and deliverance in the kingdom of God. They call us to covenant with God and each other. Of course their content is important. Without that content, they could not call us to repentance or to covenant. But what is most important is that they call to us.

---

1. See chapter 6 in this volume for a discussion of the coming of God's kingdom in this life.

But how do they do so? Since Spinoza, the most common answer to how scripture means has been that it does so in the same way as any other book. Of course there are ways in which that must be true, however books mean. But scripture isn't just "another book." It is revelation. Scripture is a text in which God reveals himself to us, and not just any text does that. Like the law of Moses, scripture points our souls to Christ (Jacob 4:5), also something that other texts do not do. Therefore, we cannot read scripture or any other revealed text in quite the same way that we read another book, for to do so is to ignore the holiness that it reveals and calls for.

However, if revealed writings do not mean as other writings do, then how *do* they mean?[2] For at least a couple of hundred years, many religious people have felt that the best response they could give to that question was, "They mean what they say literally, except when they obviously mean something more poetic," an explanation at which we may smile because of its circularity, but a common explanation nonetheless. It is common, I believe, because there is an important sense in which it is true. Nevertheless, that answer has created problems for thinking about the meaning of scripture. I believe that most of those problems stem from the fact that literalists as well as those whose work would undermine the literal historicity of scripture share an important assumption. They assume that "the most primitive meaning of a text is its only valid meaning"[3] or, at least, its most important meaning. Notoriously those in the self-importantly named Jesus Seminar have spent hours combing the New Testament texts, parsing words and phrases and what we think we know of history trying to discover the primitive meaning of the New Testament, the authentic sayings of Jesus as opposed to those which were supposedly invented

---

2. I address the issue of how scripture means more fully in chapter 8. This is an overview of the argument I make there.

3. David C Steinmetz, "The Superiority of Pre-Critical Exegesis," in *The Theological Interpretation of Scripture: Classic and Contemporary Readings*, ed. Stephen E. Fowl (Oxford: Blackwell, 1997), 26–38, especially p. 27.

by admiring disciples.[4] The biblical literalists disagree vehemently with the Jesus Seminar about what is primitive meaning and what is not. In spite of that, and it seems with neither of them having reflected on the fact, the two groups agree exactly with the insistence that the primitive meaning determines scripture's meaning.

That assumption is problematic, however, because, as the Book of Mormon demonstrates, a text is scriptural precisely because the primitivist assumption about meaning is not true. In 2 Nephi 11:2, Nephi says that he will liken the words of Isaiah to his people—even though he knows that Isaiah's words were not originally about the Lehites (see 1 Nephi 19:23; 2 Nephi 6:5, 11:8). The primitive meaning—what Isaiah's words meant for Israel when Isaiah first delivered them—is more or less irrelevant to the Lehites, but Nephi can liken the words of Isaiah to them nevertheless. Isaiah is scripturally meaningful to the people of Lehi, apart from its primitive meaning. The likening of scripture to people did not privilege its primitive meaning.

Second Nephi 6:5—"There are many things spoken by Isaiah which may be likened unto you, because ye are of the house of Israel"—might be taken to suggest that Isaiah could be likened to the Nephites because they and Israel share a common history and heritage or because the responsibilities and blessings of Israel are also theirs. However, as 2 Nephi 11:8 tells us, the words of Isaiah may be likened "unto *all* men." The interpretation of scripture that we see modeled in Nephi's reading of Isaiah is interpretation by likening, and scripture can be likened to all people.[5]

In Isaiah, the word *liken* and its cognates, such as *like*, usually translates some form of the Hebrew verb *dmh*, meaning "to share the

4. The participants in the Jesus Seminar recognize the challenge that their work presents to ordinary belief. Its founder, Robert Funk, said in his address to the first meeting of the Seminar, "We will be asking a question that borders the sacred, that even abuts blasphemy, for many in our society." Jesus Seminar home page: www.westarinstitute.org/Jesus_Seminar/jesus_seminar.html (accessed 9 March 2008).

5. I find it informative that Nephi explicitly avoids teaching his people the culture of the Jews. Evidently language, culture, and context are not always necessary for likening the scriptures. See 2 Nephi 25:2.

same attributes," as in Isaiah 14:14.[6] Using this verb, something that is like something else does not only look like that which it is like. Perhaps it does not at all look like what it is like. Indeed as Thorlief Boman reminds us, "In the historical and presumptively historical writings it is never reported how a person looked"[7] nor are biblical writers particularly interested in giving a visual description of the things they see.[8] The Isaiah sermon—which mocks the king of Babylon (sarcastically calling him "Lucifer," "Morning Star"[9]) and his pretensions of being like God—shows us that the verb *liken* means "to *be* like something else." Nephi is comparing a way of being that we find portrayed in Isaiah with the way of being of the Nephites, and not to compliment them.[10]

As Nephi suggests, the argument about the meaning of Isaiah for the Lehites is expandable: The scriptures as a whole are meaningful to *us* only because their primitive meaning is not determinative. Scripture is God's revelation to us, now, as well as to its original hearers. Its meaning, therefore, must go beyond the particular ideas and settings

---

6. G. Johannes Botterweck and Helmer Ringgren, eds., *Theological Dictionary of the Old Testament*, vol. 3, trans. John T. Willis, Geoffrey Bromiley, and David Green (Grand Rapids: Eerdmans, 1978), s.v. דמה. Interestingly, the verb can also mean "to think" or "to plan," as in Isaiah 10:7.

7. Thorlief Boman, *Hebrew Thought Compared with Greek* (New York: Norton, 1954; rev. ed., 1960), 76.

8. Boman, *Hebrew Thought Compared with Greek*, 74–76.

9. Isaiah 14:12. The Hebrew word translated "Lucifer" in the King James translation is *hêlēl* (הילל), and means "shining one" but can imply boastfulness. Francis Brown, S. R. Driver, and Charles A. Briggs, *Hebrew and English Lexicon* (Oxford: Clarendon, 1951), s.v. הילל. The name *Lucifer* means "shining one," but has Latin rather than Hebrew roots.

10. Of course we cannot be sure what the original word was that Joseph Smith translated *liken* in 1 and 2 Nephi, for though we know that Nephi was writing in reformed Egyptian (Mormon 9:32), we do not know whether that describes the characters he was using to write in Hebrew or the language in which he was writing. Nevertheless, since Nephi is an immigrant from Israel, the chances are that he and his people still speak some variant of Hebrew, particularly since he is reading and transmitting the work of Isaiah, and it is likely (though not necessary) that he wrote in the language that he spoke. With caution, we can assume that the underlying language was Hebrew. See Royal Skousen, "The Original Language of the Book of Mormon: Upstate New York Dialect, King James English, or Hebrew?" *Journal of Book of Mormon Studies* 3/1 (1994): 28–38, especially p. 38.

of the original writer. However inspired he was, he did not—could not—see all the ways in which the scriptures can be likened to each of our lives in particular. He did not see all the meaning implicate in his writing. However, he did not need to. All he needed to do was record the defective way of being of Israel (as well the possibility of its being otherwise), for we could then understand our own being as a type and a shadow of what the Lord has revealed through Israel. Just as it was for the children of Lehi, to liken scripture to ourselves is to compare the way of being that it reveals with our own way of being.

As revelations of God's interaction with his people, the scriptures come to us as a call, a call to consider another way of being than that we currently inhabit, in other words, a call to repentance. By opening a new range of possible meanings, scripture outlines an alternative way of being-in-the-world, to use the philosophical language of Martin Heidegger, Hans-Georg Gadamer, and Paul Ricoeur, a way of being-in-the-world in which God has revealed and continues to reveal himself, a way in which his self-revelation calls us to repentance.

If we think of scripture in that way, as a text in which God reveals himself and calls us to his kingdom and which, therefore, questions our mundane being-in-the-world, making it possible for us to see an alternative, the alternative made possible by Jesus Christ, then we can say at least this about interpretation: The meaning of a scriptural text is that meaning that leads us to godly life (though the relation between godly life and scriptural meaning is circular: scriptural meaning leads us to godly life, and godly life produces spiritual meaning as its fruit).[11]

Does it follow that historical meaning is irrelevant, then, or that the interpreter has free reign to impute to the scriptural text whatever comes to mind? Neither. Historical meaning is important. It is important to ask questions like "How did those who wrote the texts understand their meaning?" It is important, first, because historical

---

11. Compare Henri de Lubac, "Spiritual Understanding," in *Theological Interpretation of Scripture*, ed. Fowl, 3–25, especially p. 13.

meaning cannot be separated from scriptural meaning. The historicity of Jesus, the basic historicity of the scriptural accounts (leaving
room for variations in understanding, for editing and transmission,
etc.) is essential to the scriptural meaning of the Bible. The spiritual
claim that the New Testament makes on us is in the announcement
that Jesus the Messiah was born, suffered, died, and was resurrected.
If these claims are not historical, then our hope is vain and Jesus was
an exemplary moral teacher rather than the Savior of the world. Likewise, the historicity of the Book of Mormon is essential to its scriptural meaning. It does not mean the same spiritually if there were
no Nephites or Lamanites. The types and shadows of scripture, the
schema or patterns they offer us for reunderstanding our lives—for
repenting—mean something very different (if they mean at all) if they
are not manifest in history.

The historicity of scripture is also important because it can serve
a spiritual function. Historical understanding of the scriptures can
challenge us to question the overlay of interpretation that has accrued
to the text and become "obvious," a tradition of our fathers. For us,
such unquestioned accruals become its scriptural meaning, and they
make it difficult for us to be brought to repentance by what we read
because the text no longer challenges us when we already know what it
has to teach. When that happens, what we take to be scriptural meaning displaces the meaningfulness of scripture. By making us reconsider our traditional interpretations of the text, historical research
can help the scriptures question our understanding of ourselves and
the world, as well as the ways we comport ourselves in the world.[12]
Historical research on scripture often forces us to recognize that the
work of interpretation is to conform our ideas to scripture rather than
to force scripture to conform to our ideas. Or, better, by helping us
conform our ideas to scripture, historical research helps us conform

---

12. Some of the work of N. T. Wright is exceptional in this regard. See, for example,
his *The Challenge of Jesus: Rediscovering Who Jesus Was and Is* (Downers Grove, IL:
InterVarsity Press, 1999).

our souls to scripture. It is, therefore, a good place to begin scriptural interpretation. Nevertheless, historical meaning is secondary to scriptural meaning.

Though sometimes we may appear to think otherwise, we also do not have free rein in interpreting scripture—scripture is of no private, no merely individual, interpretation (see 2 Peter 1:20)—because the interpretation of scripture requires unity. One form of that unity is the unity of the literal and the spiritual. Just as the body and the spirit are ultimately a unit rather than two things at war with one another, the literal and the spiritual are aspects of a unit. Neither exists without the other. Each influences the other; each limits the other. Together they prevent scriptural interpretation from proceeding willy-nilly. To use an extreme example to make a point, Moroni 10 cannot be interpreted to be a recipe for fondue because the words and grammar of that chapter as well at its history do not allow for such an interpretation. Nevertheless, though unity in interpretation is important, interpretation is also manifold because meaning is implicate in the writing of the text as much as it is explicit. It does not follow that the writing itself can be ignored. Interpretation must often be rethought because there are historical textual and editorial questions to sort out (Which is the best manuscript? What was the original form of that manuscript? etc.). It also does not follow that the answers to those historical questions will tell us how to understand scripture. Every good interpretation of scripture must give careful heed to the words of scripture, to the unity of the literal and the spiritual.[13]

A second and overarching unity of our revelatory writings is the unity of Zion: We live in covenant with one another because we live in covenant with God. Within that covenant, we have recognized some revelation as scripture, as "standard works," works against which to measure ourselves, not only as individuals, but as a people. The choice of the Latter-day Saint canon has not always been an explicit choice. Sometimes, as in the case of the Bible, it has occurred through history

---

13. Chapter 8 in this volume is about that unity.

and tradition as well as by common consent. Presumably, however, these choices have come about under the influence of the Holy Ghost working in the church as a body.[14] The standard works provide unity of interpretation by serving as a common source of understanding.

However, within the unity of Zion the standard works do not stand alone. Because we have an open canon, and as part of living in covenant relation with God and one another, we recognize priesthood authority as a second unity. Prophetic voices speak to us, continuing to call us to repentance, continuing to offer us an alternative way of being. Like the standard works, they provide limits on interpretation, the limits of our common life together in Zion.

A further element of the unity of Zion in scriptural interpretation is what, in Catholicism, is called "the tradition." As we have standard works, we also have, even if not officially, what we could call standard interpretations, the interpretations we have in common. We share with one another understandings that provide limits within which scriptural meaning takes place. At the practical level, this unity is both necessary and most dangerous. The tension between our shared interpretations and the possibility that they are things overlaid on the text, things apart from their authentically scriptural meaning, is obvious. That is the tension in which much interpretation of scripture is situated, unable to distinguish easily between which traditional interpretations give us scriptural meaning and which hide that meaning,

---

14. I take it, however, that we differ from many others because, believing in an open canon and in continuing revelation, we understand that the Bible could have been otherwise. It could have included fewer or more books than it does. Its present shape is the product of social forces and decisions as well as the inspiration of the Holy Ghost. We also know that the Doctrine and Covenants could be otherwise, because we have seen it change over the life of the restored church. I assume that the Book of Mormon could have been otherwise, that its editors could have chosen to include some additional texts or to exclude something, though there are also indications that the Lord had a direct hand in selecting at least some of its texts. (See, for example, 1 Nephi 9:3 and Words of Mormon 1:9.) Thus, for Latter-day Saints, what makes something canonical is not only that it is inspired by the Holy Ghost, for there are many such revelations in addition to those canonized. Something is canonical because, from among the revelations, it has been agreed on by common consent to be a standard.

perhaps spoiling us "through philosophy and vain deceit, after the tradition of men" (Colossians 2:8).[15]

Given that tension, a member of the church may argue against our common interpretations. However, the fact that we live together, that we are covenant with one another and with God, that when it comes to scriptural meaning, our individual understanding is not primary—this means we cannot argue against common interpretations heedlessly. We need not accept everything that is commonly believed. Far from it. However, if someone does not, the burden of proof falls on that person. That burden need not be heavy. Indeed, it can be light, and carrying it can lead to the beautiful and holy. Good interpretation of our writings and beliefs is perhaps most often done by someone who accepts that burden of proof, showing us how our common interpretations have fallen short or how they can be renewed. That kind of scripture interpretation is most likely to open our understanding and allow us to liken the scriptures and our beliefs to ourselves freshly. However, we cannot interpret scripture in Zion without living in that tension between the need to renew our interpretations and the requirement that we recognize the legitimacy of what we share. To leave that tension, either to insist on the legitimacy of my private interpretations or on the absolute authority of common interpretations, with little or no regard for the other side of the tension, is to give up the desire to establish Zion. It is to fail the beauty of Zion.

Thus, scriptural meaning occurs in covenant relation. Our situatedness in that covenant and the way-of-being that it opens, the life of covenant obligation to God and our fellows, presumably determines the likening that can occur in interpretation. To interpret scripture in the covenant is to be called to be in Zion, called on by God and others who speak words of gladness, truth, and joy, and who demand that we accommodate ourselves and our interpretations to the canon, to

---

15. I understand most, if not all, references to "the philosophies of men" in LDS discourse to refer to what we might otherwise call "common sense," to the traditions of understanding that seem obvious to the world and that we often take up because we too take them to be obvious.

authority, and to the traditions of the Saints, not in some inflexible way, but by taking up the cause of Zion and seeking to establish and bring it forth in interpretation. It is to be called to the interpretation of a Christian life, as well as in the explicit interpretations of scriptural texts.

It would be inaccurate to say that I encounter God in the writings of his revelations. I encounter him in prayer and ordinance, and especially in my reception of the Holy Ghost. It would be inaccurate to say that I encounter the other person in writings, for I encounter others in my family, in the church, and in society. However, I can recollect—re-collect—my covenant relation with God and others through scripture.[16] The distance between myself and the primitive meaning of a text and the work to understand which that distance imposes on me is one way in which the obligation created in my relation to what is other than myself is manifest. The distance between my life as it is and the life to which I am called imposes a similar work and is, therefore, evidence of a similar obligation. Those distances are a matter of otherness: the Other speaking to me in scripture (the standard works), the otherness of authority (both God and those who represent him), the obligation to respond to and renew the testimonies of other persons (common consent).[17] Within the covenant, I have an obligation to make the concretized said of the scriptures into something that continues to say,[18] both for myself and for others, a saying that is enacted not only in my ideas and beliefs, but particularly in my life. Responding to the call of scripture, I must en-act the cause of Zion.

---

16. In the language of contemporary philosophy, I encounter the obligation to the Other. The work of Emmanuel Levinas is perhaps most obviously in play here, but as my earlier remark suggested, the work of Gadamer, Ricoeur and, particularly, Jean-Luc Marion has been at least as important for my reflection on these issues. And, of course, given their reliance on the work of Heidegger, that is always also in the background. For more on recollection, see chapter 1 in this volume.

17. Of course, it is not determined only by these. It is determined, foremost, in personal relations of love, both with the Divine and with other people.

18. This distinction between the saying and the said is something that I take from Levinas. Roughly defined, the said is the content of a speaking and the saying is the significance of the act of speaking. See Levinas, *Totality and Infinity: Essay on Exteriority*, trans. Alphonso Lingis (Pittsburgh: Duquesne University Press, 1969). See, for example, pages 30 and 62.

Because we have continuing revelation, within mortality there can be no end to the work of interpretation that enacts the establishment of Zion. There can also be no end to that work because we live together in an organic rather than a static whole. And there can be no end because we have not yet come to an end: as temporal, living beings, we are not always the same, unchanging from moment to moment; we live in that we continue to come to be, in that we continue to renew our life. We hopefully await the Apocalypse, the final revelation of the Son of God, his reign. Awaiting it, we must continue to renew our hope and expectation of that revelation, for ourselves and for others, by continuing to read, interpret, and reread. The medieval scriptorian's[19] motto—*lege, lege, lege, labore, ora, et relege*; "read, read, read, work, pray, and reread"—must also be ours. In that unending rereading, reinterpretation, and renewal, we find ourselves always partaking of what is new and everlasting (see D&C 132) rather than "ever learning and never able to come to the knowledge of the truth" (2 Timothy 3:7). Reading scripture we find ourselves called to and participating in Zion, called to holiness and beauty.

---

19. I use the word *scriptorian* with its common meaning, "one who copies scripture," rather than with its LDS meaning, "one who knows the scriptures well."

CHAPTER EIGHT

Scripture as Incarnation

Christian Belief and the Historicity of Scripture

The historicity of scripture is important to most Christians and, especially, to Latter-day Saints. Christians disagree among themselves about how to understand scriptural history, but few deny that, in some important sense, Christian scripture is historical. However, given the challenges to scriptural history, challenges that are especially strong for Latter-day Saints who take the Book of Mormon to be historical, what are we to make of the claim that scriptures are history? Given those challenges, is it *possible* to understand scripture as literal history? The answer to that question—positive, I will argue—lies in answering the question of what we mean by *history*, a question that becomes more difficult the more we think about it.

The way that academic historians have thought of history since the beginning of modernism (about 1500) is not the only way to think about it.[1] However, since the eighteenth century, but especially in the nineteenth and twentieth centuries, those approaching the Bible and, therefore, also Latter-day Saint scripture, have used some variation of the academic understanding of history as their entrée into the

---

1. Philosophically, modernism is a way of thinking about the world that is dominant from roughly 1500 to about 1800, though it continues as an important force into the present. (In that regard, it is important to note that for philosophy *modern* and *contemporary* are not synonyms.) However, though modernism is the dominant way of thinking during that period and though that period has given its name to modernism, what we call modernist thought is not confined to that historical period. There were modernist thinkers and elements prior to modernism and, obviously, there continue to be modernist thinkers. See Stephen Daniels, "Paramodern Strategies of Philosophical Historiography," *Epoché: A Journal for the History of Philosophy* 1/1 (1993): 41–63.

question of scriptural historicity. We understand scriptural interpretation to be a subset of scholarly historical understanding, but the science of history has raised and continues to raise a variety of questions about the historicity of scriptural accounts. For the Bible, some of those questions have been resolved to the satisfaction of believers and others remain questions. Given the unique character of the Book of Mormon, work on defending its historicity has been much less decisive. As a result, believers, especially Latter-day Saints, find ourselves having to answer the question of to what degree our scriptural accounts are historical.

In general, scholars, even believing ones, have been more or less skeptical of the historical character of scripture. However, believers (scholars and otherwise) have felt it necessary to defend the historicity of scripture with the historian's scholarly tools. Most Christians believe that the religious claims of Christianity cannot be completely separated from its historical claims, and we think that we have no way of understanding those claims except via the tools of historical scholarship. For example, few have been willing completely to give up the historicity of Jesus's life and, particularly, the historicity of his death. Even those who deny the physical character of the resurrection usually tie the idea of resurrection to an historical event, such as an experience of the first apostles.[2] We seem faced with two options for understanding scripture: On the one hand, we can accept some variety of the academic historians' approach to scripture. We may opt for the more "liberal" approach of people such as Raymond Brown or we may prefer the more "conservative" approach of Christian literalists, but we agree that scripture is historical. Believers have generally sought to show that the scriptures are accurate histories, to some degree, and they have accepted some version of the canons of historical scholarship as the canons for understanding the historicity of scripture.[3]

---

2. For example, see Thomas Sheehan, *The First Coming: How the Kingdom of God Became Christianity* (New York: Random House, 1986).

3. During the last several years there has been a sometimes rancorous discussion among Latter-day Saint scholars about how to understand history. I think the rancor of

A common alternative is to escape the problems created by accepting those canons by arguing that the scriptures are not essentially historical. On this view, rather than being accurate descriptions of historical events, the scriptures are writings that may often look like history and, in fact, may have historical elements, but they are really about something other than the events portrayed in them. These believers often argue that scriptures are not about history, but about another reality, such as a reality of archetypal meanings. Given the problems of establishing the historicity of scripture, such believers want to reject the necessity of that historicity but retain the truth of scripture: Scriptures may or may not be historical, but they are not about historical truth, they are about religious truth, these people argue. Thus, according to them, though scripture takes the guise of history, it is actually about something else, such as an ahistorical transcendent or archetypal reality.[4]

---

that discussion has died down—thank goodness—so I hope that I can take up this related question without becoming embroiled in that earlier debate. What follows is not a criticism of academic history nor historians nor their methods. To offer another understanding of what the word *history* can mean is not to suggest that there is something wrong with other meanings of the word. We make a mistake when we use a notion of history inappropriate to the context at hand, not when we use a different notion of history. That mistake, a kind of equivocation, is what I believe often happens in the debates between those who defend scriptural historicity and those who attack it, as well as between those who deal with that historicity by means of differing understandings of history. (For an important though, I believe, generally misunderstood discussion of several possibilities for history, see the second of Nietzsche's *Untimely Meditations*.)

4. One problem with this view, a problem that I cannot explore here, is that on such a view there can be nothing new in the world. What-is is always and only what has already been; everything was given "in the beginning," and nothing else can be. Though, under the influence of Greek philosophy, this understanding has been a feature of much traditional Christianity—perhaps most explicitly in Calvinism—it is a view that is out of character with Christianity, in which the hope for what is to come, what Bloch calls "the Not-Yet," plays a crucial role. See Ernst Bloch, *The Principle of Hope*, trans. Neville Plaice, Stephen Plaice, and Paul Knight (Cambridge, MA: MIT, 1986). The not-yet is a notion without which it is difficult to understand how such things as repentance and exaltation can have meaning, but if everything already has been given, then there is nothing that we can describe as genuinely not-yet. Some versions of this position are likely to seem very unorthodox to ordinary Mormons. However, the Platonic view, common among many orthodox Latter-day Saints, in which religious truth is the expression of a Platonic realm of truth—laws, principles, for example—may be subject to the same criticism.

Most Christian believers find this ahistorical resolution of the problem of scriptural historicity unacceptable, and this is doubly true for Latter-day Saint believers. For example, most Latter-day Saints find it difficult to explain and accept the Book of Mormon's account of itself and Joseph Smith's account of its origin if it is not substantially a historical document rather than an embodiment of a- or trans-historical truth. Most Latter-day Saints feel that if the Book of Mormon is not substantially historical, then much of its text—the narrative, major portion—is irrelevant to its meaning for us, and it is difficult to see how to avoid accusing Joseph Smith of fraud.

Perhaps one way to avoid that charge would be to understand the production of the Book of Mormon as the creation of myth, in the positive sense of that word which academics often use, namely a discourse that purports to give the structure of reality. As will be apparent, I am sympathetic to that understanding. Nevertheless, I think it is flawed because, as the view is usually argued, it gives up too much. Such an explanation gives up the claim of peculiar and unique truth—a truth inseparable from historical truth—that most Christians and (even more) most Latter-day Saints take to be essential to their religion and their religious experience. The historicity of origins has been an essential element of biblical religion from the beginning. To understand any of those religions *only* in terms of myth changes them and the religious experience within them to such a degree that it is not clear how those who take the mythic view can claim that they are Christians or Latter-day Saints or Jews or Muslims rather than merely religious people with no particular religious identity.

For Latter-day Saints the problem of the mythic understanding of scripture is even more severe. For it is difficult to understand such things as the hefting of the gold plates and the testimony of the various witnesses and the visits of the Angel Moroni if they are only part of the construction of a myth.[5] Mythmakers account for their

---

5. Though I am not using the word *myth* in its everyday sense—a false or fanciful story—in contrast to the way it is used in chapter 4, I do use it here to denote an account

myths as things they have received.[6] To that degree Joseph Smith's account could be construed as mythic. However, mythmakers do not consciously create the kinds of detailed, first-person accounts of that reception that Joseph Smith gives. Mythmakers give accounts in which they have received the story of someone who received the sacred objects. They have not themselves received the objects. Thus, if we explain Latter-day Saint scripture by saying that Joseph Smith was making myth rather than reporting historical experiences, it is still difficult to avoid coming to the conclusion that not only was he making myth, he was also committing fraud. The phenomenon of myth-making and the phenomenon of the origins of the LDS Church are not consonant with each other.

However, I believe that there is a more difficult problem. Beside the existential and phenomenological problems of the myth-making understanding of scripture, there is a theoretical problem: Those who argue that the authors of scripture are mythmakers assume, with the apologists and the academics, that the canons of academic history are *the* canons of history. They do not consider the possibility that there are other ways of understanding history and that, on one of those understandings, scripture is historical, literally so.

As a result of such problems, believers find it necessary to insist on the historical character of scripture, though doing so is sometimes rationally difficult; historical scholarship seldom lines up with our understanding of scripture as well as most believers would like it to. We can take various positions on the historicity of scripture, but if we are to think about that historicity, we must ask ourselves what the word *history* can mean and which of its possible meanings we can

---

that is not historically true. As I noted in the earlier discussion, the common scholarly meaning of the word *myth* does not include that it is not historically true, but I am not using the word in that sense. However, if one were to use the word in that scholarly sense, then one could take my argument to say, among other things, that scripture is myth, but the myth of scripture and its factual history are not mutually exclusive.

6. Jean-François Lyotard, *The Postmodern Explained to Children: Correspondence 1982-1985*, ed. Julian Pefanis and Morgan Thomas, trans. Don Berry and others (Minneapolis: University of Minnesota Press, 1992), 31–32.

most accurately apply to scripture. I argue that our discomfort with the various alternative attempts to deal with the historicity of scripture results from using a concept of history that is inappropriate to scripture. As a result, though I believe that the historical part of scripture is genuinely historical, I do not think the canons of contemporary historical scholarship will be much help to us in understanding scripture as history. We must reconsider what history is.

The discussion of history and its meaning, and—especially in the eighteenth and nineteenth centuries—the discussion of the historicity of scripture, have been an important part of modern intellectual history. Much of the contemporary discussion of these issues owes its form and content to those earlier debates.[7] However, though the terms *premodern* and *modern* are not unproblematic,[8] I believe that the understanding of history held by premoderns is quite different from our own, that it is a plausible alternative understanding of history, and that a contemporary rethinking of it gives us a better way to understand scripture than does a modern understanding—not just a way of understanding how premoderns understood history and scripture,

---

7. Literary criticism also owes much to those debates. Most of the varieties of positions taken in literary criticism are very much descendants of the various positions taken in the eighteenth- and early nineteenth-century debates about the Bible, and even the positions that are not directly descended from the debates two hundred years ago often rely on parts of those arguments and positions. One need only read Frei's overview of the debates about biblical meaning to see that. See Hans Frei, *The Eclipse of Biblical Narrative; A Study in Eighteenth and Nineteenth Century Hermeneutics* (New Haven: Yale University Press, 1974), especially chaps. 2–7. Much of the contemporary row over texts and meaning amounts to little more than a rehash of those earlier discussions.

8. Among other reasons, the terms are problematic because the periodization of history is a questionable and peculiarly modern practice, because the definitions of the periods take modernism as their point of reference, and because the names of the periods do not name specific periods of history so much as ways of thinking that may be more obvious in one time than another, but are rarely exclusive to any period. As I will use the terms here, *premodern* and *modern* are general terms. There were a variety of ways of understanding history prior to modernism and there are a variety of ways of understanding it in modernism. However, there is, nevertheless, a divide between the two. Thus, in spite of the difficulties of doing so, I will use the word *premodern* to refer to an understanding of history perhaps best exemplified in medieval thinking and I will use the word *modern* to refer to the "scientific" ways of understanding history that come to dominate with modernism.

but the basis for understanding our own relation to history and scripture differently than we do. Consequently, a brief comparison of modern and premodern history can serve as a starting point for thinking about alternative conceptions of history.[9]

The Modern Concept of History: Representation/Reference

Perhaps the first thing to be said about the difference between modern and premodern history is that modern history takes narratives and the events they describe to be separable from each other, but premodern history does not. The distinction is not an obvious one. In fact, even if we understand that distinction conceptually, we do not find it easy to think about scripture except by using the modern distinction. Though, in its origins, the separation of event and narrative is an academic distinction, it has become so "obvious," so "natural," that we have difficulty understanding the distinction or reading scripture in any other way. It seems inescapably true to us that there are two things, the event itself and what one can truthfully say about that event. But premodern thinking does not make that distinction, at least not in the way that modern history does.

To give an account of an event is to speak meaningfully of that event. For example, "The cat sat on the mat" is meaningful, but it does not mean much. Though we can understand it lexically and syntactically, unless that sentence is correlated to an event in some way (whether negatively or positively), it lacks fullness of meaning. If I say "The cat sat on the mat" as a description of a particular event, then I find that event meaningful, and the meaning of the sentence is a presentation of a meaning of the event. However, counterintuitively, without such presentations of meaning, whether or not explicitly put into language, there are no events. Events without meaning are strictly inconceivable; *as events, events are meaningful*. Without meaning, the

---

9. Though I do not agree with some of his conclusions, Frei's seminal work on biblical meaning and the influence of the modern understanding of history on our understanding of biblical meaning serves as my starting point.

flux of time and space is not filled with events. Without meaning, the flux is random motion of "stuff," at best.

Modernism's mistake was to think that the meaning of sentences and the events they describe is explained merely referentially. Modernism assumes that the truth of the sentence is a function of its reference to a particular event, but reference is not enough to explain the meaning of events. If there is to be some meaningful notion of truth, then the constituting and interpreting subject must be in relation to a world that is more than and, in some sense, prior to his or her perceptions and interpretations. The question is how to refer to that which is prior to perception and interpretation when it seems that we can only do so through perception and interpretation.

I am not saying that reference is impossible. After all, we do speak of things in the world, and attempts to do away with referential talk about things in the world are self-refuting (if there are such attempts).[10] The modernist mistake is not in thinking that meaning requires reference, but in thinking that reference is sufficient to explain meaning as truth. There is meaning, but it always goes beyond what one can account for merely referentially.[11]

---

10. However, whether we talk about real things in the real world in a referential way (i.e., as explained by a referential theory) remains a question. Strictly speaking, reference *per se* may be impossible, as thinkers such as Frege and Davidson argue. It does not follow that we cannot speak of the world, only that we do not do so in the way that referential theories of meaning assume that we do, namely, by correlating our meaningful sentences with states of affairs in something like a one-to-one manner. One response to the problem, a response I find interesting and perhaps compelling, is in the work of Jean-Luc Marion. See, for example, his essay, "The Event, the Phenomenon, and the Revealed," in *Transcendence in Philosophy and Religion*, ed. James E. Faulconer (Indianapolis: Indiana University Press, 2003), 87–105. Marion argues, not that reference is possible, but that we have meaningful contact with the things themselves in the world.

11. I will take up the issue of signs from a Derridean standpoint: Every system of signs depends on something outside the system, so no system of signs can completely capture that to which it refers; thus, there is always more to reality than any interpretation of it can capture, though we can give only interpretations. Nevertheless, I do not think the Derridean character of my argument is essential to it, as I will argue later. The points I take from Derrida could also be made using other contemporary philosophers, including Anglo-American ones. See Kevin Hart's *The Trespass of the Sign: Deconstruction, Theology, and Philosophy* (Cambridge: Cambridge University Press, 1989) for a readable, more

The connection between a word and the thing it refers to—in other words, meaningful reference—exists only in an act of reference, but no theory of reference can give an account of that act. Among other things, a theory of reference cannot account for the particular thing to which the meaning-act points or for the fact that it does so point in this case. Language theories can tell us how words relate to each other (in an "endless chain of signification," to use a phrase from the twentieth-century French philosopher Jacques Derrida), but given the infinite variety of possible references in any particular act of meaning, language theories cannot fully account for the success of acts in which we talk about things in the world.

Many theories mark this inability by mentioning the importance of context, but such a remark makes the Derridean point, for context does not name something to which we can refer, though at first glance it may seem to. Each reference to a context is made possible by another context which is, itself, not referred to, making any attempt to refer to context itself endless. One cannot refer to context as such; context is beyond reference, though essential to it. This means that the invocation of context in a theory of reference shows that, beside whatever the theory proposes to explain meaning, something more is needed. What I mean in a putative referential act, such as the description of an historical event, is not completely decided by the sign system (such as a natural language) that I use to make that reference or by any theory of such sign systems. It is always also decided by "something more."

We may try to specify what that something more is by mentioning the speaker's intent, the particular audience she addresses, the history of the language, the social relations in force at the time of the event, and all of the other "things" to which rhetoric attends, including the relation

---

detailed overview of Derrida's discussion of signs and for a treatment of the relevance of that discussion to religious understanding. For an excellent criticism of Derrida, see Françoise Dastur, "Heidegger and Derrida: On Play and Difference," *Epoché: A Journal for the History of Philosophy* 3/1–2 (1995): 1–23. However, her criticism does not undo this point about signs and referentiality. Eco has made an argument similar to Derrida's. See Umberto Eco, *Theory of Semiotics* (Bloomington: Indiana University Press, 1976).

of the referential object to the person making the reference (which begs the question of reference). However, though we can talk about context, about what else reference requires, there seems to be no possible science or theory of context. Beside that, the act of reference (which must, as an act, include both the object of reference and the particular, existent thing that corresponds to that object) exists within the system of signs in which the reference occurs. Thus, the referential act is not a simple connection of two autonomous things, the thing to which I refer and the reference.[12] We cannot leave language behind, even in our putative reference to what is outside language.

We must use language to speak of what is beyond language. Nevertheless, we necessarily say what is, strictly speaking, impossible to say—namely, that talk about the world and the things in the world always involves something more than language. Something more than/other than language, something that cannot be said directly, accounts for any successful talk about things. Contrary to a common American (mis)interpretation of Derrida, *the point is not that there are only texts, but that, though we can deal with only texts and text analogs,*

---

12. Thus, also, reference is inherently unstable, not only in its inability to be explained by any theory of reference, but over time. As the context of an event changes (and the event has temporal as well as momentary context), so too does the event, as anyone who genuinely believes in repentance must believe. The present can change the past or there is no difference between repentance and mere regret. This idea of backward causation sounds nonsensical to most people (though how, without it, to explain repentance as anything other than a change of mind rather than a purification remains a mystery). However, consider rhythm as an analog. The moments of a rhythm cannot be discreet like the moments in a time line. If they were, they would not be moments of a rhythm. Rhythmic moments require (already "contain") their before and their after. One hit on the head of a drum is not part of any rhythm; each beat in a rhythm is what it is only in its relation to each of the other, preceding and following beats, only as it fits into the rhythm as a whole. Consequently, as one varies a rhythm at any particular beat, the meaning of each *previous* beat changes. Since beats are defined in their relation to each other, a change in the relation between the various beats changes any beat in the past into something "new," something other than what it was. The past beat no longer exists in the same way that it did. At the time the drumhead was struck initially, the beat was one thing. However, with subsequent strikes, that past event is now something other than what it was. If events are what they are in relation to each other, then the analogy suggests that their meaning could change over time, that they, therefore, could change over time.

there is necessarily something more than any *text*.[13] Ironically, modernism rather than Derrida insists that there is nothing other than the text: By assuming that, in principle, it is possible, or at least desirable, for human beings to give a final, complete description of the world, modernism makes an identity of its ultimate, though ideal, text and the world described by that text. In contrast, Derrida denies the possibility of that identification. Something always remains beyond the text—beyond explanation—something that explains the text in question but is not explained by that text.

The empiricism of modernism (not the only kind of empiricism) imitates the Sophists of classical Greece, for it pins its hopes for understanding on a supposed ability to fix the connections between ideas and words, on the one hand, and things on the other. However, as Catherine Pickstock notes, it is not only impossible to achieve fixity in that connection, it is dishonest to seek for it: "Human life is always in the midst of things; the clarity of empiricist conclusions is an illusion fostered by the falsely isolated and inert nature of its artificial

---

13. Explaining Derrida's position, John Caputo says: "Derrida does not deny but delimits reference; what he denies is reference-without-difference. Without *différance* [Derrida's technical term for what happens in acts of reference: the sign differs from its object and defers complete identification, never completely corresponding to its object]. *Différance* does not lock us up inside anything. On the contrary, *différance* is a doorway, a threshold (*limen*), a door through which everything outgoing (reference, messages sent, etc.) and incoming (messages received, perceptions, etc.) must pass. **A threshold supposes both an inside and an outside.** . . . On this accounting, proper names refer *in actu exercitu*, in the exercised act, in actual use, in the concrete happening or the factual event. . . . It is a wonder, a little difficult to account for, but it happens. . . . [It is] something that philosophy is forced to swallow while being unable to digest" (John D. Caputo, *Against Ethics: Contributions to a Poetics of Obligation with Constant Reference to Deconstruction* [Bloomington: Indiana University Press, 1993], 76–77; boldface added.) The misunderstanding that attributes to Derrida the claim that there is nothing external to language is common, so common that it has become the "common sense" of those who criticize Derrida, as well as many of those who praise him. Nevertheless, it is mistaken, as a careful reading of Derrida, in the context of his background in Husserl and Heidegger, will show. Out of ignorance, some continue to make and repeat this mistake because it has become so common. Others, such as Huston Smith, seem to do so more willfully. See Huston Smith, "The Religious Significance of Postmodernism: A Rejoinder," *Faith and Philosophy* 12/3 (1995): 409–22.

findings."[14] In contrast, "the genuine 'fixity' parodied by the Sophists can be attained only in the unshakeable conviction of a certain way of life." In other words, as Aristotle argues in *Nicomachean Ethics,* the alternative to the fixity of ideas is fixity of character, the fixity of a lived life, a fixity that cannot be reduced to a fixed connection between ideas and things. By ignoring that alternative, when modernism discovers that it cannot nail things down as it wishes, that crucifixion is no more appropriate for ideas and values than it is for human beings, it concludes that nihilism is the only alternative.[15]

For history, as for any other discipline, the question that a nonmodern understanding of signs and reference raises is, "What else is involved in producing the 'text' of our understanding of history?" According to what we choose, we will get different ways of understanding history. And, though we can and must adjudicate between the various ways of understanding history, there is no way to do so "purely"—in other words, without referring to such things as various authorities; our goals and traditions; social, scholastic, and other conventions; social relations; and so on. As Friedrich Nietzsche saw clearly (in the second of his *Untimely Meditations*), we must take into account the lives and ways of life into which such histories enter. We cannot name, once and for all, what the "what else" of language or even of an individual language act is. Contrary to the expectations of the Enlightenment, we have no Archimedean point from which we can leverage our decision for or against a particular understanding of the world, much less of history.

It is important to note, however, that the consequence of the absence of such a risk-free leverage or standpoint does not result in absolute relativity and, therefore, in the meaninglessness of our decisions.

---

14. Catherine Pickstock, *After Writing: On the Liturgical Consummation of Philosophy* (Oxford: Blackwell, 1998), 19.

15. This explains why so many who read the work of thinkers such as Derrida, Lyotard, Levinas, and others cannot see anything in them but nihilism: since such thinkers reject modernism's understanding of fixity, those readers assume that the thinkers in question must argue for no fixity at all.

That relativist consequence would follow only if, contrary to fact, we have only two options: mathematical certainty or absolute relativity.[16] Philosophers such as Plato and Aristotle, among the ancients, and Hannah Arendt, in this century, have offered other options. However, we need not know the work of these philosophers to see that we can break the horns of the dilemma with other options. The necessity of faith (though not necessarily religious faith) shows that there are more than those two options.[17]

Since the eighteenth century, both those who criticize scripture as history and those who defend it have assumed the modernist understanding of the connection between history and meaning, though usually only implicitly. I argue that, in spite of themselves, eighteenth-century biblical critics give up the Bible as a sacred text—even, implicitly, those who wished to defend it as sacred. They assume that there is a universal, language-free view available to them (at least in principle) and that the scriptures refer to or depict that universal view more or less accurately.[18] They assume that events exist prior to and independent of the meanings of those events, and that the better a historical

---

16. Those who assume that the absence of a risk-free, universal viewpoint results in thoroughgoing relativism share with the Enlightenment the assumption that meaning is either constituted as the Enlightenment says it is or there is no meaning. With most contemporary philosophers, I deny that assumption. As a consequence, vicious relativism does not necessarily follow from denying an Archimedean leverage point for understanding and interpretation.

17. For example, echoing what other contemporary philosophers have also said, Derrida says: "There is no morality without faith, faith in the other. There is no social experience without bearing witness, without attestation, the recognition of a dimension of trust and faith. This is not a religious point; it is the general structure of experience" (Derrida, private discussion, Paris, 1 March 1996). The first of the *Lectures on Faith* made a similar point more than one hundred years ago, and it presumably echoes what the Prophet Joseph Smith believed. Joseph Smith might reply to Derrida: "True, it is the general structure of experience, but that is a religious point, for religion gives the general structure to experience."

18. Such a view may be consequent on the traditional Christian understanding of God: As an unembodied being, God is omnipresent. For such an omnipresent being, knowledge is aperspectival, i.e., universal. Thus, as the Renaissance and Enlightenment argument goes, since we are made in God's image, to the degree possible our knowledge also should be aperspectival and universal. However, one can believe in God's knowledge, understanding, and omniscience without assuming that they are to be understood

text is, the more accurately it describes the independent event. By agreeing to the modernist assumption about how meaning is fixed, even defenders of the Bible conflate historical understanding with an accurate, referential description of events. They assume that meaning, biblical or otherwise, is essentially referential/representative and that only a rational method can give us understanding of historical texts, such as the Bible. By making the question of scriptural truth—scriptural literalness—a merely referential question (in other words, by understanding meaning via a referential theory and by applying that understanding to scripture), both the religious and the critics of religion turn religion into a set of beliefs to which one assents because one takes them to be referentially valid. But to paraphrase James, the devils also refer, and tremble (see James 2:19).

A Premodern Concept of History: Incarnation

In contrast, premodern thinkers take the Bible not as an accurate reference to either history or another reality (though they do not deny that we can speak of the world), but as the incarnation (or enactment) of a symbolic ordering.[19] Work in the anthropology of religion,

---

in these universal, aperspectival terms. Much of David Paulsen's work is dedicated to showing the alternative.

19. The concept of a symbolic ordering is not a rigorous concept, but I do not think it a difficult concept to understand. I think its meaning will become clear as I use the term in context. However, let me try to say something for those who would like more of an explanation. For background in understanding my discussion of symbolic ordering, one should read sections 31 and 32 of Heidegger's *Being and Time* (and perhaps the material leading up to those sections). See *Being and Time*, trans. John Macquarrie and Edward Robinson (New York: Harper, 1962). There he discusses understanding and the necessity of preunderstanding to understanding and interpretation. (By *understanding* Heidegger means something like "implicit understanding," and by *interpretation* he means the explication of understanding.) The correlate discussion of prejudice in Hans-Georg Gadamer's *Truth and Method*, trans. Joel Wein, 2nd rev. ed. (New York: Continuum, 1993), 265–300, and the discussion of prefiguration (also called *mimesis₁*) in Paul Ricoeur's *Time and Narrative, Volume 1*, trans. Kathleen McLaughlin and David Pellauer (Chicago: University of Chicago, 1984), 1–64, might be helpful. (Both Gadamer and Ricoeur rely heavily on Heidegger's work.) Charles Guignon's book may also be helpful: *Heidegger and the Problem of Knowledge* (Indianapolis: Hackett, 1983). Briefly put, what we think of as understanding requires preunderstanding; preunderstanding gives us our possibilities for understanding. As we have understood since Plato, our understanding of the world

such as that of Mircea Eliade, suggests that we misunderstand religion when we understand it as essentially a set of beliefs.[20] In contrast,
when we see what such anthropological work shows us, we discover
that religion is an ordering of the world in and through symbols. Beliefs are consequent on that ordering, not constitutive of it. Thus, a
Catholic, a Southern Baptist, and a Latter-day Saint differ from one
another, not so much because they hold different beliefs (though they
do), but because they are involved in different ways of ordering the
world symbolically (though, given that they are all Christians, there
is considerable overlap in the orderings manifest in their lives). The
most obvious place to find symbolic ordering is in the rituals of religions and in their sacred objects, though symbolic ordering also

---

cannot begin from zero, *ex nihilo*. Something, some way in which the world gives itself
to us prior to reflection, makes reflective understanding possible. But the world does not
give itself as the bare presence of mere things. It always—always already—gives itself to
us in shape and relations, in a figure. The world gives itself to us, prereflectively, as con-
figured in various ways. One fundamental preunderstanding is the configuration of the
world (anciently, the *kosmos*), within which one finds oneself oriented in the world: an
ordering gives the possibilities for understanding by configuring the possible relations
of the world. Various things can serve to order the *kosmos*, language and mathematics,
for example. A symbolic ordering is a preunderstanding in which symbols and symbols
systems (as opposed to sign systems) are fundamental, though not exclusive, to the configuration in which one finds oneself oriented.

20. This reduction of religion to sets of beliefs is also consequent on the traditional
understanding of God and the way that understanding led to the Enlightenment: On a
voluntaristic Christian view, God's will is coextensive with his knowledge, which is ideal
and at least a representation of the world. Thus, since humans image God, human knowledge (i.e., representation of the ideal), like God's knowledge, is prior to or fundamental
to human action and life. (This explains why Western thought consistently values theory
over praxis.) On a voluntarist view, religious beliefs are representations to ourselves of the
religious aspect of the ideal world. As such, they make it possible for us to act in religious
ways. Therefore, beliefs are fundamental to religion. We generally take recognition of and
adherence to a particular set of beliefs to be identical with being an adherent of that religion. (Note that it is possible to understand a good deal of modernism as an outgrowth of
voluntarism in theology. For an argument to this effect, see Klaus Held, "Civic Prudence
in Machiavelli: Toward the Paradigm Transformation in Philosophy in the Transition to
Modernity," in *The Ancients and the Moderns*, ed. Reginald Lilly [Bloomington: Indiana
University Press, 1996], 115–29.) To take religion to be a matter of symbolic ordering is to
reject this understanding of the connection between religion and belief. (Of course, I do
not necessarily reject everything about voluntarism, only those features that make belief
and representation fundamental to action in the way that voluntarism does.)

encompasses more ordinary aspects of life, including such things as peculiar idioms and patterns of deference—and assertions of belief. Especially in religion, systems and sets of beliefs are part of the orders in question, but they are not foundational to those orders. To be religious, therefore, is not to assent to particular propositions or assertions, though that assent follows from the fact that one is religious. Instead, to be religious is to recognize—to reverence—the holy and to live in a world of which the contents, including beliefs, are ordered by the holy.[21] For the religious, the holy is the ordering principle, the "form" of the world, to use a term important to Plato, Aristotle, and all of medieval philosophy.[22] For premodern thought, both religious and

---

21. I am hesitant to define what I mean by *holy*. I fear a kind of definitional blasphemy, but I can say that it has to do with what is excessive—in other words, abundant, and determinative: the holy "transcends" the world of our experience and our ability to explain (though it transcends without having to be, itself, in or of another quasi-Platonic metaphysical realm) and it "explains" the world (by grounding that world, though—again—it is not a ground outside or beyond the world). Those curious about how to think such transcendence and ground might find Heidegger's *Principle of Reason,* trans. Reginald Lilly (Bloomington: Indiana University Press, 1991), interesting. Though that book is not about the holy, it does deal with transcendence without making transcendence otherworldly. The question of transcendence has become central to much contemporary European philosophy, so much so that some philosophers have complained of a "theological turn" in French thought. See Dominique Janicaud, *The Theological Turn of French Phenomenology,* in Dominique Janicaud and others, *Phenomenology and the "Theological Turn": The French Debate,* trans. Bernard G. Prusak and Jeffrey L. Klosky (New York: Fordham University Press, 2000), 16–103.

22. I use the language of form and content here for heuristic reasons. As we usually understand that language, it requires another world to which this world refers; that is, something like a metatheory of representation. However, one need not be a Platonist or a representationalist to find the language of form meaningful and helpful. For the ancients, form is that in which the real shows itself, presents itself. That is the point, and the point need not be understood in representational terms, as Aristotle well shows. Put otherwise: the language of form and content can be helpful, though the danger is that we will understand that language via a theory of representation or something like it. The work of Heidegger, for example, is amenable to this way of thinking. I believe that Wittgenstein's work is similarly amenable to form and content language, though of course neither Heidegger nor Wittgenstein would use the word *form* in its Platonic sense because of the metaphysical, representational, baggage that the word carries with it. Heidegger speaks of horizons, Wittgenstein of forms of life. In what follows, I will discuss how form can be that in which the real shows itself without assuming that the form must have some existence independent of that which it informs.

nonreligious, the real is primarily "formal." There not only can be, but must be, a variety of manifestations of what I here call form, but each is an instance of the "same thing." The form of something is the real manifesting itself in the world. For religious premoderns, the holy is the real manifest in the symbolic order of things—it is the form not just of individual things but of things as a whole—and religion gives us that form/order.

It is important to note that rational ordering and symbolic ordering are not necessarily at odds with one another. Within a symbolic order, rational discourse is one of the forms in which the real is manifest. Therefore, it is not opposed to symbolic ordering, but a possible part of any symbolic order. In contrast, in a rational ordering, symbolic discourse cannot be made an instance of reason, except as a parasitic form of reference; in other words, as ambiguous or "poetic" speech.[23] As a result, though within a symbolic ordering there is no necessary opposition between the rational and the symbolic, that opposition may be necessary to a rational order.[24] There is an asymmetry between symbolic order and rational order, an asymmetry that is to the advantage of symbolic order.

Living as we do in an age when modernism is the common sense for perhaps most human beings (at least those under the sway of progress and its Euro-American manifestation), the holy is no longer what orders the world as a whole. When we are asked to talk or think about religion, we usually do so as if religion were one of several regions of life. On this view, there are many regions of my life: the world of work, the political world, the family, the world of morality, the academic and scholarly world, the economic region, the world of leisure, and so on.

---

23. John Searle's work is an interesting and relevant example of the attempt to take the language of symbolic ordering as parasitic. See, for example, *Speech Acts: An Essay in the Philosophy of Language* (Cambridge: Cambridge University Press, 1969).

24. Ironically, however, the exclusion of symbolic ordering from the rational is self-defeating since rational language cannot avoid the intrusion of the symbolic via such features of language as metaphor: we no longer understand words such as *inference* and phrases such as *follows from* out of the metaphors that inform them, but if all metaphorical language were removed, even the language of logic, like all language, would cease to function.

Religion is one of these regions of our lives, and some people's lives may have no such region. Though we engage in activities that involve the various regions of our lives, we assume that each is, strictly speaking, separate from the others, though possibly overlapping; in themselves, each region is on an equal footing with the others, and each region is differentiated in value from any other only by my valuing of it, in other words by my interests, desires, or needs.[25]

In contrast, for the premodern, religion is not one of several possible regions of my life. Instead, it is the field within which any other regions or aspects are marked out and related to each other. Religion is that which makes regions possible and which enacts the world as a whole, giving it unity, order, and meaning in and through symbols. To use Platonic language, religion manifests the "form" of the world. On this view, we can still speak of regions of human endeavor and interest, but ultimately those regions, such as economics or morality or politics, get their meaning in themselves and in their relations to each other, as well as their relative weight and importance from religion, rather than from our valuing.

If we understand religion this way, then I think we must conclude that the religious and the critics of religion implicitly agreed to give up the Bible as a sacred text when they agreed to take it as a referential text like any other referential text rather than as a symbolically ordering one. For to understand the Bible by means of a referential theory is to take it as a manifestation of one region of human experience among others. It is to take it as something on a conceptual and ontological par with other of its regions, rather than as something incomparable because it is a revelation of what gives meaning to any possible region of life as life's enactment. The eighteenth- and nineteenth-century interest in reading the Bible with the methods that one would use to read any other book was, implicitly, a recognition that the Bible was

---

25. Some may expand on this, not placing the value in the individual, but in the group. However, the basic structure remains the same: the distinction between regions and the value of each is determined subjectively or intersubjectively.

no longer *the* text about human existence, but one of many texts, each referring to or describing more or less accurately a different dimension or region of human reality.

The disagreement between Catholicism and the Reformation over the nature of symbols is one locus of this difference between symbolic ordering and reference. The doctrine of transubstantiation is the most obvious instance of this difference in the understanding of symbols. Because those outside the Roman Catholic tradition do not accept that doctrine, they also often reject the idea that symbols are incarnations rather than mere references. However, one need not accept transubstantiation—at least not as it is usually understood—to accept that symbols in general are incarnations.

As the roots of the word *transubstantiation* imply, the problem with the doctrine for those who are not Roman Catholics is that it requires one to believe that the substance of the Eucharist has become, essentially and substantially, the actual flesh and blood of Jesus Christ. Such an understanding of the Eucharist is the consequence, on the one hand, of believing that symbols are incarnations, and, on the other, of having an Aristotelian/Thomistic metaphysics of substance and, therefore, a commensurate explanation of what it means for a symbol to be an incarnation.[26]

---

26. This is not to say that the dogma of transubstantiation begins with Aquinas. Rather, he formulates philosophically the justification for a teaching that has been generally argued for (though not always required to be believed) since at least the tenth century and that was made dogmatic only with the Fourth Lateran Council (1215). The Thomist interpretation of Aristotle's doctrine of substance takes substance to be that which exists in itself or that which remains what it is, though it might have differing qualities at different moments. (For more on substance, see Aristotle's *Categories*.) The second of these characterizations of substance makes possible the doctrine of transubstantiation as usually understood in the dogma of the Catholic Church: the bread takes on the metaphysical substance of Christ's body, though in doing so it has different qualities than it does in the person of Jesus Christ. However, one caveat: Pickstock takes a position very much like that of Marion (*God Without Being*, trans. Thomas A. Carlson [Chicago: University of Chicago, 1991]), arguing cogently and more fully than he that the Thomist interpretation of transubstantiation is not what makes that doctrine implausible. Rather, the implausibility results from the metaphysics of Duns Scotus and the consequent spatialization of ontology: Before Scotus, the sacrament of the Eucharist was understood as the embodied, temporal link of the past to the present and to the future. As such, it

However, one could believe that symbols are incarnations without accepting an Aristotelian-Thomistic metaphysics of substance and the explanations of incarnation that follow from it. The tight connection between the two ideas is only an historical one. Those who accepted the first of these ideas, incarnation, but not the second, Aristotelian metaphysics, would not hold to the doctrine of transubstantiation in the dogmatic sense. Even Catholics have other alternatives for understanding the doctrine of transubstantiation, non-Thomistic, Augustinian ones.[27] Thus, Marion argues that the bread and wine (or water for Latter-day Saints) are incarnations of Christ without arguing that they become, in metaphysical substance, his body and blood; he

---

connected the meaning of the past event of the atonement to the coming event of the Apocalypse, through the present. Therefore, the Eucharist was the embodied *presenting* of the atonement, an act. See Pickstock, *After Writing,* 160–65. In contrast, under Scotus's influence, the Eucharist later "instantiated a transposition from a *temporal* distribution (which linked sacramentally the past and present to the eschatological future), to a *spatial* one, according to which the sacramental 'action' became less a non-identical repetition continuous with the 'original' event and more a simple, positive, authoritative 'miracle' in the present'" (Pickstock, *After Writing,* 160), the presence of a thing. On the pre-Scotus reading, "that which exists in itself" is dynamic rather than static, more like an event than a thing. See Heidegger's *Aristotle's Metaphysics θ 1-3: On the Essence and Actuality of Force,* trans. Walter Brogan and Peter Warnek (Bloomington: Indiana University Press, 1995), for a discussion of this way of understanding Aristotle and, thus, also Aquinas. Thus, Pickstock reads Aquinas's pre-Scotus explanation of the Eucharist and transubstantiation as escaping my criticism, above, though her understanding of Aquinas's explanation fits well with my understanding of how ordinances, symbols, and texts work in the premodern world. Whatever one might think is the most coherent explanation of the doctrine of transubstantiation, my point is that medieval Christians rejected the modernist assumption that the most important symbol in Christianity, the eucharistic wafer and wine, are material things that *merely* direct our attention to something immaterial and invisible. Their understanding of the Eucharist implicitly rejects any simple version of reference, and that rejection can be generalized to their understanding of symbols and to the meaning of texts, as I argue we must do to understand the literal character of scripture.

27. We have seen Pickstock's explanation. Marion explains the Eucharist, neither as a mere "perceptible medium for a wholly intellectual or representational process" nor as "an imposture of idolatry" by which "the community would seek to place 'God' at its disposition like a thing," but as an incarnation of the eucharistic gift, as a temporalizing memorial, a physical memorial that orders the present and, in doing so, grants the future: "The Eucharist anticipates what we will be, will see, will love: *figura nostra,* the figure of what we will be, but above all ourselves, facing the gift that we cannot yet welcome, so, in the strict sense, that we cannot yet figure it" (Marion, *God Without Being,* 166–67).

argues for transubstantiation without arguing for that which most of us associate with transubstantiation and which non-Catholics find religiously and philosophically objectionable. Marion does so with an understanding similar to that we see in Eliade and others like Pickstock: symbols are incarnate orderings of our world.

One way to understand Marion's point better is to consider that early Christians also did not take the Eucharist as a mere reminder, but as a corporate (in other words, an embodied, incarnate) act, an enactment of a way of life. For early Christians, the Eucharist is something the church does and becomes rather than merely something by which the individual signifies and recalls. To remember the sacrifice of Jesus is to take part in a community and the life of that community. It is to incarnate the divine community—the body of Christ (see 1 Corinthians 12:27 and Ephesians 4:12)—and to become incarnate in it, not merely to recall a past event. (If the sacrament were merely a matter of recall, one could effectively perform the sacramental ritual by passing out slips of paper on which was written, "Remember Christ and your relation to him"—or even with an e-mail message to that effect or a note in one's tackle box.) For early Christians and, presumably, for contemporary ones, to partake in the elements of the Eucharist was to be and become something—to be made something ("incarnated" in the divine community, Zion) in and through ritual—not merely to recall a past event.[28] Of course, one cannot become what one must without recalling that past event at some times, but the point stands that the ritual's function cannot be understood only in terms of recollection. Marion's point about how the Eucharist temporalizes—incarnates, putting us into the world in a particular way—is similar.

In contrast, the Reformation understanding of symbols breaks the *incarnans* of the symbol (the material of the symbol) from the *incarnatum* (that which is manifest in the symbol). In doing so, it makes

---

28. Gregory Dix, *The Shape of the Liturgy* (London: Adam and Charles Black, 1945), 29ff., 78ff.

the relation of symbol and what it manifests a matter merely of reference.[29] Rejecting the Reformation, Catholicism continues to insist that the *incarnans* and the *incarnatum* cannot be separated: the *incarnans* is more than something that helps us think about the *incarnatum*. Certainly one need not be a Catholic or believe that the bread of the sacrament becomes the actual body of Christ to think that this insistence has something valuable to say. The issue is not one of Catholics versus Protestants, especially for those like ourselves who are neither. The point is that, contrary to the modernist understanding, religions do not take symbols merely to be referential; they understand them as something more (even when their theologies deny that they do, as in much Protestantism). Contemporary philosophical arguments about meaning and reference point in the direction of a need for something more. The anthropology of religions suggests that we must understand that religion requires more than referentially valid beliefs. The Catholic tradition has called this something more *incarnation*, a term that I adopt as informative, though I will supplement that term with another, *enactment*. To be incarnate is to *be*, materially, a manifestation of, an instance of, what is, supposedly, only referred to. On this way of thinking, the symbol is what it incarnates (or what "in-forms" it, if we use Platonic language) rather than merely a representation of or reference to it. To use the language of Aristotle, to be incarnate is to en-act that to which we might think the thing refers.[30] My claim is that we can understand scripture as an incarnation or enactment of history rather than a representation of it.

Catholicism has given the most thought to how to understand sacred things, including rituals and symbols, in terms of enactment. However, that tradition fails to attend fully to scripture. The Reformation reverses this problem, giving attention to scripture but rejecting

29. Thus, one takes a Reformation view when one understands scripture as a more or less successful attempt to describe events accurately *and* when one takes it to be essentially ahistorical and referential to something transcendent.
30. Note that the literal meaning of *actual* is "enacted." To be something is to enact something.

the understanding of ritual and sacrament as incarnation. And this is true even though the Reformation and Christian humanism also speak of the Bible as an incarnation of Christ, as Erasmus does in speaking of the text as the body of Christ.[31] In spite of what might appear to be incarnational language in Reformation works, we can see the shift from enacted incarnation to representation in the seventeenth-century debates over theater (a debate between written text—representation—and enactment). As Richard Helgerson says:

> Where print fixes the author and frees the reader, performance [in my terms, enactment] does the reverse. It frees the performer and fixes—transfixes—the audience. Performance allows the self a Protean adaptability, but skillfully managed, it overwhelms its audience, rendering it captive to impressions that defy interpretation. For over a millennium the Western community of Christian believers was held in at least a semblance of unity, despite theological difference and hierarchical schism, by the power of ritual performance, only to disintegrate into countless mutually hostile churches when the printed word replaced performed ritual as the primary source of authority.[32]

One could make many points from this observation, from points about the importance of the temple to an explanation of why priesthood authority, something enacted rather than spoken or written down, loses its importance in Reformation belief. However, for our purposes, the point is that the rise of Protestantism involved a shift from scripture as incarnation (enacted presentation) to scripture as written re-presentation.

Having rejected the enactment of incarnation, the Reformation finds itself in trouble when it tries to preserve the sacred character of

---

31. Cited in Richard Helgerson, "Milton Reads the King's Book: Print, Performance, and the Making of a Bourgeois Idol," *Criticism* 29/1 (1987): 1–25, at p. 4.
32. Cited in Helgerson, "Milton Reads the King's Book," 6.

scripture, even though it insists on that. By the eighteenth century, the Reformation relies on referential theories of meaning, with the consequence that scripture, too, loses its sacred character. By itself, writing cannot do the work that the Reformation places on its back; it always falls short of re-presenting its object.[33] Though individual Protestants and Protestant churches may think of scripture otherwise, in principle it ceases to be sacred.[34] For the Reformation, scripture refers to what is sacred, but it is not itself an incarnation of what is sacred. This is because the Reformation gives up the possibility of understanding symbols as incarnations and replaces the incarnational understanding of symbols with the modern theory of reference that comes to the fore.

Thus, the key to the alternative understanding of history that I think saves us from the dilemma of academic history, on the one hand, and ahistory, on the other, is to understand the scriptures as incarnational: *the scriptures are literal history, but their history is incarnational rather than representational.* One can still reasonably ask, however, what it means to speak of incarnation.

To better understand what it means to say that a symbol (and, therefore, also a religious text) is an incarnation, consider an example from the contemporary Belgian philosopher, Paul Moyaert:[35] When Moyaert's father died, he inherited his father's cup. The cup, which he uses for his coffee every morning, has a surplus value. It cannot be reduced to instrumental values. For example, it cannot be reduced to an instrument for helping Moyaert recall his father. If it were, such a

---

33. Writing falls short when it assumes that the relation between the written word is simple reference rather than enactment, for it will always fail to reach that which it supposedly represents because, as only reference, it removes itself from the *act* in which genuine reference occurs. Reference is an act, not a relation. Writing must be read and interpreted for it to be enacted.

34. Ironically, I take it that the nineteenth- and twentieth-century conservative Christian interpretations of *sola scriptura* are the consequence of the fact that scripture has lost its sacred character—an insistence on its sacred character when the rational underpinnings for thinking it sacred have disappeared.

35. The example comes from a lecture by Moyaert, Catholic University of Leuven, 8 January 1996. I have used a variation of the same example in chapter 1 in this volume.

perspective would make the cup, as symbol, only a means for having a particular mental attitude, such as contemplative recollection or psychological reverence for his father. That kind of understanding of the cup will not do. Among other things, it robs the cup of its symbolic value by making it possible that anything, even something that Moyaert chose arbitrarily, could serve the same purpose. If a symbol were only something for creating a mental attitude, then Moyaert could choose a pebble from the street in front of his house to remind him of his father, but it is no coincidence that symbols do not come into being in such an arbitrary fashion. They are not mere keepsakes (and even the keepsake is rarely, if ever, arbitrary or merely subjective).

The cup is not just a tool for recollecting; the surplus value of the cup comes from the fact that Moyaert's father touched it. Thus, its character as a symbol is a matter of contiguity rather than representation or instrumentality. However, when Moyaert uses the cup, it is not that, by doing so, he touches his father *in absentia*. The cup is not a substitute for his father—another reason that it is not essentially a reminder. Though the cup can remind him, often Moyaert uses it without explicitly recalling his father. Instead, the cup is a symbol of Moyaert's father because it does something for Moyaert in spite of himself: even when he is not thinking of his father, the cup demands Moyaert's reverence; it connects Moyaert to his father even when Moyaert is not conscious of his father. In a small way, the cup gives a symbolic order to Moyaert's world, an order that relates him to his father and to the rest of the world, an order that cannot be reduced to his intentions to recall his father. It is as if the cup remembers Moyaert's father for Moyaert.[36]

Thus, not only does the cup not refer to or even represent Moyaert's father, it does not take his place. In a very real sense, it takes

---

36. It is not central to the thesis of this paper, but I should note that, as I say in chapter 1, I distinguish memory from recall. Recall is a psychological event. Memory is what we share and participate in. As such, it gives us direction (intention) beyond our subjective intentions, often intentions we do not know. It also creates expectations of us that are beyond our will. Though the cup remembers for Moyaert, it may not always or ever recall for him.

Moyaert's place rather than his father's. In that sense, Moyaert is willing to grant something like but not identical to consciousness—within
the symbolic order—to his father's cup. This approaches what we see
described in anthropological encounters with so-called "primitive"
religions: symbols are objects that do something in spite of my intentions; they do something that we otherwise could attribute only to human beings. In this sense, religion is magical—though we must avoid
equating magic with naive or bad science.[37] The cup is an incarnation
rather than a reference; it gives a symbolic order to Moyaert's world
rather than a rational one, and the cup gives order by embodying that
order in the lived world that it orders.

It is important to emphasize that this result—that symbols oper-
ate in a "magical" way—is because the reverence that characterizes
life in a symbolic ordering is not a matter of consciousness. Of course
conscious reverence for the sacred is possible. However, one could
not have the mental attitude of reverence without already being in a
symbolic ordering, an ordering that gives one the possibility of conscious reverence, at least partly by manifesting objects that demand
reverence. The symbolic order gives objects as objects of reverence,
so to be within the symbolic order is to *be* reverent, to attend to the
sacred, whether or not one is explicitly conscious of and attentive to
that order. For to be within a symbolic ordering is to be ordered by,
to have the world ordered by, that symbolic ordering. The objects and
possibilities of the world, especially but not only ritual objects and
possibilities, are related to each other in and through the fact that they
manifest the ordering of the symbolic; the symbolic ordering gives
them their place and their relations in the world, and it makes possible
our understanding. And in ritual acts, one's own body, as well as the
objects to which one attends, are loci for such incarnations of the sym-

---

37. For an interesting discussion of symbolic ordering and its power—in the context
of witchcraft rather than magic—see Jeanne Favret-Saada, *Deadly Words*, trans. Catherine Cullen (Cambridge: Cambridge University Press, 1980). The introduction to that
book also shows why symbolic ordering cannot be reduced to primitive science.

bolic. Symbolic relations do not come from mental acts and attitudes; they make acts and attitudes, such as conscious reverence, possible.

One way to state my thesis is to say that scripture is incarnation and religion is sacred ordering. Thus, difficulties occur when, with the onset of modernism, scripture becomes, like any other book, something that is understood merely referentially, and religion ceases to be thought of as *the* ordering power of the world and becomes one sphere of interest among many, a sphere that must be ordered by something else. For modernism, that "something else" is reason, though for Christian premoderns, the ordering power is the incarnate Divine— and this difference in the ordering "principle" produces the chasm (and the common antipathy) between the two.

We see a symptom of this loss of symbolic ordering in Descartes' *Discourse on the Method of Rightly Conducting the Reason* (published in 1637). In the *Discourse*, Descartes tells us that he needs something by which to adjudicate between the various plausible opinions he learned in the schools. Finding nothing, he takes up the method of geometry, namely formal reason. In addition, Descartes confines religion to the region of morals. He not only speaks of the moral truths of his country and Catholicism (truths that he accepts as provisional),[38] he also mentions the truths of faith.[39] Nevertheless, Descartes does no more than mention the truths of faith. Rather than being that which orders the regions of our lives, for Descartes, religion is one region of human life among other possible regions, a region that can be ignored or set to the side as one goes about laying a foundation for understanding the world and its various regions.[40] Descartes finds himself in a chaos in which it seems that nothing can be known or trusted.[41] Prior to the Reformation, the Catholic Church had given the world

---

38. Descartes, *Discourse on the Method of Rightly Conducting the Reason*, part III ¶1.

39. Descartes, *Discourse on the Method*, part III ¶6.

40. Interestingly, Descartes reduces the religious region of human experience to the moral, a reduction that begins at about his time and grows more prevalent until, today, the identity of religion and morality is common sense—in spite of Nietzsche's pointed and accurate attacks on such religion. Such common sense robs religion of its vitality.

41. Descartes, *Discourse on the Method*, part I.

its order, but that order has failed for Descartes. Thus, if there is to be something other than chaos—in Descartes' terms, if knowledge is possible—then something other than religion must order life as a whole, including religion. For Descartes, religion has ceased to give order to the world and has become one of its regions. His project in *Discourse* and in *Meditations on First Philosophy* is to allow reason to order life by giving us the method for conducting/ordering reason; in other words, by showing us that reason can order itself.[42]

That Descartes believes we need a method for ordering reason is evidence that the symbolic ordering no longer has force: Descartes confuses our tool for dealing with the various regions of existence, namely reason, for the ordering authority of the world. He makes it clear that he has settled on a method for conducting reason and finding truth because he has no way of choosing between the various opinions of his predecessors: finding nothing that orders reason, Descartes must give a rational method for ordering it. Yet the necessity of grounding reason on itself (method) would never have occurred to an ancient Greek or a medieval Christian, Jew, or Muslim because, whatever the many differences between them, for each, the exercise of reason occurs within an ordering that is prior to and fundamental to reason. For them, whether it is *physis* or Divine creation, reason has a ground that is, on a modern view, nonrational.[43] Even those thinkers, such as the Averroists, for whom the truths of reason and the truths of faith are ultimately commensurable, do not assume that something is true because it is rational. Instead, something is rational because it is true. That reversal of the relation between truth and reason is signifi-

---

42. As Emmanuel Levinas shows in *Totality and Infinity: An Essay on Exteriority,* trans. Alphonso Lingis (Pittsburgh: Duquesne University Press, 1969), 48ff., Descartes' attempt relies on the necessity of something beyond the rational (see *Meditations* III). Nevertheless, Descartes seems not to have understood the degree to which the necessity of recourse to the extrarational Infinite undercuts his methodological claims. Even if he did understand that, it is certainly the case that those following him did not.

43. Of course, if one does not have the narrower definition of reason that modernism adopts, then it becomes possible to identify the ground of reason (in that word's modern sense) with reason itself, as ancients and medievals usually do.

cant. It marks the huge difference between the way that the ancients and the medievals see the world, on the one hand, and the way that we see the world once modernism arrives.

For premodern thinkers, reason's being is granted by the truth of the symbolic ordering, even if the rational order and the symbolic order are ultimately identical. Thus, for those in the centuries before modernism, there had been means for adjudicating between various plausible opinions. For Christians, the Catholic Church—its authority, its doctrines and practices, its institutional structure—provided those means and order came to the world through them. Descartes' inability to adjudicate between differing opinions and his subsequent search for a method shows us that by Descartes' time a radical shift had already taken place, a shift away from an understanding that finds the use of reason within what is given by a symbolic ordering. Prior to modernism, the world had been given order by the Divine and reason was a tool for dealing with and in that order, though not itself the source of order. However, the loss of the Divine as a ground left reason and the world without moorings and, so, required something like the four-part rational method that Descartes prescribes.[44] Reason filled the vacuum created when religion ceased to order life.

This loss of the Divine as a ground shows up in the difference between modern and premodern understandings of certainty. Prior to modernism, Christian certainty was the certainty of salvation, a certainty *given* by the life of faith, a certainty available to all who lived that life. Thus, though Christians had certainty, that certainty did not include a complete apprehension of the rational (in other words, of the mind of God). With modernism the ground shifts: since certainty is no longer given, it must be achieved; one must have a method for gaining certainty, rules for what to do to get it.

Since, as we see in Descartes, the method for achieving certainty is rational, the rational is thought of as self-revealing. Based on the biblical teaching that humans are made in God's image (Genesis 1:26

---

44. Descartes, *Discourse on the Method,* part II ¶¶7–10.

and Moses 2:27), human reason is rethought and at least implicitly modeled on the mind of God, a mind that has come to be understood as, strictly speaking, capable of only purely theoretic understanding. As a result, modernism assumes that the use of the proper method, a self-grounding method, will (in principle) lead one to the complete capture, the complete apprehension, of the rational (which, though no longer identical to the mind of God, continues to be thought in the same terms: for example, as self-revealing and atemporal). This shift changes the meaning of everything—the rational, certainty, method, knowledge—in such a way that the premodern understanding becomes inaccessible to thought, incomprehensible, at best naive and primitive.[45]

One way to see the difference between a modern and a premodern understanding of religion is to focus on the question of signs. In latter-day scripture, the Lord says to Adam:

> Behold, all things have their likeness, and all things are created and made to bear record of me, both things which are temporal, and things which are spiritual; things which are in the heavens above, and things which are on the earth, and things which are in the earth, and things which are under the earth, both above and beneath: all things bear record of me. (Moses 6:63)

---

45. In spite of the way that, for heuristic reasons, I have described the change from premodernism to modernism and in spite of the way that modern thinkers often portrayed and understood themselves, modernism was no sudden and absolute rupture with its past. Such things as Greek *epistēmē* combined with the Christian idea of an external nature over which humans rule, the certainty of salvation, ascetic "methods" for achieving salvation, and voluntarism are important antecedents of modernism. Nevertheless, with modernism's explicit rejection of its roots and its move to the subject (individual consciousness) as fundamental, a very new understanding of things and the world entered into European history. For more on the antecedents of modernism, see Louis Dupré, *Passage to Modernity: An Essay in the Hermeneutics of Nature and Culture* (New Haven: Yale University Press, 1993), and Pickstock, *After Writing*.

We often read this passage and similar ones as if it speaks of signs referentially. However, there are problems with that view.[46] The understanding that this citation exemplifies was a common one among ancient thinkers, including Augustine, so consider his reflection on signs and on the claim in question. In one obvious reading, Augustine is said to argue that signs are essentially referential. The referential character of signs seems difficult to avoid in *Christian Doctrine* 1.2 and 2, where Augustine seems to give a standard, modern theory of signs, a referential theory: words are signs of other things; we use words to refer to things. However, it is important to notice that in Augustine's discussion God is not a creature, so (in Augustine's understanding) he is not a thing. We cannot refer to God.[47] Nevertheless, all things, particularly corporeal things, point to God.[48] It follows that all things point to God, though none refer to him. Either God is an exception, or some ways of signifying point at that which they intend, but they do not refer.

In addition, Augustine explicitly compares the Incarnation with speech,[49] but the Incarnation cannot be understood as a merely referential event. Thus, though every thing (every creature; every created thing) is a sign, the final object of signs, which makes all other signs possible as signs, is no thing (because it is no creature), and cannot be referred to. The consequence is that, for Augustine (and I think also for the scriptural passage in question), we cannot understand signs merely referentially; referential theories of signs are only partial theories. Something more is needed, namely God (for Augustine) and I would add "also other intelligences."

Notice also that, according to traditional Christian doctrine, after the fall of Adam, human beings are unable to see God directly, a thought often expressed for Latter-day Saints in the idea that we

---

46. One problem is that, as I argue in chapter 7 in this volume, *likeness* in scripture seems to suggest likeness of being rather than likeness merely of appearance or qualities.
47. Augustine, *Christian Doctrine* 1.5.
48. Augustine, *Christian Doctrine* 1.6.
49. Augustine, *Christian Doctrine* 1.13.

cannot see God "with natural eyes."[50] From this comes the traditional Christian view that language—veiling and obscuring as it may be in some sense—is not only a consequence of the fall, it is a blessing. Language gives human beings our only access to the Divine, which otherwise would blind us. If, as modernism suggests, the words that refer to God and divine things were mere signs, tools for thinking about something else, just tools for referring to something else, then for them to function as signs we would also have to have direct access to the referent, to God, which is impossible. Merely referential signs require that what they refer to must be available to the person who understands them.

Consider a simple sign: my driver's license. My license has a name, a number, and a picture. They each refer to me and together they represent me. To understand this reference and representation—for any one of them or all of them as a group to function as a sign—a person taking my license as a sign must have access not only to these signs, but also to that which they refer. In principle, a person must be able to encounter me independent of those signs. He or she must be able to see, hear, or touch me independent of my license. Without that, the license cannot refer to me because the merely referential sign is a substitute for the thing signified, the license is a substitute for my person. Imagine a case in which someone says, "This license has a referent, but the picture is not the picture of the person it refers to, the number is not that person's number, and the name on it is not the referent's name." No one would take the person's claim seriously. As merely references, signs function only if that to which they refer is also independently accessible to those who read them.

If we understand symbols as a kind of referential sign, then we understand signs of God as substitutes for him and, therefore, we assume implicitly that we have direct access to him. However, signs of God do not work that way, for if they refer, they do so across a chasm with

---

50. In latter-day scripture, see Moses 1:11 and Doctrine and Covenants 58:3, as well as 2 Corinthians 12:1–4.

"nothing available" on the other side. Of course, religious people will deny that nothing is available on the other side, but that makes my point rather than contradicts it. The religious can see and listen to and be commanded by the Being to whom the religious symbol refers, not because it refers in the same way that an ordinary sign does (in other words to something public, something that anyone can see or hear independent of the sign), but because, being enlightened fundamentally by the Divine rather than by reason,[51] they see the "other side" in and through the symbol.[52]

Though there are a variety of positions among premodern thinkers regarding signs, I think we can characterize them as generally taking the words of scripture not to be merely referential signs of a divine reality (though they may have what we could call a referential component). Instead of referring to the Divine as do ordinary signs, the words of scripture are an embodiment of the Divine, an incarnation; they embody the divine order of that to which, on a modern view, they seem only to refer.[53] Thus, according to Carol Harrison, in spite of the homonymy, instead of translating Augustine's word *signum* as "sign," we should understand it to mean *sacramentum*, itself a translation of *mystērion*: what is secret or hidden.[54] And we must remember that the *mystērion* is not just temporarily hidden. It is hidden in principle; in

51. Which, of course, is not to say that they are not, secondarily, also enlightened by reason.

52. The difference between what Augustine and Aquinas mean by *enlightenment* and what the moderns mean is another way to mark the difference between the medieval and the modern. The former has to do with the gift of seeing the sacred in the temporal, seeing the sacred order of the temporal; the latter has to do with using reason critically. For the former, see Augustine's *The Literal Meaning of Genesis*; for the latter, see Kant, "What Is Enlightenment?" in *Kant Selections*, ed. Lewis W. Beck (New York: Macmillan, 1988), 462–67.

53. The incarnationist view of scripture is not confined to Christianity. Speaking of the medieval Jewish mystical understanding of Torah, Fishbane says, "On this view, the Bible . . . is ontologically unique principally because it is nothing less than a dimension of divinity itself." Michael Fishbane, *The Garments of Torah: Essays in Biblical Hermeneutics* (Bloomington: Indiana University Press, 1989), 35.

54. Carol Harrison, *Beauty and Revelation in the Thought of Saint Augustine* (Oxford: Clarendon, 1992), 85, 203.

other words, it is invisible to human or "natural" eyes. We see it only
by revelation. *the mysteries or hidden things of the kingdom of God*

On such thinking, the visible—the elements and objects of the
created world, the history of the world, our lives together—bears (incarnates, enacts) rather than refers to spiritual reality. It bears and
enacts it as depth and richness—as mystery in the strict, positive sense
of that word, "a secret"—just as the human body bears and enacts the
depth and richness and mystery of the person. For a Muslim, a Jew,
or a Christian, the full history of the world is necessarily a history
understood under the order of divine creation. Thus, strictly speaking, the actual, literal history of the world is invisible *except* as the
symbolic ordering of creation embodies and reveals it. Any other history is an abstraction from that literal history. For the religions of the
Bible and Qur'an, scripture is an important incarnation of the divine
ordering (as are also ordinance, priesthood authority, tradition, and
so on). Because it is symbolic, scripture embodies what reference cannot yield, what is in itself unrepresentable because it is excessive of
reference. Scripture embodies and bodies forth the divine ordering of
the world and its events. For premoderns, that embodiment is history,
literal history, not the accurate reference to and description of events
that have no order or meaning other than the chronology of time and
the relations of reason.[55]

For Christians, the Incarnation of Christ is the perfect instance of
the conjunction of *factum* and *sacramentum*: Christ is neither a rep-

---

55. Suppose, however, that one cannot accept the argument that symbols are best understood incarnationally, that one still feels that symbols must be understood as references,
as a kind of sign. Even then, it is impossible for us to refer adequately and accurately to the
history of the world. Human understanding may hold some few points of that history together, but it cannot hold them together as a whole, especially not an ordered whole. For human understanding, the *kosmos* becomes, at best, a blur of amorphous shapes in an ancient
mirror. (See 1 Corinthians 13:12.) If the *kosmos* can be comprehended, only God can do so.
Therefore, even if scripture were referential rather than incarnational, for a believer only
the divine revelation of history—in other words, scripture—could be an accurate reference
to and representation of that history as a whole, something that scientific history neither
attempts nor wishes to give. The events of history can be understood only as they fit into the
whole of which they are a part. Thus, even the particular events of a divine history could

resentation of divine reality nor a reference to it. He is not something given to help us recall God.[56] He *is* that divine reality perceptible to human beings. As such, he is also the perfect analogy for scripture: "In the case of Scripture, the visible, created, temporal order cannot simply be shunned as an ambiguous, misleading imitation of a spiritual truth which is better grasped by the mind. Rather, . . . Scripture is the 'incarnate' form of the Christian revelation."[57] Similarly, New Testament statements about the church being the body of Christ suggest that one encounters Christ *in* the church. The church is an incarnation of Christ, not a simple signifier of or reference to him—an incarnation in the sense I have discussed earlier, namely something that materially manifests or enacts a symbolic ordering, here, that of Christ.

Though this language of incarnation, as when we speak of the church as the incarnation of Christ, is scriptural,[58] it strikes Latter-day Saints as odd. It is sufficiently odd for a Mormon audience that we assume it to be, perhaps, metaphorical or a matter of simile: we want to say, "the church is like the body of Christ," though that is not a particularly informative clause. The problem is that, given Standard English usage, we think of incarnation as an event in which something that is without a body becomes manifest in something embodied. Therefore, we speak of that event as "the incarnation of *x*, *y*, or *z*," where the variables stand for the unembodied thing in question. Since Christ is embodied, it is not clear how he could become incarnate in the church. In fact, according to our standard usage, to say that he does suggests that he is not already incarnate himself.[59] No surprise

not be understood except from within the perspective of a divine revelation, the perspective purportedly offered by scripture and a perspective purposefully and necessarily unavailable within the parameters of modern historiography.

56. For Latter-day Saints, the comparison is even closer: the Son is an incarnation of the Father without being the same person as the Father.

57. Harrison, *Beauty and Revelation*, 81.

58. For example, 1 Corinthians 12:27; Ephesians 4:12.

59. Alternatively, it suggests something that we find too mysterious, something like the traditional interpretation of the doctrine of transubstantiation.

that we are confused by talk of the church being the body of Christ, or by this discussion of scripture as incarnation.

However, consider that Joseph Smith says, "There is no such thing as immaterial matter. All spirit is matter."[60] According to his teachings, my body is not the incarnation of something non-bodily, for the spirit is also incarnate. In fact, there are no non-incarnate entities.[61] This suggests that we cannot understand incarnation as something unembodied becoming embodied. What, then, can we mean by *incarnation*?

Our common usage and the history of thought about incarnation make it difficult for us to think of incarnation in terms consonant with the Prophet's teaching. His teaching flies in the face of that usage and history. Nevertheless I do not think we are faced with an insurmountable difficulty. We must think carefully about embodiment. We must ask what it means to say that we "have" a body, given that we cannot mean that something unembodied possesses or inhabits something embodied and we do not explain that usage when we speak of one kind of body (a spirit body) possessing another (a physical body).[62] Though this is not as simple as it first might seem (thinking otherwise than our usual prejudgments and understandings is often difficult, even when we know they are wrong), there are philosophers, such as Maurice Merleau-Ponty, who may help us begin to do this thinking. Put broadly, Merleau-Ponty argues that to be embodied is to inhabit (to "enact," if you will) a world in a particular way:[63] "We must . . .

---

60. *Teachings of the Prophet Joseph Smith*, comp. Joseph Fielding Smith (Salt Lake City: Deseret Book, 1938), 301.

61. This is how I read the Prophet's seemingly tautologous statement that there is no immaterial matter.

62. Talk of spirit bodies possessing physical bodies does not explain what it means to have a body since, according to LDS doctrine, spirits, too, have material bodies. They too are incarnate.

63. One reason that I find Merleau-Ponty's discussion helpful is that it echoes Paul's way of talking about what it means to be a Christian. See, for example, Romans 7 and 8, where it is clear that the change that occurs in a Christian is not a change of characteristics, but a change of being. (Compare 7:22–23 with 8:8–9.) For Paul, the division is not between inner and outer, or mind/spirit and body, but between living by the Spirit and living according to one's will—that is, living according to the world. For Paul, to be a Christian is to inhabit the world in a particular way, not to subscribe to a particular set

avoid saying that our body is *in* space, or *in* time. It *inhabits* space and time";[64] "To be a body is to be tied to a certain world."[65] Taking off from Merleau-Ponty's insight, perhaps we can say that the body is one's attitude (in the literal sense—"fittedness; disposition; posture"— rather than in mentalistic terms) and attitudinizing in the world. The body is the position one takes in the world, where *position* refers not only to a spatio-temporal position that we can fix by specifying a series of coordinates, but also to one's temporal relations to other things, persons, and so on—one's orientation. We have a body like we have an idea or a fear, not as a possession, but as the way in which things appear to me and the way in which I project myself in living and in relating to other persons and other things.[66] Consciousness is part of my bodily attitude, but not the sum of it.

Given this thinking about incarnation, we can expand it to think about incarnation in general: to speak of something as an incarnation is not to say that something else, something nonmaterial, has come to be material in it. It is to say that a particular attitude, a particular way of being situated in and among the things there are, comes to be manifest, or enacted, in it. Of course, to be situated in the world in a particular way is always, necessarily, also to be situated with regard to what there is. There is no "pure, unembodied" enactment or presentation. In a strictly scientific attitude (an attitude that scientists need not take except when they are explicitly doing science, an attitude that is not the same as their mental attitude or personal beliefs) there is no relation to God. The scientific region, the region in which one investigates bodies using the assumptions, methods, and background of

of beliefs (though beliefs will follow from the fact that one inhabits the world as a Christian—see note 20). See also 1 Corinthians 1:26–29, especially v. 28, where Paul speaks of the Saints as "non-being" (*mē on*), suggesting that the difference between Christians and non-Christians is a matter of their *being* rather than the propositions to which each adheres.

64. Maurice Merleau-Ponty, *The Phenomenology of Perception*, trans. Colin Smith (New York: Routledge & Kegan Paul, 1962), 139.

65. Merleau-Ponty, *Phenomenology of Perception,* 148.

66. Merleau-Ponty, *Phenomenology of Perception,* 174 n. 1.

science is necessarily godless.[67] Scientific objects, themselves impoverished, in other words abstracted objects, incarnate the work and understanding of that region. Other objects incarnate other regions and orderings.[68] Thus, to say that the church is an incarnation of Christ is to say that in the church one finds oneself situated and oriented in the world in a way given by Christ toward things revealed by Christ as they are revealed by him: one finds oneself in a world that Christ has enacted, and that enacts its relation to him as Creator. Similarly, to say that scripture or an ordinance is an incarnation is to say that, in the material existence of these things—as scripture and ordinance rather than as abstracted to merely so-called objective qualities—we are given an orientation in the world: relations to things, meanings and values of things, the existence and nonexistence of things.

As incarnations in a symbolic ordering, symbols are opaque beings rather than signs with multiple reference. The use of the word *incarnation* to describe the being of entities that give symbolic order is not accidental, for signs are like the living, enacting body, as Augustine explicitly says: "How did He come except that 'the Word was made flesh, and dwelt among us?' It is as when we speak."[69] The opacity of the living human body, the density and richness that, in principle, cannot be made transparent, means that no one, final description of a human being is possible. This opacity need not be something arcane

---

67. This is not to criticize scientists for that attitude or to suggest that God ought to be part of science. A great many other important things also do not exist in a world inhabited scientifically, things such as morality and value or, of less consequence, good taste in food or clothing. That absence is the consequence of the specialized incarnation required of science and is only a problem if scientists (or more often those who idolize science because they know too little of it) forget that such a specialized incarnation is not the only one, the best one, or the final one. God is equally—and unproblematically—absent from other regions, such as mathematics and military strategy. See also pages 167–68 of this chapter, pages 72–74 of chapter 4 in this volume, and Heidegger's "The Age of the World Picture," in *The Question Concerning Technology and Other Essays*, trans. William Lovitt (New York: Harper Colophon, 1977), 115–54 and "Science and Reflection" in *Question Concerning Technology*, 155–82.

68. Moyaert's discussion of symbols—see pages 174–76—is a discussion of symbols as incarnations.

69. Augustine, *Christian Doctrine* 1.13.

or complex. Seeing it and understanding it does not require great eru-
dition on the one hand or mumbo jumbo on the other. For example,
the opacity of living persons, an opacity consequent on their embodiment, both physical and spiritual, is an ordinary, everyday experience:
a person cannot be reduced to one "meaning" or perspective, though
a person has meaning and one has perspectives on any person.[70] One
could argue that nonhuman objects, both animate and inanimate, are
similarly dense. The incarnational character of scripture makes it also
dense and opaque—embodied—but the opacity of scripture is different from the unclarity of a poorly formed assertion.

Assertions that can have more than one meaning are unclear because they are faulty as assertions. They are ambiguous at best. However, it follows that all language ought to be clear in the same way that
assertions are clear only if all language is best understood as asser-
tional and referential. If scripture is not to be understood, fundamentally, by means of a referential theory of meaning, then one cannot
criticize it as if it were a set of referential assertions. Scriptural opacity
and depth are different from ambiguity. One cannot reduce the density of scripture to multiplicity of reference, as do most of the critics of
the Bible and most of its defenders.

Both poetry and scripture attend to what is excessive of language
and attention; both are matters of reverence for what exceeds and explains us. There is not enough space here to decide how they are related. It is enough to notice that they at least overlap, and that overlap
helps us see how religious language differs from merely referential language. In the languages of both poetry and religion, I intend what is
beyond my understanding, though often by means of something that
does not, especially at first glance, itself transcend my gaze. I intend

70. I have in mind here Edmund Husserl's concept of *Abschattungen*, "profiles." *Ideas: General Introduction to Pure Phenomenology*, trans. W. R. Boyce Gibson (London: Collier Macmillan, 1962), 117–20. We know an object only in its profiles, but it is always excessive of those profiles as well as of any imaginative combination of profiles (and it is important to recall that a combination of profiles is always the result of an act of imagination; the scientific objectivity of a thing is the work of imagination rather than perception).

what transcends my intention. Thus, in both poetry and religion one speaks, but not to make everything transparent and easily accessible. In fact, among other things, in both one denies, by one's way of speaking, by the language itself and its "content" (as if the two could be separated), the transparency of what one intends and one's ability to master it or fully intend it. Religious and poetic languages show us that meaning is not reducible to reference, for they mean without being able fully to refer, without trying to refer. They mean by incarnating that which they mean rather than merely referring to it.

The languages of poetry and religion incarnate things that one is mastered by rather than master of. In those languages, what I mean—what my words and thoughts supposedly intend—outstrips what I understand, outstrips what *I* mean. The object of my intention is excessive of my intention, of any possible intention.[71] However, what exceeds my meaning is not another meaning, not something to be said "in other words." The abundance of meaning does not suggest that, given sufficient time, I will be able to say everything, that the abundance will disappear.[72] Thus, what I intend in poetry or religion is never an object in the strict sense of that term ("something placed or thrown before me, clear to my sight and examination"), making the word *intention* itself problematic, though it will do for now.[73] Because of this abundance or excess, the languages of prophecy and poetry do not dissimulate an adequacy and clarity of understanding that belie the truth of what they say. They are not the clear and distinct languages that Descartes proposes for modernism *because* they remain true to that of which they speak. For prophecy and poetry, as

---

71. See note 40.

72. The Enlightenment had this overcoming of all abundance and excess as its goal. In Derridean terms, it aimed at the identity of text and world. However, the excess of meaning is a function of the embodiment of the world and ourselves, and it makes continued speaking and relation possible. Thus, the implicit goal of the Enlightenment was the destruction of the body by the reduction of everything to certainty—absolute irrelation and silence; absolute death.

73. Both Levinas's and Marion's discussions of intention are instructive (Levinas, *Totality and Infinity*, 23, 27–29, 49, 122–30, 204–9, 257–61, 294–95; Marion, *God Without Being*, 18–23).

the twentieth-century German thinker Walter Benjamin says, "Truth is not 'an unveiling that destroys the secret,' but the revelation that does it justice."[74]

It may seem that this discussion of the abundance of scriptural language implies that scripture is necessarily obscure, but that does not follow. The alternative to understanding the opacity of scripture as multiple references is not to understand it as obscure; scriptural language is neither essentially obscure nor essentially meaningless. Just as opacity and the abundance that opacity makes possible are not the same as unclarity, they are not the same as obscurity. Isaiah is not more of a prophet than Mark or Nephi because he is more difficult to read; the abundance, depth, and richness of incarnation should not be confused with obscurity.[75] Any

---

74. Walter Benjamin, *The Origin of German Tragic Drama*, trans. John Osborne (New York: Verso, 1977), 31; translation revised. See also the text that Benjamin may have in mind, namely Nietzsche's preface to the second edition of *The Gay Science*, section four, where Nietzsche compares the will to see everything to Egyptian boys who desecrate temples: "We no longer believe that truth remains truth when one pulls off the veils: we have lived too much to believe this. Today it seems to us a matter of propriety that one would not to wish to see everything naked, to be present at everything, or to understand and 'know' everything." Perhaps this is a way of explaining the Savior's remark in Matthew 13:13: "I speak to them in parables: because they seeing see not; and hearing they hear not, neither do they understand." That idea is an important part of the Christian tradition, though it is often a scandal to believers as well as nonbelievers. The traditional explanation for parables and parabolic language is: "The motives for symbolism are secrecy and revelation, as accommodated to the abilities of the interpreters. God uses symbols so that 'the most sacred things are not easily handled by the profane but are revealed instead to the real lovers of holiness' (1105C, 283)." Pseudo-Dionysius, quoted in Paul Rorem, *Pseudo-Dionysius: A Commentary on the Texts and an Introduction to Their Influence* (Oxford: Oxford University Press, 1993), 25. For more on Pseudo-Dionysius, see chapter 6, note 40. My argument suggests that perhaps, instead, parables are to be explained as the only possible response to those who demand that the language of religion be "clear and distinct." Parables demand that their hearers deal with them as something containing a secret, but a secret that, it turns out, cannot simply be removed. (Of course, the two explanations are not mutually exclusive.) Note also that the view I propose contests Kermode's explanation of the secrecy of parables and, therefore, of what it means to understand a narrative. See Frank Kermode, *The Genesis of Secrecy: On the Interpretation of Narrative* (Cambridge, MA: Harvard University Press, 1979).

75. Of course, these remarks do not imply that we ought to avoid clear and distinct language. Our preference for such language is not merely contingent. Taking the identity of intention and expression to be an ultimate good for writing is an outgrowth of our Cartesian goal of mastery over everything with no remainder, the transparency of the

religious person has had the experience of discovering new meaning in texts that she has read before, often many times. That is a phenomenon of abundance, of the excess of meaning—of the incarnation of scripture— not a phenomenon of ambiguity or obscurity. Religious ordinances are a perfect example of the kind of abundance that we find in religion and scripture. In religious rituals, in other words in symbolic ordering enacted in ritual objects and on my body, my words and actions intend more than I, as an individual human being, can possibly intend, though they can and often are themselves quite simple and straightforward.[76]

To take scripture as incarnational is neither to conflate historical understanding and accurate description nor to take scripture to be essentially referential. Neither is it to take scripture to be merely metaphorical or poetic (in the impoverished, everyday sense of that word). To see scripture as incarnational, as opaque and revelatory, is to see it as telling the *literal* truth, as giving the literal history of the world. As Frank Kermode says, speaking accurately of incarnational interpretations (though he does not recognize them as incarnational): "The spiritual sense so authorized [in other words, within the structure of the medieval Catholic Church, official as well as unofficial] was the true literal sense."[77]

This identification of "spiritual sense" and "literal sense" is surprising to contemporary ears. After all, we take the literal truth to be

---

world. However, the identity of intention and expression is sometimes a good: when that identity *is* possible, then our language ought to embody it. If our language does not, it fails. It is inadequate. Nevertheless, languages other than the language of clarity are also possible, even necessary. (For one thing, if they are not possible, then it is not clear how to avoid making the desire for knowledge a desire, ultimately, for annihilation.)

76. The Latter-day Saint and Catholic recognition of the need for ordinances and for authority in ordinances is a recognition of the inadequacy of individual intentions when it comes to understanding or invoking the Divine. In general, Protestantism disagrees on this point, but its disagreement runs the risk of reducing religion to the thoughts and feelings of the individual, to only a psychological attitude. See my "A New Way of Looking at Scripture," *Sunstone,* August 1995, 78–84. Though the title is unfortunate—not of my choosing—that piece contains a sketch of an argument for the necessity of authority. See also Marion, *God Without Being,* 153ff., from which I have adapted that argument.

77. However, Kermode misunderstands the relation of the Roman Catholic Church to medieval scripture interpretation, accepting without question the modernist view of

the truth that most accurately describes or refers to what happened, independent of any symbolic ordering, and we take the "spiritual sense" to be something beyond the literal. We take the spiritual sense to be "merely" symbolic. Premoderns, however, do not disjoin the literal and the spiritual. For them, the word *literal* means something quite different. For them, it means, "what the letters, in other words, the words, say," rather than, "what an objective report would say." The sentences, "What *x* says" and "what *x* describes accurately," do not mean the same, even if the first is a description. Even a careless reading of medieval discussions of scriptural exegesis will show that the medievals' interest was not in deciding what the scriptures portray, but in what they say. They do not take the scriptures to be picturing something for us, but to be telling us the truth of the world, of its things, its events, and its people, a truth that cannot be told apart from its situation in a divine, symbolic ordering made manifest in human history.

Of course, that is not to deny that the scriptures tell about events that actually happened. They are about real people and real events. What I propose is not a way to reduce the premodern understanding of history to a modern view, to one that denies the historicity of scripture by taking scripture to refer to a transcendent, nonhistorical reality. I am not arguing that the scriptures only *seem* to be historical. Premodern interpreters of the Bible understand the scriptures to be about actual events. For them, what the scriptures say includes portrayal of and talk about real things. However, premodern interpreters do not think it sufficient (or possible) to portray the real events of real history without letting us see them in the light of that which gives them their significance—their reality, the enactment of which they

---

the matter: he applies the distinction between what the texts are about and what they mean, and he criticizes biblical texts for their failure to describe events accurately. As a result, he does not seem to understand the incarnational character of premodern interpretation or its communal character. He also misunderstands Heidegger's discussion of interpretation.

are part—as history, namely the symbolic order that they incarnate. Without that light, portrayals cannot be accurate.

A bare description of the physical movements of certain persons at a certain time is not history. "Person A raised his left hand, turning it clockwise so that .03 milliliters of a liquid poured from a vial in that hand into a receptacle situated midway between A and B" does not mean the same as "Henry poured poison into Richard's cup." Only the latter could be a historical claim (and even the former is no bare description).

History is not possible without meaning and significance, perhaps not even mere chronicle is. The question is where that meaning and significance derive from. For premodern Bible interpreters, the divine order that events incarnate give them their meaning. A literal history, therefore, necessarily incorporates and reveals that order. Any history that does not incorporate it is incomplete and, therefore, inaccurate.[78] It is inaccurate because it does not embody the divine order that makes it what it is. That means that premodern literal histories—the accurate portrayals of what happened, if one continues to insist on referential language—will differ significantly from literal histories told under the aspect of a different order, such as that of the rationalism of modernism.

As already noted, modernism, too, requires that meaning be "added" to otherwise bare events so that we can understand them. In modernism, too, something besides our accounts orders those accounts and stabilizes meaning. However, with the Enlightenment, modernism does not recognize a divine order as the source of order and stability. Modernist history intentionally and necessarily ignores any divine ordering of history, taking up, instead, the order of causation as understood scientifically. This is not a matter of perversity or

---

78. However, we must remember that we decide accuracy relative to the region or order within which a description occurs and to the purposes for which it is given. A scientific description would be inaccurate in a scriptural text; a scriptural description would be inaccurate in a scientific text. In neither case could one rectify the inaccuracy of the description by saying more, by giving more detail, by looking more closely, by correcting one's "mistakes," for the inaccuracy is a function of the relation between the description, the place in and purpose for which it is given, and the order which gives it meaning rather than only a function of the descriptive skill of the person offering the description.

antitheism on the part of modern historians. There are sound, methodological reasons for such an assumption in academic history, as there are in the "hard" sciences.[79] Nevertheless, it follows that modernist historians cannot mean by the word *history* what premoderns mean, and modernist criticisms of premodern histories, such as the histories we find in scripture, beg the question. In modernist history, reason rather than the Divine gives the ultimate order of things, so reason becomes the arbiter of any claims about divine order, rather than the reverse. From the modernist point of view, history and scriptural accounts are incompatible. From the scriptural point of view, they may be incompatible, but the latter may instead encompass the former.

In conclusion and summary: If we understand scripture by means of a referential theory of history, then we assume that there is an original event that we represent (re-present) in language; on that view, a historian repeats the original event by constructing a description that represents the event as fully and accurately as possible. However, such a theory of history is problematic, for to the degree that a historian can be successful, there is, ironically, no real history, only the repetition of something that is always the same. One explanation for the unending necessity of writing histories that represent an original event might be that, though there is an original event that we describe in our histories and for which there is, in principle, one complete description, our language, methods, and so on are finite. Thus, we do not come to an end of giving the one, complete description. However, in addition to the problem already mentioned (namely that such a theory seems to deny history even as it describes it), we can ask this question: How can one justify the claim that there is such an event and that there is one ideal description of that event without encountering the very difficulty one is trying to avoid? With what language does one understand and discuss the event that is in continual need of redescription? How

---

79. For a discussion of some of these reasons, see Heidegger's "The Age of the World Picture," and chapter 4 in this volume.

is it available to the historian apart from the finite language that he or she uses to describe it? The only possible answer seems to be that historians are engaged not only in the accurate description of events, but that they are so engaged based on some kind of intuition (in the strict, philosophical sense) of something that is, in principle, not ultimately capturable in human expression.

Because of this difficulty, some conclude that, even if we begin with the view that there is only one, ultimate description of an event, we are driven to conclude that there is nothing to history except what we say about it. Recognizing the problematic character of claims to intuitions of something ultimately ungraspable, they take what they think is the only remaining position: history is only a socially determined, infinitely redescribable matter, a matter of what we have to say about it and no more. Though that position and variations of it have become fashionable, it is a position fraught with problems, among them, that to say something is a human construction, even that it is necessarily a human construction, is not to say that it is *only* a human construction. I think that the position also entails that the person coming to this conclusion is self-contradictory, arguing for radical historicism and invoking a principle that is not to be understood from a radical historicist position. In short, in spite of the current popularity of this response to the problem, I think it is less sound than the flawed, referential position against which it responds.

I too conclude that writing history involves an intuition of something more than what we can say. However, it is difficult to know what it means to say that. For example, I do not think the usual referential theories, which gloss over the problem, are adequate. I have attempted to give one answer, though not the only one, to that question:[80] Scriptural history is a matter of divine incarnation. And, I am supposing that academic history is another kind of history, a kind that answers very differently the question of what more there is to history than what

---

80. It should be clear that I do not think there is only one way to do history properly.

we can say, a way that is, therefore, strictly speaking, not comparable to scriptural history because it incarnates something very different.

On the view for which I argue, one can understand scriptural history using as a starting point a premodern understanding of what makes history. For premoderns, genuine, literal history is essentially symbolic, in other words, incarnational. For moderns, it is essentially referential. With the rise of modernism, symbols came to be understood as references (even if complex ones), and, therefore, so did the Bible: scripture is a more or less accurate depiction of events that exist independent of other considerations. (And whether one takes them to be more or less accurate depends on one's religious disposition.) Premoderns, however, understand the Bible figurally or typologically: as incarnating a symbolic order and as giving an order to life through its symbolic work.[81] To say that premoderns understand scripture typologically is not to say that premoderns understand the Bible to refer to another reality or to be merely fictions. In fact, exactly the opposite is true: for premoderns, history understood apart from revelation is a fiction, a necessary and convenient one for some purposes, perhaps, but nevertheless a fiction. It does not give us the fullness of the events of history. Like moderns, those reading as premoderns understand that scripture orders human history by giving it a shape—a figure. However, they disagree with the moderns about what gives that shape. For premoderns, the revelation of scripture gives history meaning, without which there would be no real history, only chronology, if that.

For example, for medieval Christians the life of Christ as revealed in scripture is a figure or type that we can use to understand the scriptures as a whole and, therefore, history and our place in it. It is not

---

81. As the "Concluding More Scientific Postscript" to this essay notes, prior to Christianity, pagans had a merely cyclical view of history. It might have no meaning beyond the cycle itself, or it might, as in Platonism, only have meaning to the degree that one could leave it behind, or it might, as in Stoicism, have only the meaning possible in detachment. But even though paganism did not have a figural understanding of history, as did Christianity, it also did not have any notion of history as we understand it. See David Bentley Hart, *Atheist Delusions: The Christian Revolution and Its Fashionable Enemies* (New Haven: Yale University Press, 2009), 200–201.

that Christ did not live or that the story of his life is "merely symbolic" of some other reality. Instead, truly to understand the life of Christ is to understand it as a life that literally (in other words, in the way that the texts say it) is a figure of our lives and history. Thus, to read the story of Israel's exodus from Egypt, forty years in the wilderness, and entry into the promised land as a figure of the granting of salvation, our continuing sinfulness, and the promise of possible blessedness—in other words, as it shows us our relation to Christ—is not to impose an additional meaning onto the story of Israel. Contra some Jewish thinkers, neither is it to reduce the children of Israel to mere shadows, references to another reality. Instead, it is to see the biblical story of Israel as an incarnation of the symbolic order of which we, being religious, find ourselves to be part.

Those who read the Bible as an incarnation do not reduce its texts to what is described as only symbolic, for the literal/symbolic disjunction is not a disjunction for them. For premoderns, reading the story of Moses and Israel typologically, figurally, anagogically, allegorically is not what one does *instead of* or *in addition to* reading literally. Such readings are part and parcel of a literal reading. Premodern understanding does not reduce the scriptural story to a reference to or representation of something else, though it also does not deny that there may be an important representative element in scripture. Instead, premoderns believe that understanding the story of Israel is essential to understanding history—actual history, the real events of the world—as incarnation, a continuing incarnation, as types and shadows, to use the language of the Book of Mormon (for example, Mosiah 3:15). It is to understand history as having an order and the events of history as related to each other within that ordering (an ordering that does not exist independent of events, but that cannot be reduced to those events as "bare" events). It is to understand history as part of a symbolic ordering; an ordering that is given not only in scripture, but also (perhaps most importantly) in ritual—ritual objects and ritual language—as well as in the moments of history themselves. Thus, for premoderns, the biblical narrative is literal history; the literal truth, the truth "by the letter," is that told in the letters and words of the text as revealing and embodying the order given by God. The literal truth is the truth constituted in and through the text as incarnation, not the supposed truth supposedly only referred to by those letters and words.

In spite of appearances or what we might say when we are asked to talk about scriptural history without having reflected sufficiently on our experience with it, I think that most Latter-day Saints read scripture as an incarnation of a symbolic ordering.[82] We may often do so confusedly and inconsistently, but we do. That is why we feel compelled to defend the historicity of the scriptures, whether we do so naively or with a full range of scholarly, theoretical, and interpretational tools at our disposal. This is especially true for adherents, such as us, of religions in which symbols and symbolic acts figure prominently. The informality of Latter-day Saint sacrament meetings may make us think otherwise, but the church's all-encompassing social structure and the importance of temple liturgy show that Latter-day Saints' lives, like the lives of other religious people and perhaps more than many, continue to be ordered symbolically.

For the most part, we have lost, forgotten, or never had the vocabulary and concepts for talking about our participation in a symbolic order and our reading of scripture as part of that participation. As a result, when called on to talk about scripture or to teach lessons from it or to speak reflectively about it, we resort to language and methods that ignore the symbolically ordered character of our lives and that deny the incarnate character of scripture by making it merely referential. The fact that we mix implicit attention to scripture as symbolic ordering with an insistence on simple reference often confuses our reading. Nevertheless, it remains possible not only to continue to read

---

82. Many non-Mormon Christians probably also continue to read symbolically, especially those often thought of as literalists or conservative.

scripture as incarnational rather than merely referential, but to do so more explicitly than we have done.

Concluding More Scientific Postscript

Several years after this essay was originally published, for the most part I continue to understand scripture along the lines it sketches, but I have come to realize that I did not sufficiently differentiate two ways of making sense of the premodern understanding of the world: I collapsed the Greek and pagan Near Eastern way of understanding the world with the Jewish and Christian way. Were I to explain my failure in terms of those on whom I have depended intellectually, I would say that I leaned too heavily on the work of Mircea Eliade.[83] As a result, I did not notice important differences between those two ways of understanding.[84]

There are important similarities between the two ways. Because of those similarities I could make the argument I did, and because of them I believe it still works. But there are also important differences between them (differences which, for my purposes here, I will grossly oversimplify). Perhaps the first thing to notice is that the archaic understanding of the world takes it as a cosmos, an ordered and beautiful whole. (The Greek word *kosmos*, from which we get our word *cosmos*, first referred to jewelry.)[85] For the Greeks the cosmos may have come

---

83. I still think that Eliade's work on premodern thought can be quite helpful to us as we try to make sense of texts that have come to us from long ago. Reading his work, such as *The Sacred and the Profane* (New York: Harcourt, 1959) and *Myth and Reality* (New York: Harper & Row, 1963), has helped me think profitably about scripture and my experience in the temple. Nevertheless, it is essential to notice that Eliade's description of the ways that scripture works is not only incomplete because it does not (and could not, of course) include an understanding of the restored gospel, it is also incomplete as a scholarly treatment of comparative religion, as I will describe in what follows.

84. I first noticed those differences when I read Paul Ricoeur, "Manifestation and Proclamation," in *Figuring the Sacred: Religion, Narrative, and Imagination*, ed. Mark I. Wallace, trans. David Pellauer (Minneapolis, MN: Fortress, 1995), 48–67.

85. Rémi Brague, *The Wisdom of the World: The Human Experience of the Universe in Western Thought*, trans. Teresa Lavender Fagan (Chicago: University of Chicago Press, 2003), 19–20. Brague's book is excellent for understanding the complexity of the question of how the ancients of various Western cultures understood that which surrounded them. Indeed, had I been paying better attention, I would have noticed when I first read Brague's book in 2001 what I have only now come to see.

into being or it may have always existed, but it was rarely the product of a creator.[86] Perhaps more importantly, the cosmos was understood cyclically: it has passed through cycles comparable to spring, summer, winter, and fall, and it will continue to pass through them. Myth gives us an understanding of the cycles, and religious ritual reenacts them and may even insure them, but there is no historical vector in myth nor its ritual. In this way of understanding, time amounts merely to the repetition of what has already occurred.

Jewish and, later, Christian understanding is similar, but it differs significantly on at least the two respects I have mentioned: it takes the world to be the creation of God (rather than a cosmos), and it insists that there is a historical aspect to its stories (rather than that they are merely cycles in an eternal round). Instead of the ordered and beautiful, perhaps eternal, cosmos, we have the ordered and beautiful creation of God. Instead of the endless repetition of the cycles of nature, we have ongoing history (with a beginning, a middle—the incarnation—and an end) within which we can see the imprint of God's patterns.[87]

For the understanding of the incarnational nature of scripture, the second of these is most important. On the Jewish view, time moves. Even if the types that God has prefigured show themselves in moments of history, showing us the way that some events are "the same" as others—for example, the fall and expulsion from the Garden, with its attendant promise of blessed life to come; Abraham leaving Ur to wander in the wilderness before he enters the promised land; Israel's exodus from Egypt, wandering in the wilderness, and crossing into the promised land; Lehi's family's flight from Jerusalem, wandering in the wilderness and ocean, and arrival in the new promised land; the Saints' flight from Illinois to Utah; the experience of every repentant sinner—these moments, all shadows of what Christ's life, and indeed the plan of salvation, prefigure are not merely a repetition of the same

---

86. The demiurge of Plato's *Timaeus* is a notable exception.

87. See chapter 6 in this volume for a discussion of types and shadows, with their antitypes or prefigures (what I have here called "patterns").

thing each time. The incarnation of a divine pattern in history rather than the reoccurrence of the same event is the difference between the Judeo-Christian understanding of itself and the archaic self-understanding. In contrast with both, modern history preserves and amplifies the notion of history, but rarely if ever has a serious notion of the cyclical (as in pagan cosmology) or the symbolically ordered (as in Judeo-Christian cosmology). Understanding scripture requires that we set aside our modern prejudices about how to understand history in order to read the histories of ancient writers, as Nephi suggests, with the understanding of the Jews (2 Nephi 25:5)—and, I would add, the early Christians.

CHAPTER NINE

ON SCRIPTURE,
OR IDOLATRY VERSUS TRUE RELIGION

Ancient Israel was often called away from idolatry. Perhaps no theme is more common in the Old Testament than that Israel must give up idolatry. Michael Fishbane has argued that the heart of Judaism is its rejection of idolatry and the worldview of idolatry, the rejection of "idolatrous metaphysics."[1] We hear that theme much less in modern Israel. Usually when we hear someone speak of idolatry today, that person does so primarily in terms of materialism or something like it; we think our idolatry is primarily metaphorical. Real idolatry is something done only by other people—perhaps in ancient times, perhaps more primitive than we, at least more exotic. However, it is naive to assume that ancient Israel was susceptible to real idolatry and we are not. What idolatry is and how we avoid it remain questions, and they are as much questions for us as they were for ancient Israel.

If we look closely, we see that at least three things mark the difference between pure religion—in Latter-day Saint terms, Zion—and idolatry. First, pure religion is founding but ultimately not founded. It is originary in that those "within" it are constantly reborn, constantly re-originated. But pure religion has no *theos*, no metaphysical foundation.[2] If it did, it would have an idol rather than a God. The word *theos*

---

1. Michael Fishbane, "Israel and the 'Mothers,'" in *The Garments of Torah: Essays in Biblical Hermeneutics* (Bloomington: Indiana University Press, 1989), 49–63.
2. The Greek word *theos* has more than one meaning. I am not using the word here in the same way that I do in chapter 5 in this volume. There *theos* has the sense it has in the New Testament and the Septuagint: the God of Israel. I will explain the different, philosophical meaning that it has here.

is the Greek word for "god," and it is the word that Aristotle uses for the ultimate being in his metaphysics, a usage determinative for the rest of the Western intellectual tradition. Traditional metaphysical systems, religious or not, each have something like the Aristotelean *theos* as their foundation or goal. Each assumes a *theos*, in Aristotle's terms, as the basis for what-is, whether that *theos* is God or something else. In the terms of the twentieth-century German philosopher, Martin Heidegger,[3] each is onto-theological. Given that traditional usage, I will use the word *theos* here to designate any such metaphysical being or any other being that performs the same structural function as Aristotle's *theos*: the thing that accounts for or encompasses all other things.

In contrast, rather than a *theos* that acts as a foundation or goal, pure religion finds its origin in our relation to a beneficent, living Person rather than a metaphysical origin: the God of Israel. Thus, the religions that have their origin in the Bible, which of course includes the Latter-day Saints, are strictly speaking metaphysically a-theistic: their scriptures deny the unmoved and unmoving god (whether it is called *theos*, Law, or Reason), whatever their theologies might assert. Latter-day Saint doctrine, by asserting not only that God is a beneficent, living Person (a claim with which all Christians will agree), but also an embodied one (a claim that shocks most informed non–LDS Christians), insists on that denial. The Latter-day Saint claim implicitly denies any foundation, at least as that word is used in the tradition.

There is a sense in which God remains a foundation in Latter-day Saint thinking. We do, after all, refer to him as the Creator. However, the sense in which he is foundational is quite different for us than the sense of *foundation* in the onto-theological tradition. We believe that the God of Abraham, Isaac, and Jacob is a person—not a foundation, except to the degree that a person can be said to be a foundation (see 1 Corinthians 3:11). He is not, however, a metaphysical foundation.

---

3. For more on Heidegger, see chapter 2, note 62, in this volume.

For more than twenty-five thousand years, however, when Western thinkers have reflected on religion philosophically or theologically, they have often assumed that to speak of God is to speak in terms of a metaphysical foundation, in terms of a *theos*.[4] The language of foundations and the *theos* are virtually everywhere in our culture, even in our discussions of our particular religious experiences, and Latter-day Saints have not been immune to that way of talking. Our thinking and speaking about our belief is sometimes not consonant with our belief itself. In spite of what we intend, the language we share with others and the assumptions common to that language infiltrate our discussions because they come to us naturally. They are the common sense of our culture and, so, something about which we give little thought—but we do not yet have another language to use. The question is, if we reject the assumption that we must speak of God as a metaphysical *theos*, what can we say of our relation to the person who is God? In other words, how can we make sense of the world and its Creator if we reject the philosophical understanding of the world and of its Creator as metaphysical foundation? What is the alternative to idolatry, given that our reflective religious language is permeated by traditional understanding? Where can we find a language suitable to our religious experience and understanding?

Among others, the work of the contemporary French Lithuanian philosopher, Emmanuel Levinas, provides some outlines of part of a philosophical answer. Levinas shows us much about our relations to one another, focusing for example, on the family as the model for

---

4. There are ways of reading pre-modern theology (and perhaps much modern theology) as escaping this criticism. For example, Catherine Pickstock makes an argument that the metaphysical/theological understanding of religion is a result of the thinking of the thirteenth-century thinker, Duns Scotus. See her *After Writing: On the Liturgical Consummation of Philosophy* (Oxford: Blackwell, 1998), 121–40. This means that prior to the thirteenth century, reflection on God is more or less nonmetaphysical. Pickstock's argument is an important one, but for reasons of brevity, I will continue the rhetorical device of assuming that theology has more or less consistently assumed a *theos*.

human being.[5] I cannot accurately précis Levinas's work here,[6] but among other things, in it we see how the other person gives the self itself, its ego. Levinas shows, convincingly I believe, that I am not, fundamentally, an entity existing on my own and beholden to no one. Rather, my very existence as an autonomous, self-aware entity is a response to my relation to another person or persons who initiated my response. And my continuation as a person, as a self, is based on my continuing relation to others. The result is that the self and the growth of the self—its repentance—have their origins from the other person.

But though the self and its repentance originate from the other person, the other person is no foundation in any usual sense of that term. And in the philosophical and theological sense of the term, the other person is no founder. The other is a person, a creator, not a thing, and the founding occurs in ethical demand, in the face-to-face of Joseph Smith before God, not in ontology. Persons, specifically other persons, rather than metaphysical or some other kind of principles, are fundamental. Persons can found us, but they are not themselves a foundation. They are living, continuing persons, not static, impersonal, dead foundations. As a consequence we could go so far as to say, shockingly, that in a strict philosophical sense, pure and true religion is nihilistic, but that is only to say that it is not idolatrous, having no onto-theological foundation. True religion posits no ultimate thing; instead it is response to an Ultimate Person.

Second, because pure religion is not metaphysically founded, because it has no *theos*, it recognizes no power before which it must bow—though it bows. True religion bows before ethical demand—the

---

5. Emmanuel Levinas, *Totality and Infinity: An Essay on Exteriority,* trans. Alphonso Lingis (Pittsburgh: Duquesne University Press, 1969), discusses the relevant points most directly—the section on fecundity comes immediately to mind—but *Otherwise than Being or Beyond Essence,* trans. A. Lingis (The Hague: Martinus Nijhoff, 1981), also has a number of important—though incredibly difficult—discussions of these points.

6. For an overview, see my "Emmanuel Levinas," in *Twentieth-Century European Cultural Theorists,* Dictionary of Literary Biography, 2nd ser. (Bloomfield Hills, MI: Gale, 2004), 285–95. See also, Colin Davis, *Levinas: An Introduction* (Notre Dame: Notre Dame University Press, 1996), or Simonne Plourde, *Emmanuel Lévinas, altérité et responsabilité: Guide de lecture* (Paris: Cerf, 1996).

relation of one person to another rather than rules for moral conduct[7]—not superior and potentially threatening power.[8] True religion
is a-theistic in refusing to bow before the supposed power of the idolatrous god, the *theos* of traditional philosophy and theology, with its
Santa-Claus promises and implicit threats.[9] Instead it bows before the
God it loves and respects.

A third difference between true and idolatrous religion, between
Zion and "the world," is that because the obedience of true religion is
a matter of service rather than appeasement, true religion is, at one
and the same time, both obedient and beyond any law. It is obedient
to the ethical demand that occurs when the other person disrupts my
totalizing, comprehending, dominating relation to the world. In other
words, true religion occurs when I respond to the obligation I have
to another person (including God) rather than to my reasoned and
coherent understanding of that person.

If I respond to my understanding of the world and of the other
person's place in that world rather than to the other person herself, I
do not respond to the other. I respond only to myself: I have come to
an understanding of things and I respond to that understanding, *my
understanding* rather than the other person whose life impinges on
me. In contrast, ethical obligation requires that I respond to something that is other than myself, something I am unlikely fully to understand intellectually. I must respond to what is outside of myself, to
what is beyond my ability to grasp, comprehend, and dominate (even
intellectually) or thematize. Law is always at least a thematization of
the ethical obligation I experience: to universalize what I learn in my
relation to others is to make a theme of that relation. Therefore, as

7. This is the way that Levinas uses the term, and understanding him requires that
we not forget that his use is not what we usually expect.

8. Though true religion sometimes uses the word *power*, I think that use refers not
to the power found and feared in idolatrous religion, but to the power of the ethical
command.

9. See Paul Ricoeur, "Religion, Atheism, and Faith," in Alasdair MacIntyre and Paul
Ricoeur, *The Religious Significance of Atheism* (New York: Columbia University Press,
1969), 58–98.

universalization, in principle law always occurs within my compre-
hension and even under my domination. As the product of human
understanding, thematizing is something that human beings can in
principle dominate.[10]

We cannot escape the thematizing of law if we continue to speak
to one another, for example when we admonish another or apologize
for our behavior. We should not escape it. Not only is it not wrong to
thematize, it is essential that we do. Not only human justice, but also
teaching, require thematizing, for example. Nevertheless, ultimately
pure religion goes beyond any thematizing of the demands made
upon me by the other person. Pure religion is beyond any mere law:
"Therefore, my brothers, you too are dead to the law" (Romans 7:4).
That is inconceivable within idolatry, and is nihilistic to those who
insist that there must be a *theos*.

Of course, the nihilism of being without foundation and beyond
the law has nothing at all to do with a nihilism that rejects law of any
kind and opts for chaos. As mentioned, an ethical demand can occur
only where there is also a thematizing of that demand. It may be impossible for me to experience the ethical obligation and, at the same
time, not to thematize that obligation in consciousness. Consequently,
ethical demand may never be separable from law—so much so that
the law is essential to the demand; the law is a blessing, an appearance
of the command of God, though not the same as that command. The
ethical demand, God's ongoing command—its appear*ing* rather than
its appear*ance*—always exceeds any thematizing in which it occurs.
No law captures the ethical demand that it thematizes. In true religion
the moral law is not that by which humans become calculable. Instead, it is that in which we fulfill the ethical obligation that confronts
us, an ethical obligation that always exceeds and makes possible any
moral law in which it is necessarily embodied.

---

10. Of course, the irony with which the atonement deals is that we do not dominate
the law and, in fact, find ourselves spiritually incapable of doing so: "What I would, that
I do not" (Romans 7:15).

But if no law is sufficient, if true religion cannot be reduced to a law, what remains for us to do? To quote someone now defunct, "What will become of us?" How do we speak of this description of our being, of fundamental ethics, of Zion, of the fact that we are *already* in Zion? How do we speak of nonidolatrous, in other words, true, religion? And where do we find such a speaking?

At first glance, it seems that the failure of philosophy and its issuance in the nihilism of onto-theology—its reliance on the idol of the *theos*, which turns out to be nothing and nothingness—means that we cannot expect philosophy to take account of its failure and to remedy itself. As often conceived, philosophy is incapable of saying what needs to be said. In fact, as traditionally conceived, philosophy is essentially totalizing. As it is often taught, I find it difficult to doubt that philosophy is ultimately bankrupt.

But that is not to say that all philosophers or philosophies have been totalizers. In general, great philosophers are great precisely because their work did not and, for the most part, still does not fit within the traditional, totalizing conception of philosophy.[11] The tradition tames the great philosophers for its own totalizing use, but the tamed philosopher is not the great philosopher. There may be other possibilities for philosophy than those of the tradition. Perhaps Heidegger or Ludwig Wittgenstein provides the beginnings of an alternative. Perhaps some of the work of Edmond Jabès, Jacques Derrida, Jean-François Lyotard, Levinas, or others points in the direction of an alternative. Perhaps a fresh reading of Plato or Aristotle or Augustine will teach us much. Or perhaps a careful return to our own tradition—which includes and overlays the philosophical tradition—will do the job.

Thus, though it is not clear what we are to do philosophically in face of the totalitarian character of traditional philosophy, it is clear that, in some sense, philosophy will probably remain. In his discussion of this

---

11. Though I have used Aristotle as a bogeyman earlier, I think what I say here applies at least as much to him as to any other philosopher.

point Levinas insists that a role for philosophy remains, a role that does not rely on the merely deconstructive or rhetorical.[12] In spite of his criticisms of philosophy, Levinas consciously remains a philosopher. The bankruptcy of philosophy is not a given, however common it may be.

But whatever we eventually decide about philosophy, Levinas shows us that when we see the priority of ethics to ontology—in LDS terms, when we genuinely come to believe that persons are prior to principles—then from the beginning, our question is not "What is it?" (as philosophy has traditionally asked), but "What must be done?" There are ostensibly any number of ways one could take up this question. Perhaps, as Levinas, Derrida, Luce Irigaray, and others indicate, some of these ways are philosophical. But, however other many ways there might be, I believe that sacred scripture is such a speaking. In fact, I think it is the most important of such ways because it is the "most ethical," asking us to listen not only to others, but to *the* Other Person. Scripture is a speaking that has the virtue of being considerably more accessible to most of us than the work of writers like Heidegger, Derrida, and Levinas—and it is always better written.

As much as I am enamored of contemporary philosophy, as much as I find contemporary Continental philosophy not only interesting and useful but morally compelling, I nonetheless find scripture more appealing and more accessible than contemporary philosophy, and more morally compelling. But more than that, I find scripture more genuinely revelatory. Paul Ricoeur notes that the philosopher can be no preacher,[13] and Heidegger has made a similar point.[14] The philosopher must wait for the prophet. Heidegger and Derrida may help us wait for the prophets.[15] Levinas may announce the necessity of the

12. Cf. Levinas, *Otherwise than Being,* 182–83.

13. Ricoeur, "Religion, Atheism, and Faith," 30.

14. See, for example, Martin Heidegger, "Phenomenology and Theology," in *The Piety of Thinking,* trans. James G. Hart and John C. Maraldo (Bloomington: Indiana University Press, 1976), 5–21.

15. Marlène Zarader, *La Dette Impensée: Heidegger et l'Héritage Hébraïque* (Paris: Seuil, 1990), does an excellent job of showing how Heidegger's work depends, probably without him being conscious of it, on his understanding of the Bible and of prophecy.

prophet. I believe these thinkers have helped me hear the prophets' voices. But they can do no more than that. They cannot even be John the Baptist for us, announcing the prophet. Only in the living prophets and in scripture can I find the announcement, the call, of what philosophy has helped me wait for. In spite of the possibility that, turned against itself, philosophy may be able to say something about Zion, I believe that only in the prophets will we be returned to what is beyond philosophy, namely to Zion.

But though many, if not most, Latter-day Saints are committed to the idea that scripture is more important and more revelatory than philosophy, it is also true that our mental commitment runs aground on our everyday practices. We know what it means to take philosophy seriously. We do not usually know what it means to take the scriptures seriously.

We usually read scripture as if it were naive philosophy and ontology, looking for the principle of principles, for the *theos* that stands behind what we are reading, asking constantly the question, "What is it?"—even when we want to ask the question, "What must be done?" We are taught to read scripture that way from our births, both inside and outside the church. That way of reading scripture is something we share with many, especially the majority of those in the evangelical, charismatic, and other conservative Christian traditions. Like the image of good traditional philosophers, those who read the scriptures in this way take the gospel to be a set of doctrinal propositions that one is to learn, and they take the scriptures to be a record of those principles and propositions behind which the "theological" gospel hides. When we read scripture this way, it is as if we assume that God is simply a poor writer—or that he chooses poor mouthpieces—and finds himself unable to lay out clearly and distinctly, in an ordered fashion, the principles he wants to teach us. With amazing hubris, we assume it is our job to do the work he was unable to do, the work of making everything clear, distinct, and orderly.

But scripture need not be read that way. In the New Testament, the word *gospel* refers much more to the proclamation of the gospel than to the content of that proclamation, though the content is certainly not irrelevant. Nothing can be proclaimed if the act of proclaiming has no content. Levinas explains this by distinguishing between the saying and the said: the saying is the event; the said is the objectification of the event of saying, its transcription, whether in writing, memory, or a recording. There can be no saying without a resultant said, but it is a mistake to think that the two are the same. A parent's command, "Do the dishes," can vary wildly in meaning. It could be a gentle reminder or a stern warning. It could, however, be part of a joke. Even if we were to transcribe more of the context of that command, it would be possible to understand it in at least somewhat different ways, and we would fail to capture aspects that the child hearing the command would have known in the moment of the event. The said reflects but does not capture the saying. The saying is in the said only as a trace, as something we can hear, but never see because when we try to look directly at it, we see only its after-image. Similarly, there could be no proclamation of the gospel if there were not a content of the gospel. However, as used in the New Testament and, therefore, as it also informs our later uses, the word *gospel* puts its emphasis on the saying, not the said. What is most important is the preaching, the call to repentance which is in the scriptures as a trace. Reading the scriptures requires likening them to ourselves, because it requires us to read them as a saying—an event in which we are addressed—rather than a said. If we read the scriptures as scriptures, the written record becomes an address, the preaching of the gospel.

When the scriptures proclaim, they disrupt what we are, what we have made ourselves. They invite our response, our repentance. As saying, scripture speaks the ethical rupture of my constant though implicit claim to autonomy. Scripture ruptures the interiority I prize so much, my consciousness and self-consciousness. Scripture disrupts the natural and necessary movement of consciousness into itself and its principles, into its understanding, and it does so by calling me outside of myself. Scripture calls me out of the solipsistic universe toward which I tend in reason, and in doing so it calls me to my obligation to the Divine and to my fellows. It disrupts my focus on principle by pointing out that my field of vision, as *my* field, excludes the other person, something that is not mine in that field. The speaking of scripture opens me to that rupture of my solipsism and, so, to the understanding, as King Benjamin says, "That [I] must repent of [my] sins and forsake them, and humble [myself] before God; and ask in sincerity of heart that he would forgive [me]" (Mosiah 4:10).

It follows that scripture can and should be read ethically—as a saying in which I encounter my obligation to others and God—rather than philosophically. Scripture reading can be the response to the saying of the ethical rupture, rather than the thematizing said of principle and ontology. To use Levinas's language because it is useful, scripture reading and study can be an encounter with the unsaying saying of the other person, rather than the said of the same.

Unlike most of what is done in philosophy, scripture does not demand violence in response to violence, though it often reveals violence. Scripture does not take up philosophy against itself, so unlike the current criticisms of philosophy, including my own, scripture is not guilty of parricide. When not taken up as a defective or naive form of philosophy, scripture engenders. It replaces murder and scapegoating (the desire that everything be totalized in some static Parmenidean One Thing) with the call for fecundity: "Be fruitful, and multiply, and replenish the earth" (Genesis 1:28). When read as ethical demand, scripture disrupts my interiority with exteriority. It disrupts the universal and the merely moral (using Nietzsche's sense of that word),[16] the desire for the *theos*. In doing so, scripture opens the

---

16. Nietzsche was certainly no Christian. Nevertheless, no one was more aware of the limits and defects of conventional, merely rote Christianity than he. So, his work, though no guide for life, can help us see the problems to which the gospel is an answer. In Romans Paul teaches that the law by itself is dead, and he urges us to find newness of life by accepting the Holy Spirit, the origin of the law. Nietzsche shows us that religion

ethical demand and makes generation and continued life possible as well as necessary. In scripture and with the prophets, I stand before the other person, exposed and called upon prior to being anything at all. In fact, whatever I am is a consequence of my position before the other person. The ethical response to the ethical demand is the desire for the other person rather than for the *theos,* which dissimulates and displaces the other person, as in idolatry. Desire for the other person and the concomitant rupture of interiority by the other person are what philosophy has called community. They are what the scriptures call Zion. Zion is always already here; it is already amongst us—within us—though not our creation:

> And when he was questioned by the Pharisees concerning when the kingdom of God is to come, he answered them and said, "The kingdom of God does not come with careful watching, neither will they say 'Look here!' or 'There!' For behold, the kingdom of God is within you." (Luke 17:20–21)

For the most part, philosophy demands that we watch carefully. Sometimes it demands nothing else. Usually it *can* demand nothing else. Philosophy is primarily, but perhaps not necessarily, oriented toward vision and the unifying perspective of vision. That is what the said requires, the seeing of reading. In contrast, scripture speaks the a priori character of Zion and its demand for our ethical response. It speaks and asks us to listen, to hearken. Scripture calls us back to the Zion in which we are constituted; it calls us to a continuation of that Zion.

It is possible to end this discussion here, with an abstract, philosophical appeal to the nonphilosophical. But surely that self-deconstructing appeal is insufficient. So as a gesture, but no more than a gesture, in the direction of allowing scripture to speak the ethical

---

as mere convention is dead and dangerous to our souls, a point very similar to, if not the same as, Paul's. But Nietzsche, though raised in a Christian family, was unable to see the possibility of life by the Spirit and, so, could recommend nothing better than an aesthetic life.

demand, let me outline "disruptive" readings of two scriptural stories, attempting to show some of the ways in which I hear the other person exceeding principle and mere being in these stories. I have fuller expositions of these stories in another place awaiting completion.[17] But these outlines should serve to show some of what I find in an ethical rather than philosophical reading of scripture. Because they are outlines, these readings will ignore the attention to textual details that scripture calls for. They will remain philosophical in spite of themselves. But I think they will be enough to show that an ethical reading of scripture is possible. I hope they will at least indicate that such a reading can be fruitful.

The first story is that of the creation, a story that focuses explicitly on ethical relation rather than ontology. First notice Genesis 1:1, 26; and 3:22 (compare Moses 2:1, 26; 3:28; and Abraham 4–5):

> In the beginning God created the heaven and the earth. (Genesis 1:1)

> And God said, Let us make man in our image, after our likeness. (Genesis 1:26)

> And the Lord God said, Behold, the man is become as one of us, to know good and evil. (Genesis 3:22)

God's oneness is the unity of Zion, a unity of multiple individuals who remain individual in their unity. God's unity is not the unity of an overarching, metaphysical *theos*, for, as Latter-day Saints have pointed

---

17. For a more complete, but still incomplete, reading of the first of these stories, see my "Adam and Eve—Community: Reading Genesis 2–3," *Journal of Philosophy and Scripture* 1/1 (2003): 2–14; http://www.philosophyandscripture.org/Archives/Issue1-1/ James_Faulconer/james_faulconer.html (accessed 8 May 2009). A fuller version of the Abraham and Isaac story can be found in James E. Faulconer, "The Past and Future Community: Abraham and Isaac; Sarah and Rebekah, . . ." *Levinas Studies: An Annual Review* 3 (2008): 79–100. In addition, I have a similar reading of a third story, that of Moses and Israel. It can be found in "Philosophy and Transcendence: Religion and the Possibility of Justice," in *Transcendence in Religion and Philosophy*, ed. James E. Faulconer (Indianapolis: Indiana University Press, 2003), 70–84.

out for years, God is spoken of in the multiple, not the singular. He is not alone in any sense.

Latter-day Saints often use the language of the tradition to speak of God, as well as the assumptions of the philosophical/theological tradition to understand the scriptures. Therefore, they often assume, although usually only implicitly and unconsciously, either that God is the principle of principles or that he exists in virtue of his compliance with such a principle or set of principles. But because this assumption is a postulation of the *theos*, in making it, we implicitly deny God's multiplicity and the possibility of divine togetherness. In other words, the assumption denies Zion because it takes God to be ultimately alone. However, in spite of that, the Latter-day Saint God is everywhere implicated in multiplicity. As so implicated, the one God cannot be the principle of principles. As those who accuse the Latter-day Saints of heresy recognize quickly, a God who cannot avoid multiplicity breaks the bond between unity and being, destroying recourse to God as *theos*. If traditional belief is the standard, we are heretics and should be happy to be heretics. Being called a heretic by those who have false beliefs is not a problem. However, that heresy is not only a revealed truth and, so a better standard, it is also a philosophical advantage.

As both one and multiple, God can be the Other of ethical relation, for every ethical relation implies not the I and Thou of Martin Buber, but the Thou and we.[18] Truth is reason—measure, account—and "I've a Mother there"—and a Brother, and brothers and sisters. The creation story, beginning in Genesis 1 and ending with Genesis 4:1, is the story of multiplicity and the other person, the story of a living and loving parent who creates, never from some null point, never alone. It is not a philosophical story of how a Parmenidean One generated the many.

---

18. Levinas, *Totality and Infinity*, 68–69, 155. Levinas is deeply indebted to Buber, but nevertheless critical. He criticizes Buber in several essays. For an example, see Emmanuel Levinas, "Martin Buber and the Theory of Knowledge," in *Proper Names*, trans. Michael B. Smith (Stanford: Stanford University Press, 1996), 17–35.

The multiplicity of the Other is recapitulated in the story of Adam and Eve. Genesis 2:18 (Moses 3:18; Abraham 5:14) literally speaks of Woman as "the one who stands over against—across from—Adam," though our translation of the Hebrew is "help meet," in other words the appropriate helper. But Woman is an appropriate help to Man, not by being another hand, or an extra arm, or an additional set of eyes; Woman is not an addition to Man, not an ordinary supplement, if a supplement at all. She is neither his subordinate nor his alter ego. She cannot be reduced either to him or to some third term that encapsulates them both. Woman is the appropriate helper to Man by standing opposite him, making ethical relation possible by being another to whom he can be related and, in doing so, giving Man his identity. If we read imaginatively, we can see that Woman is not simply an extension of Man, she is "the mother of *all* living" (Genesis 3:20; compare Moses 4:26). In fact, in the Genesis version of the story, as long as Woman can be thought of as an extension of Man, she remains uncreated; she has no name. She is named only when she has ceased to be such an extension. Neither she nor he was fully a person until the fall was accomplished. Their lives together as independent beings standing opposite one another makes their lives as human beings possible. Together, as those standing "across from" one another, rather than as mirror images of each other, they make the lives of others possible, as we see in Genesis 4:1 (compare Moses 5:2). The first thing that the Bible tells us after it tells us of the expulsion from the garden is "And Adam knew Eve his wife; and she conceived, and bare Cain." Fecundity, sexuality, fraternity and sorority—Zion—are functions of alterity, not functions of identity and sameness.

Note also that the knowledge which Man and Woman gain in the creation story is explicitly ethical knowledge, knowledge-with rather than knowledge-about. We see this illustrated in the way in which Man comes to know of his need for Woman: He does not know that he needs another person because God tells him that he does; he does not come to conclude that he needs a partner by logical deduction. His knowledge of Woman's necessity is not propositional. Man comes to know that need, a need beyond simple want or lack, only through his relation to the Divine and through the experience engendered in that experience. He learns of the need for Woman by assisting in the creation of animals and discovering that there is nothing that is paired with him, nothing opposite him, no appropriate helper: "And Adam gave names to all cattle, and to the fowl of the air, and to every beast of the field; but for Adam there was not found an help meet for him" (Genesis 2:18–23; compare Moses 3:18–23 and Abraham 5:14–21).

Likewise, having eaten of the tree of the knowledge of good and evil—having the knowledge of the Gods (explicitly ethical knowledge)—Adam and Eve are like the Gods at the same time that they are set across from them: "Behold the man is become as one of us, to know good and evil" (Genesis 3:22; compare Moses 4:28). Divine knowledge makes Adam and Eve in the image of the Gods at the same time that it makes the Gods truly Other. The story of Adam and Eve is the story of the necessity of the other person—a sexed other—with whom one can stand before God, as a god, in ethical labor and ethical knowledge. It is a story that undoes philosophical knowledge in favor of personal and even sexual knowledge.[19] It is a story that demands ethical response. The story of Adam and Eve disrupts our totalizing knowledge of each other and of God and demands, instead, that we hear the ethical demand.

The question of the story is not, "*What* art thou?" (as much philosophy and all psychology supposes), but "*Where* art thou?" (Genesis 3:9; Moses 4:15). And the "where" of this question supposes neither a geographic position nor a Heideggerian site in being. Instead it asks about the ethical where: standing before me, face-to-face, God asks "Where are you?" The question of the story of Adam and Eve is explicitly the question of ethics—of relation to the Other—not ontology.

Man's answer to the question, however, is not straightforward (as Abraham's will later be). Rather than "Here am I" (compare

---

19. See Genesis 4:1 and Moses 5:2 where *know* is no euphemism.

Genesis 22:1), Man responds with an excuse for hiding: "I heard thy voice in the garden, and I was afraid, because I was naked; and I hid myself" (Genesis 3:10; compare Moses 4:16). Guilt and shame come because the possibility of community is also the possibility of alienation. In this case, by choosing knowledge—ethical knowledge—Man and Woman have chosen both. They have chosen alienation from God because only in doing so is human community possible.

There is separation, difference between each and between each and God, and that separation is necessary if the otherness of either of them, or of God, is to have meaning. Man and Woman must be separated from the Divine if they are to image the Divine, but separation necessarily carries with it the possibility of alienation. However, they also learn that their separation from one another, their difference, is the ground of human and divine community. Without that, community would not be possible. If our imaging of God did not include our otherness, we could only be like him; we could not be individuals. But if we could not be individuals, then we would not be like him. We could not be at all. Thus, though the absolute, transcendent otherness of God would make human being impossible; otherness is nevertheless necessary, namely the otherness of persons, both divine and human.

After revealing themselves to God in response to his call, Woman is told that the consequence of her knowledge of good and evil is pain, and Man is told that the consequence of his knowledge is labor. But these are not two distinct things. The fact that the pain of childbirth is, in English, called *labor* is helpful. The words are also closely related in Hebrew. Thus God does not say essentially different things to Man and Woman. What he says to one he says to both.

The pain of childbirth is a particularly appropriate beginning. For both creation and relation are represented in it. Knowledge, the knowledge of good and evil, the knowledge that brings mortality, makes pain—the pain of bringing forth community—possible. To escape that pain would be to cease to be human. And, implicitly, the escape from pain is impossible even for God. Being in relation to us, he cannot escape the pain that is necessarily part of having created us. God too must weep (see John 11:35 and Moses 7:29–31).

Labor too is an essential part of human-being. Man and Woman were required to dress the garden and keep it (Genesis 2:15; compare Moses 3:15), but they were not able to do so meaningfully. True, they could work in it, but their work would have been unconscious and self-gratifying toil. True labor is done only in relation to another (and it must include the otherness and depth of the other). Only in labor rather than toil can one have human being. The Hebrew word for work, *avodah*, can equally well be translated "service." As is pain, labor is concomitant with creation and required by relation.

The first part of Genesis 4:1, "Adam knew Eve his wife," is a summary of the creation of humans, the final act of the creation story: they have received knowledge by which they can be in relation to one another, and through those relations they can be fruitful. Implicit in all of this is the grounding in the Divine: "I have gotten a man from the Lord" (Genesis 4:1; compare Moses 5:2). The story of creation in Genesis lays the foundation for an understanding of the relationship of humans in community by pointing to Man and Woman as unique individuals bound to each other, and *in virtue of what it means to be human*, to all others. To be human is to be in community, though not always the community of God.

From this theme springs a major theme of biblical writers, namely the return to true community.[20] In order for such a return to occur, humans must recognize themselves as created in the express image of God: unique, potentially fruitful, knowing good from evil by intimate association, and capable of action. Perhaps more than anything else, they must recognize themselves as bound to each other by their being, by the pain and labor—each both positive and negative—of human relation.

---

20. Cf. Isaiah and his call to come forth from physical and spiritual Babylon so Israel can return to their calling as the people of God.

The second story I would like briefly to consider is also the story of ethical response and the relation to other persons. It is the story of Abraham and Isaac. That story begins when Abram is set apart from his country, his kindred, and his father's house—in an order the reverse of geographic order (Genesis 12:1). Chronologically and geographically, one must leave one's father's house first, then one's kindred, and finally one's country. However, Genesis reverses that order. Abram's leave-taking is not merely a chronological and geographic leave-taking. He takes his leave spiritually. Given that he is defined by country, kindred, and father, Abram becomes other than himself and other than his family. Why? In order to make family and Zion possible. Abram's blessing has its origin in his otherness rather than in his identity.

However, having been cut off from his family, having become other, as I read the story, Abram searches for a *theos*. He seeks to create Zion himself, to force it. He thinks of the promised seed as something he can bring about, so he agrees to create that promised posterity with Hagar. In doing so, he implicitly assumes that the other person is not really other: one son is as good as another; for the purposes of the blessing that has become abstract, one wife is as good as another. The otherness of Abram's promise is totalizable by his will; he believes that the future promised in the original disruption is to be brought about by totalizing, by taking control, by his will.

In spite of Abram's attempts to control, his search for the community founded on a *theos* is interrupted. First it is interrupted by his forced dismissal of Ishmael and Hagar. Then, after the covenant marked by his name change, Abraham's attempt to control is interrupted by a call that implicitly asks, as Adam was asked, where he is, a call that erupts in the command to sacrifice Isaac (Genesis 22:1). However, unlike Adam, Abraham responds to this interruptive call with "Here I am"—"Behold me here" or "Ready."

Within the space opened by God's call, Abraham is finally able to be separated from his son, and his son is finally able to be separated from him. The totality that Abraham has willed is finally broken. The binding of the sacrifice, the binding that separates father and son at the altar on Moriah, separates Isaac from Abraham. The community can no longer be the product of Abraham's endeavor because the means of that production is no longer his. It has been taken away by the command to sacrifice his son. Isaac is now genuinely an *other* person to him, given by God in the disruption of Abraham's security. Isaac is an other whose existence before Abraham makes an ethical demand on Abraham. Isaac is one to whom Abraham must respond as another person rather than as a possession. Isaac is one whom, in Abraham's confrontation with the dizzying command of the Divine Other, Abraham is called to serve. In separating father and son, the sacrificial binding binds father to son in Zion.

With the turn toward the ram in the thicket, the promise of posterity can be fulfilled; in that turn it *is* fulfilled. Thus, as soon as the sacrifice is over, the text tells of the birth of Isaac's wife, Rebekah, the other person who marks the beginning of Abraham's posterity (Genesis 22:20–24). Though Abraham's trial begins with him alone, speaking not even to his wife, this second separation, the one that occurs through the binding and turning from sacrifice—separation from both wife and son as individuals rather than extensions of himself—results in the biding and the binding of Zion. Through Rebekah, not one of Abraham's possessions, the second separation results in the fruitfulness of Abraham's covenant. That binding, Zion, is a binding of individuals who stand "over against" each other as do Adam and Eve.

The binding of the sacrificial victim at Moriah results in the binding of Zion, but this binding is not the application of a universal principle. As Søren Kierkegaard argues in *Fear and Trembling*,[21] Abraham's response defies all merely universal principles. Instead, it is the ethical response to the other person that makes possible continued relation to the other person, the continuation of otherness and response. In the beginning, Abram's response is the welcome of the power of the

---

21. Søren Kierkegaard, *Fear and Trembling* (New York: Penguin Books, 1985).

Divine Other. In the end, Abraham's response is the welcome of the filial other and the Divine Other himself.

Though both these stories are stories of unity, they both warn us against looking for the unity of Zion in unity of being, in a totality. In a certain sense, both tell the same story, the story of our fruitful separation (difference), from each other and from God, in Zion. Both are stories of welcoming the other in a relation that seals individuals to each other as individuals. Both call us to our lives before each other. Both make the ethical demand. Both deconstruct totality in favor of Zion.

Both these stories do what I believe all scripture does. They do not describe the life that is required, nor do they give us its principles. Scripture is not guilty of idolatry, though as readers of scripture we often are. Rather than doing philosophy, these stories call to us and disrupt the lazy and unethical comfort of our being-at-home with ourselves and our present situation. In them we hear that Zion is not to be found by looking because it is already here, though we often cannot see it. As I assume do also other scriptural stories, the stories of Adam and Eve and of Abraham and Isaac call us back to where we already are so we can be there for the first time and so we can continue to be there, constantly reborn into Zion.

CHAPTER TEN

Breathing:
Romans 8:1–17

〜

I am going to mingle scripture with the philosophies of men—not because I am unaware of the danger, but precisely because *I am* aware. Scripture gets mingled with philosophy all the time in places such as Sunday School, priesthood and Relief Society, Seminary, and religion classes at BYU and in our institutes of religion. The problem is not so much the mingling. That is inevitable if we speak reflectively of scripture. The problem is our ignorance of that mingling, our assumption that we are not mingling scripture with philosophy when, in fact, we are. Much of what we say about the gospel is simply late nineteenth-century philosophies of men rather than contemporary philosophies of men: Newtonian science mixed, oddly, with a little Comptean positivism, and a dash of idealism thrown in for good measure.

Here I wish to mingle the first seventeen verses of Romans 8 with philosophical reflection. Set against the backdrop of chapter 7, these verses tell of "life in Christ" or "the indwelling Spirit." As a response to the problem described in chapter 7, these verses offer a powerful understanding of what Christian obedience means, an understanding too often misunderstood or ignored by Latter-day Saints. From what I hear from fellow Saints—from what I catch myself thinking—we can well afford to be reminded of these verses and their solution to the problem of human frailty. I hope my mingling of philosophy and scripture will help breathe new life into these verses for those who find themselves still in chapter 7, still living the life in which one intends to be a Christian, but has not yet succeeded. I hope that what I say will help us recover from the suffocation we sometimes think we find in our religious lives.

Romans 7 shows us how, even with the best of intentions, we fail to do good: We know that the law is spiritual: but I am carnal, sold against my will into slavery to sin: "For that which I do I allow not: for what I would, that do I not; but what I hate, that do I. . . . For the good that I would I do not: but the evil which I would not, that I do" (Romans 7:14, 15, 19). Paul describes an ordinary failure, though a tragic one: the inability to do good steadfastly. We have all had the experience: I do something wrong and hate the fact that I have done it. I resolve to do differently and, for a while, I succeed. Eventually, how-ever, I fail. It often seems as if the more determined my resolve, the less capable I am of doing what I believe to be right. In the face of this problem, we comfort ourselves with a variety of excuses: "One step at a time is good enough; nobody's perfect"; "As long as I'm trying, that's what counts." But such excuses fly in the face of the demand made of us by the gospel, and we know it. We also know that our intentions to obey the law are not good enough to guarantee that we will obey. Among the many results are depression, on the one hand, and hypoc-risy, on the other.

If we give up our excuses, the horror of Romans 7 is excruciat-ing. Paul rivals anything Jean-Paul Sartre or Jean Genet has ever writ-ten about the excruciating impossibility of moral action. What Paul writes demands that we acknowledge the problem of our inability to do good—or that we wish it away, ignoring what he describes or twisting it and turning it so he says something else. But the phenomenon will not go away. Sooner or later anyone who sincerely tries to do good will be brought to acknowledge what Paul has described here. And the conso-lations we proffer each other are small consolations because, on the one hand, they deny the humanity of the Savior and, on the other hand, they deny his divine power to save us in this world as well as the next. If we are lucky, that consolation eventually evaporates in the face of our own evil. If we are not lucky, we continue on, chanting "All is well in

Zion; yea, Zion prospereth, all is well" (2 Nephi 28:21), and humming, "if it so be that we are guilty, God will beat us with a few stripes, and at last we shall be saved in the kingdom of God" (2 Nephi 28:8).

Our finitude seems to be the problem. The law is infinite. Therefore, it always exceeds my finite will and grasp. I cannot do what is demanded because it is beyond my power to do so. The law requires too much of me. At the heart of Romans, chapter 7 describes the human condition as tragic failure in the classical sense of "tragic," the failure of our finitude. In it we find a picture of the would-be Christian as a Sophoclean hero, struggling to do good in the face of an absolute inability ultimately to do good: it is not that we do not obey the law, it is that we cannot obey it for any length of time or with any consistency because the law is too much for us. In the face of that inability, we struggle to do good anyway. We are infinitely resigned to our fate, though our resignation is pathetic.

I hope to show that the answer to this problem is a commonplace: the problem described in chapter 7 is a consequence of the fact that the person described in that chapter depends ultimately on only herself. She depends upon herself to do the good, and we all know that we cannot depend on ourselves alone. If we are to do good, we must depend on the Spirit instead.

I am not going to add anything to that commonplace. It is true; what could be added? But in spite of its truth, everything about us says otherwise. It may be a commonplace that we must depend on the Spirit, but that commonplace is contradicted by the very structure that our history has given to ordinary experience: the structure of our culture, the structure of our language and ways of being. These are what I believe almost naturally. At least these things seem so obvious to us that they seem natural. We are sometimes warned against "the philosophies of men," and I think this supposedly natural belief in what our culture and history has taught us is often what is intended by that phrase. As a consequence, though we pay lip service to the commonplace that we ought to live by the Spirit, I do not think we often fully believe it, and I think we often contradict it in spite of ourselves.

Philosophers like the seventeenth-century thinker René Descartes have a penchant for clarity and distinctness. Others, like the twentieth-century Austro-British thinker, Ludwig Wittgenstein, want to dissolve philosophical problems. They want to "show the fly the way out of the bottle,"[1] so it will be bothered no more. In spite of that, philosophers are notorious for making the simple difficult. I am more in sympathy with Wittgenstein than Descartes, but my sympathy lies most with Søren Kierkegaard, a nineteenth-century Dane, and one of the most breathtaking philosophers to have lived. In *Johannes Climacus*, Kierkegaard reports that according to Climacus, the pseudonymous author of Kierkegaard's most important work, *Concluding Unscientific Postscript*, difficulty is the point of philosophy.[2]

That is what I propose to do here, to make more difficult the commonplace that we must depend on the Spirit. Such difficulty is not for everyone. Those with the faith of a child certainly do not need it. Neither do those with the more mature faith of a second naivete,[3] those who have passed from childhood through the trials of adolescence, where we confront the reality of evil and our finitude, and into the maturity of genuine faith. But many of us remain religious adolescents. Many of us are beyond the faith of our childhood but still hoping for naivete to return in its mature form. We spiritual adolescents need things to be more difficult. We need philosophy because it may help us on our path toward mature naivete by awakening us from our dogmatic slumber or from the skepticism to which we are so often reduced when we awake from dogmatic slumber and find ourselves in

---

1. Ludwig Wittgenstein, *Philosophical Investigations*, trans. G. E. M. Anscomb (London: Blackwell, 1958), ¶309.

2. Søren Kierkegaard, *Johannes Climacus, or De omnibus dubitandum est*, in *Philosophical Fragments and Johannes Climacus*, trans. Edna H. Hong and Howard V. Hong (Princeton: Princeton University Press, 1885), 113–73 at 137–38. And we must not forget that Climacus, like many of us, does not understand Christianity, though he writes about its central problem.

3. See the introduction in this volume for more on first and second naivete.

the dark. This essay is for this latter group, for those like myself who are on the way toward second naivete.

Some who know my work will recognize the melody of the song I am about to sing as a beginning because it is one I've sung before. It is a simple song about the history of Western thought, and it goes like this: From the beginning, Western thought has insisted on unity. We have inherited this emphasis on unity from the early Greeks, who might have offered this argument: Whatever is ultimate must be unitary. Why? Well, suppose it is not. Suppose there are two ultimate things. If there are, how are they related to each other such that they are the ultimate source of everything else? If there is nothing that brings them together, then there is no world, and we know there is a world. So there must be something that brings them together, something common to each. But if there is something common to each, then that thing, whatever it is, produces the one world from the two things that we assumed were ultimate. In that case, it seems reasonable to say that whatever uses the two things to make our world is more metaphysically fundamental, more ultimate, than the two things. In other words, if we suppose there are two ultimate things, we come to the conclusion that there is really only one.

Reasoning this way, everything must finally work out to one thing, not two. There is only one reality; there can be only one ultimate explanation for any event or thing. That assumption is at the heart of Western intellectual history. It has made science possible. We have always sought for some unified and enclosed system that would give the systematic and coherent law of reality without reference to anything outside it. As important as this assumption has been for the development of science, it has been less salubrious for our understanding of moral action.

The supposition of one ultimate means that there can be only one origin for good. Either that one origin is me or it is something outside of me. In other words, either I am the unified and enclosed system that makes good possible, or something outside of me is. If I am the origin, fine (though we have the problem described in Romans 7, the problem of my finitude and the infinity of the law). If it is something outside of me, then either I encompass it or it encompasses me, since we have to have closure in order to have unity. Unless I can encompass the grounds for moral behavior, taking control over them, unless they can become part of me, it seems they can never be any more than an authority before which I must bow in acquiescence, which is hardly a description of moral action. Most of us find it hard to imagine that moral action is possible from any other origin than the ego, the "I think." Following the vocabulary of Emmanuel Levinas,[4] I will call this recourse to the individual as the source of moral behavior, autonomy, self-rule.

In autonomy, the individual must depend on himself to do the truly good. I believe Bertrand Russell described the problem of doing good in something like this way: "You can choose what you desire, but you cannot choose your desires." In other words, to most of us it is clear that we can do what we desire to do. But what about what we do not desire to do? If I want to do what is right, I can, but suppose I do not want to do the good thing? How could I choose to do it? What sense would it make for someone to say to me, "But you *should* want to do it"? How can I choose to want something? It appears that either I want it or I do not. Russell's problem is a genuine conundrum for any discussion of moral behavior, but Paul goes Russell one better: even if you do desire to do something, you cannot be assured that you will, especially if what you desire is to do good. It is not just that sometimes we want the wrong thing and, so, choose what is wrong. We sometimes do the bad thing in spite of ourselves. Sometimes we desire to do the right thing yet do the wrong thing.[5]

---

4. Emmanuel Levinas, *Totality and Infinity: An Essay on Exteriority*, trans. Alphonso Lingis (Pittsburgh: Duquesne University Press, 1969).

5. Some try to avoid this by arguing that we must have wanted the wrong thing more than the right thing if that is what we chose. But that goes directly against our experience of our behavior.

As Western thought is often understood, the only alternative to the self-assertion of enclosure and autonomy is suicide or genocide, though usually intellectual rather than physical suicide or genocide. This alternative agrees that unity and closure are necessary, but it sees the shortcomings and inability of the individual. Thus, it says that the unitary, closed origin of good is outside of me and that I must become part of it, if I am to do good. Rather than encompassing what is outside of my autonomous self, taking control of it, I must be encompassed by it. I must give up my individuality and freedom, my autonomy, to the control of a closed totality that is bigger than I am. I must disappear into this larger autonomy. Some ideas of God require this kind of self-annihilation. This has also been the Marxist alternative. This way of seeing things comes in a variety of guises. Without taking the time to explain why, let me say simply that I believe this alternative to autonomy fails even more fully than the historically more common individualistic alternative. It fails primarily because, though it is not individualistic, this alternative continues to assert the primacy of autonomy: divine, social, historical, or state power, but totality, enclosure, system, and power anyway. Autonomy is the rule, whether it is individual autonomy or the autonomy of history, the State, or a false god.

The individual is almost always assumed to be the ontological and ethical origin of the good. It may be that an origin outside the individual is posited. But the individual can do good only because he includes that origin within himself. On this view, an act is only an ethical act if it is the internalized free choice of an individual. Many of the ways we think about ethics assume the primacy of the individual and of freedom. We say, for example, that unless the command I obey is mine, I cannot be ethical. We struggle to teach our children that they must learn to choose for themselves, that their ethical behavior must come from within. In our academic discussions of ethics, the broadly appealing ethics of Kant are an excellent example of our understanding of the relation of the good to the individual.

For most of us, most of the time, recourse to the individual seems the only possibility. With the fool, Polonius, we tell ourselves, "To thine own self be true."[6] However, Romans 7 is a *reductio ad absurdum* of the desire to bring about the good by grasping it, willing it, mastering it—by interiorizing it and then acting from that interiority freely. Reliance on oneself seems unavoidable, but reliance on oneself ends in Sophoclean tragedy, at best. As Proverbs says, "He that trusteth in his own heart is a fool" (Proverbs 28:25). Is there a way of maintaining individuality and having something other than myself as an adequate source of the ability to do good without committing a kind of suicide, without giving up all semblance of individuality? Are my only choices the tragedy of being a free individual but unable, ultimately, to do good or, in contrast, being subject to some force exterior to me and, so, able to do good, but no longer an individual in any meaningful sense? Paul's answer is yes. But his answer does not mean what we think it does. To make sense of his answer we must think quite differently than we are accustomed to thinking. The Christian alternative cannot easily be found within the structure of Western thought, though it can be found there if one goes looking.

A beginning of this Christian rethinking of weakness of the will is to be found in asking, "What if the law is not the kind of thing ever to be willed or grasped? What if doing good is neither one of my powers nor a power to which I must accede because it is not a power of any kind? What if willing and grasping are themselves the problem because they convert doing good into a question of control?" Though Romans 7 shows us that autonomy—free self-rule—cannot bring about the good, and it shows us the tragedy of autonomy, it does not show us that there is no good or that we cannot do it—unless we also assume, as we often do and as we think we must, that autonomy is the only grounds for the possibility of the good.

Paul proposes that, in spite of what logically seems to be the case at first glance, there is an alternative assumption. Romans 8 comes as

---

6. Shakespeare, *Hamlet,* act 1, scene 3.

an answer to the Sophoclean problem by showing another kind of law and another kind of obedience: We need not trust in our own hearts, nor must we be swallowed up in something beyond ourselves. If Romans 7 shows us the problem of autonomy, then Romans 8 shows us heteronomy, obedience to a law that is not mine to grasp, appropriate, and master because it is the law of the Other. It shows us obedience to a law with which I do not have to struggle and which I do not have to make mine. In fact, the law of Romans 8 cannot be made mine or anyone's, even by an act of will, so there can be no question of struggle with it. Neither is it a matter of ceasing to exist in the face of the new law by becoming one with something outside of myself. The law of Romans 8—if, indeed, it continues to make sense to call law what calls for the Christian's obedience—is outside the Parmenidean logic of unity. Rather than the dominance and necessity of ultimate unity, we will see Paul propose another way of thinking about the world and the possibility of good: the moral law is always the rule of another, never self-rule, but it is not subjugation to or absorption into another. Romans 8 shows us life in Christ Jesus, a life in which we remain individual while we are obligated but not subjected to the Other Person and other persons. In chapter 8 we will see life in the Spirit.

Verses One and Two

> [1]This means there is now no condemnation for those whose being is in Christ Jesus, [2]for the law of the Spirit of life in Christ Jesus has freed me from the law of sin and death.

Paul ends chapter 7 jubilantly: "Thanks be to God through Jesus Christ our Lord! So, by myself I serve the law of God only in my thoughts, while with the flesh I serve the law of sin" (Romans 7:25). His jubilation comes before his summation of the problem, but that summation is followed by verse 1 of chapter 8.[7] Paul's jubilation, joy

---

7. The chapter division, created more than a thousand years after Paul wrote his letter, is unfortunate because it divides the single thought that extends across Romans

in the face of the tragedy he has just described, is possible because those who have their existence, not in themselves, but in the Other—in the Divine Other—those whose life is not merely a life of autonomy, do not find themselves judged and separated from the Good. They are not doomed, for their being is neither in-itself nor for-itself. It is being-in-and-for-another, but not an other that absorbs and digests everything but itself. Rather than the closed, solid, impenetrable Parmenidean being presumed in the history of Western philosophy, for those in Christ, being is founded in what exceeds them and calls them. The choices that seem so inevitable from within autonomy fade away because we are not autonomous—and neither, as we will see, are we subjugated.

Life in the Other, heteronomous law, frees us from the alienation of simple autonomy, an alienation from God and even from ourselves, because heteronomous life is incompatible with merely autonomous life. If we live heteronomously, our lives are fuller because we are not confined to the boundaries of our selves. Our lives are always a matter of excess and extravagance, the excess and extravagance of what is other than us, of what cannot be subsumed or systematized in autonomy. We can and must create order. However, order and the Greek *logos* (rather than Christian one) are not fundamental. Instead, order and rationality come from the abundance of life as a loving response to it. Life creates order and rationality; they do not make life what it is. Order and rationality are a response to the fact that not everything is contained within the ego, to the fact that something challenges the I's claim to autonomy, namely the Other. They are the human response to an ethical demand, the demand that we explain ourselves, that we accommodate our existence to the existence of others.[8] According to a common reading, as a history of autonomy, Western philosophy has held its breath for 2,500 years.[9] Its spirit has been its own (autonomy)

7:25 and Romans 8:1 into two pieces, causing us to miss the fact that they are part of the same thought.

8. See Levinas, *Totality and Infinity*, 201.

9. There are, of course, better readings of that history.

and not the Holy Spirit (heteronomy). Enclosed within itself, Western philosophy has breathed nothing but itself. In fact, it has not even desired to breath something other than itself. Many of our metaphors for knowledge are metaphors of vision: "I see what you mean." As those metaphors illustrate, Western philosophy has thought seeing to be so important that it has, more often than not, not even thought about breathing. Even Hegel's *Phenomenology of Spirit*, though a frank admission of the need for Spirit and breath in thought, ends up an exercise in holding one's breath—suffocation—because it never opens itself to anything exterior. In spite of itself, like the usual reading of the previous history of philosophy, Hegel's *Phenomenology* is an account of breathing in an ultimately closed space, the space of the totality of knowledge, the Absolute.

Christianity proposes something else. It proposes that, like Adam, the dust of our autonomous, dead flesh cannot make itself live, but it can be brought to life if we receive the breath of God. Having the Spirit, breathing, is always a matter of exteriority and exposure; to breathe is necessarily to allow what is exterior to come in. It is to expose the interior of my lungs, the very center of my interiority, to the exterior. In place of the suffocation and appropriation found in the autonomous self, Christianity reveals exposure to the Other through the Spirit, through life-giving breath. Life in another, namely Christ, frees us from death and suffocation, for that life gives us our breath. The solution to the problem we have seen—either self-enclosed, tragically heroic morality or self-annihilation in the Absolute—is found in the Spirit, in bringing the Other into our autonomous, enclosed world and fracturing our autonomy by that entry. The Spirit, the breath of God, is not another enclosure in which our enclosure is subsumed. The Spirit is not another all-encompassing law to which I must submit. If it were, it would be only another death. The alternative to the death found in self-rule would be only the death of annihilation in the Other. Instead of being a modification of the enclosed self or an enclosure into which the self must enter, the law of the Spirit is a breach in enclosure, the destruction of autonomy, the destruction of the law of power. Breathing is not a matter of bringing everything into ourselves. Neither is it a matter of giving ourselves over so completely to what is exterior to us that we lose our identity. I cannot breathe if I do not have a body into which the Spirit can enter, a body separate from the Spirit; I must remain an individual if I am to receive the Spirit. But breathing breaks the solidity of the wall supposed between myself and my exterior. I cannot breath if enclosure is the rule. Breathing the breath of life, "having the Spirit," requires the exposure of my interiority to the exterior.

Jesus spoke to Nicodemus of salvation in the Spirit. Presumably, Nicodemus was an obedient man. Many presume that he was a member of the Sanhedrin, and whether he was or not, it is clear that he was an upstanding and exemplary member of his community, one of the rulers (see John 3:1). But in spite of his self-discipline and uprightness in the law, Jesus told him he must be transformed, reborn, and Nicodemus could not understand how that could be. We can imagine him asking, "What remains for me to do? I am not yet perfect, but I try very hard to do all that the law requires." In answer Jesus said:

> That which is born of the flesh is flesh; and that which is born of the Spirit is spirit. Marvel not that I said unto thee, Ye must be born again. The wind bloweth where it listeth, and thou hearest the sound thereof, but canst not tell whence it cometh, and whither it goeth: so is every one that is born of the Spirit. (John 3:6–8)

By itself, the flesh is not the living, human body; it is the autonomous body, the unbreathing, uninspired body. Merely autonomous life is suffocation. Rebirth requires breath and wind. Without that, rebirth would be stillbirth. Only the end of autonomy, the entry into the individual by the Other, can bring birth about.

The entry of the Spirit, the breach in autonomy by the breath of God, is life, deliverance from mere flesh by the revivification of that flesh. But the Spirit that revivifies is not to be mastered, and it is not something to be mastered by. The law of the Spirit gives life, but it cannot be reduced to a set of rules or written down in an agenda. Rebirth is not a goal to be planned for and attained. One cannot master the wind, the breath. But neither is one mastered by it; the Spirit is not a ruler, at least not of the kind to which we are accustomed. Life is not a matter of mastery, either of self or by another. Life, heteronomous life, the only real life, is a matter of openness and exposure to the Other. It is a matter of breathing. It is a matter of accepting the breath of life.

To open oneself to the breath of life is to be freed from death. To breathe is no longer to suffocate. Exposure to the Other brings freedom from alienation and death, though that freedom is threatening because it is exposure, because I must trust in someone other than myself and because it is always possible, at least in principle, that the Other to whom I am exposed can kill me. Those who would live must give up holding their breath, breathing only their own flesh. They must breathe the breath of another, the breath of Christ Jesus.

Verses Three and Four

> [3]What the law was powerless to do, because of the weakness of flesh, God did, sending his own Son in the likeness of sinful flesh for a sin offering, thereby condemning us in the flesh, [4]so that the just demands of the law might be satisfied in us, who conduct ourselves not according to the flesh, but according to the Spirit.

Autonomous life, mere dead—because unbreathing, uninspired—flesh, is weak. Without the breath of life, it is powerless. Perhaps that is why autonomy makes such an issue of power. Romans 7 shows that autonomy is unable to do what it desires to do, namely bring about the good. But the Father, by sending his Son among us, was able to reveal the barrenness of mere autonomy and, thus, to condemn it so that we can live justly.

For the Father, too, the law is a matter of heteronomy. He is not a merely autonomous being who demands that we submit our autonomy to his. The law of God is heteronomous through and through, not the submission of one autonomy to another. The law that the Father offers does not substitute his autonomy for ours. He does not condemn us by making a demand of us with which we must struggle or by issuing a decree to which we must submit. Rather, we are condemned by the very fact that in response to our autonomous demand for freedom (which turns out to be only alienation), he freely offers himself and his Son. Without recourse to any "need" for freedom, he exposes himself and his Son to us and our injustice. Indeed, his exposure of himself is proof that he is not the autonomous being pictured by the tradition, for an autonomous being cannot expose himself. In principle, cannot. In exposing himself and his Son, the Father reveals the alienation inherent in our autonomy and freedom. His free gift reveals the paucity of our freedom, a freedom of needs and demands. In turn, that revelation of freedom makes another freedom—freedom in Christ— possible, a freedom of grace and love.

God's offer of the Son, therefore, is anything but the offer of a scapegoat. He does not offer his Son in response to some demand for vengeance and retribution, whether that demand is a particular demand or a metaphysical one. To do so would be to authorize such demands. To do so would be to put an end to the possibility of justice. It would be to give power to injustice by acknowledging it and acquiescing to it. Instead, the Father puts an end to any such demand by offering his Son and himself in response to our injustice. He does not put an end to our injustice; he offers even the Divine to us in our injustice. There is no hint of autonomy, self-sufficiency, or misconceived freedom in the offer. They are beside the point.

We popularly speak of the atonement as a matter of fulfilling the demands of some impartial and even hateful metaphysical principle of justice. The contemporary thinker René Girard has argued convincingly that such a conception is pagan, not Christian, and that the message of Christianity is not that there was an ultimate scapegoat, but that scapegoating is avoidable and must be avoided.[10] Christ has called both himself and the Holy Spirit, "the Paraclete"—not just the Comforter, though that translation is meaningful and important, but the one who stands beside another, the advocate, the defense attorney (see John 14:16; see also 1 John 2:1). Jesus offers himself in our defense—against our autonomous selves rather than against some metaphysical principle of justice to which he must bow. He offers himself so that we will be able to meet the demands that justice makes of us. Heteronomous law is the life of Christ.

The offering Christ makes is in the incarnation. By being embodied, the Son offers us his breath that we may breathe. Unembodied, God would remain merely autonomous, either enclosed within himself and, therefore, never able to obligate us by offering himself to us, or so open and amorphous as to be meaningless. A breath without a body is not even a breath. God's offering is the body and the blood of his Son; it is his breath, his life.

Paul says that the incarnation presents the Son in the likeness of sinful flesh, suggesting to some that his life among us was only an appearance. Some gnostics of the first- and second-century church believed as much, and it was against this denial of the incarnation of Christ in a body like our own that the early church fathers fought tenaciously.[11] Today, if we speak of Christ as half human and half Divine rather than fully human and, at the same time, fully Divine, I think we make a gnostic suggestion. But the gnostic assumption is a misreading. Christ did appear among us in the flesh, but his flesh was not sinful, autonomous flesh, though it may have seemed to be so. We mistake individuality and embodiment for autonomy, thinking they

---

10. René Girard, *Violence and the Sacred*, trans. Patrick Gregory (Baltimore: Johns Hopkins University Press, 1978).

11. See Michel Henry, *L'Incarnation, Une phénoménologie de la chair* (Paris: Seuil, 2000), especially pp. 14–19, for a good synopsis of the relevant issues. Though we think of the Council of Nicea as deciding the nature of the Godhead, its most important issue was the refutation of the gnostic idea that the Son was not embodied.

are necessarily identical. He was, indeed, an embodied individual, but he did not live autonomously, and by not doing so, he both showed us the possibility of living justly and condemned us for not doing so. By living as an individual human, Christ demonstrated that alienation is not essential to individuality, and he showed that the freedom of arbitrariness and individuality, as well as the search for mastery and domination—even of the self—is beside the point.

Justice is possible for and by those who breathe. It is a matter of exhalation as well as inhalation, of expiration as well as inspiration. But justice is not a matter of either mastery or submission. It is a matter of meeting our obligations, obligations to the Other incurred because of his sacrifice. Justice is not a matter of disciplining ourselves to follow a rule imposed on us, but of being infused with the offering of Christ. It is a matter of breathing in the breath which he expires and returning that breath to another. It is a matter of being, ourselves, a paraclete rather than a judge. It is a matter of finding our being, not in ourselves, but in others.

If we live autonomously, we cannot meet the just demands of the law, because we cannot breathe. Bounded flesh cannot reach beyond itself, cannot get outside itself, so it cannot do justice, no matter how hard it tries. But the living law is contrary to the dead and breathless freedom demanded in autonomy and required in response to the law of autonomy. Because the autonomous individual reacts allergically to anything exterior to himself, assuming that it demands his subjugation, he insists on the freedom of autonomy (and, often, in subjugating what is other than himself). As a result, he takes his obligation to the Son to be nothing more than a threat: "Do what I say, or die." Even if the autonomous person desires to do otherwise, once the law is a threat, he cannot obey it with any consistency. Sooner or later, he will assert his own existence in the face of that threat. Sooner or later he will act unjustly. But the person needs no self-defense, for the law he perceives as a threat is really the manifestation of the Paraclete. It is really what breaks the boundary of his flesh so that the breath of life may enter, a breath that makes justice possible.

Thus, the irony is that the Son's demand is not the demand of another autonomy threatening a person's autonomy. It is odd even to call it a demand, since, though the person feels obligated, the Son does not demand. He is Other than the person, and that otherness is a threat. But the threat is only a threat to the person's continued, dead existence. It is a threat only to a suffocating life that breathes only flesh and never Spirit. Rather than standing before a person making a demand for the sake of his own autonomy, the Son stands beside the person and beside any to whom the person would be unjust, always already breathing the breath of life into them, always already disrupting the person's claim to autonomy and opening the possibility of justice. The disruption of autonomy by heteronomy does not negate or overcome autonomy's freedom. Freedom in the sense we usually understand that term simply ceases to be an issue.

Experience (with the emphasis on the *ex*), not freedom, is the issue in heteronomy. As the twentieth-century German philosopher Hans-Georg Gadamer argues, experience is always of the individual, never the universal,[12] so it cannot be reduced to autonomy, to some systematic, complete, and in-itself whole. As he also argues, experience is essentially negative: "Every experience worthy of the name crosses out our expectation."[13] We are never left the same after an experience. Experience is always of what is other than the sameness we expect.

When Odysseus leaves Ithaca to travel in the world, one can argue that he seeks knowledge, not experience. He wishes to see much and to hear some, but he returns to the same place from which he left, essentially unchanged. For all of his sightseeing, he remains the same. Though he appears to have ventured into what is exterior to him, he

---

12. Hans-Georg Gadamer, *Wahrheit und Methode* (Tübingen: J. C. B. Mohr, 1960, 1975), 334; Gadamer, *Truth and Method*, trans. rev. Joel Weinsheimer and Donald G. Marshall, 2nd rev. ed. (New York: Continuum, 1975, 2004), 346.

13. Gadamer, *Wahrheit und Methode*, 338; Gadamer, *Truth and Method*, 350, trans. Weinsheimer and Marshall.

has not really done so. He has had no *e*xperience. If I may coin a word, we might say he has had only *in*perience. He has lived freely. He has seen and done much. But he has encompassed what he has encountered, brought it into himself, to return home with it as booty. He now owns more; he has appropriated events and places far from Ithaca, but he is himself the same. As the homecoming scene of the *Odyssey* emphasizes, the Odysseus who returns to Ithaca is exactly the same individual as the one who left. Odysseus needs no paraclete, for he can defend himself; what he does comes from within himself and, in the long run, is what he chooses to do; what he encounters does not change him, but he takes possession of it. Odysseus is the model of an autonomous individual.

Abraham is different.[14] As Abram he leaves his country, his kin, and his father's house, never to return. One might presume he is alienated, but his separation from country, kin, and house are to bring about justice: "In thee shall all families of the earth be blessed" (Genesis 12:3). Abram is separated, but not alienated. The very point of his separation is ethical life, justice.

Later Abram's autonomy is interrupted once again by the command to be circumcised and his change of name to Abraham: he does not return; his identity does not remain the same. In circumcision the organ of regeneration is interrupted and exposed as a sign of Abraham's exposure and obligation to God, an obligation to be fecund, an obligation that is never merely individual and that cannot be mastered or, as Abraham discovers, planned. The question of Abraham's freedom—a question that cannot be avoided from within autonomy— never comes up. He is the one with whom God has covenanted for the blessing of the world. He is, therefore, obliged, but not subjugated. In fact, in being obliged to God and the entire world, Abraham is a ruler, not a subject (see Genesis 17:6–8). Abraham stands for the world as a

---

14. I owe this comparison of Odysseus and Abraham to a suggestion made by Emmanuel Levinas, *Totality and Infinity*, 271.

lawyer stands for his client; he becomes its paraclete. By being obliged to God, he becomes a defender and a blessing, and in that he rules.

The point of the Divine sacrifice is the satisfaction of justice. The law demands that we be just, but, of ourselves, we are unable to do so because we are unable to escape ourselves. Tragic heroism is the only possibility. But when the breath of life, the Spirit, is breathed into us in covenant, then we are alive and able to be just. We escape our lives, but not through ourselves. The interruption of our autonomy by the Other comes in order to bring about justice, perhaps justice for ourselves, though it is difficult to imagine how one who is autonomous can demand justice for herself, and one who lives heteronomously would have no need to make such a demand. Certainly the interruption of our autonomy comes in order to bring the blessing of justice for all the world. It comes to make possible ethical life, life *with* one another rather than lives of domination and cruelty.

Verses Five through Eight

> [5]Those who have their being towards the flesh aspire to the things of the flesh; those who have their being towards the Spirit, the things of the Spirit. [6]For, to aspire to the flesh is death, but aspiration to the Spirit is life and peace, [7]because an aspiration to the flesh is hatred of God, not being subject to God's law, or even having the power to be subject to him; [8]those who are in the flesh are powerless to please God.

If autonomous being is fundamental, if we are, like Parmenides' "Entity"—enclosed and enclosing solid bodies, without interstices and unbreached by the influx of breath—then we can aspire to nothing not already contained in those bodies of solid flesh. We can breathe only ourselves, and we must quickly suffocate. In contrast, if our being is predicated on what is exterior to us, on what is prior to that being, if our flesh is infused with the breath of life, then we can aspire to life. We become living bodies.

Aspiration toward only ourselves is expiration, not aspiration. To breathe only flesh is to be dead, and to be dead is to be in opposition to life and the giver of life. In contrast, to aspire toward the Other, to aspire to inspiration, is to aspire to life and peace. This is because death—autonomy—is alienation from God. Autonomy is not only not to be under the law of God, it is to be unable to be under that law because the very thing that constitutes the law, namely heteronomy and the breath of life that it brings, is absent.

When we are autonomous, we see the question of ethics as a question of power: do we have the power to do good? But to reduce the question of the good to a question of power is to reduce ethics to agonistics. War is the outcome of autonomy, and this is true whether we speak of the autonomy of the self or the autonomy of some overarching entity to which we are subject. If I am complete in myself, then anything exterior to me is a threat. Anything other than myself must be subdued or I must give in to it, but in either case, the only possible attitude is one of battle and struggle, the struggle to the death that Hegel portrays in the fourth chapter of *The Phenomenology of Spirit*.[15] For this reason, the autonomous self can have no relation to the law but one of struggle, and most of us—indeed, all—are all too familiar with that struggle.

In such a situation, peace is impossible, even if it were possible finally to win the struggle with the law. For peace is not simply the cessation of war. To have won the war, finally to have disciplined the self or to have submitted to the will of another, to have destroyed the enemy or to have been destroyed, is not to have found peace. Peace and war are not opposites; they are incommensurables. Since autonomy is an insistence on the enclosed self and the enclosure of everything in the self, it is the sin of Cain, murder for gain. It is the destruction of the

---

15. G. W. F. Hegel, *The Phenomenology of Spirit*, trans. A. V. Miller (Oxford: Oxford University Press, 1977). Hegel, too, sees that the only way out of the struggle is to give it up. Significantly, he argues that servitude rather than mastery will allow us to have the selfhood we sought in mastery. Nevertheless, in his argument "Spirit" never gets outside itself. It is condemned never to breathe.

otherness of what is not the same (what is not enclosed within the autonomous entity) for the benefit of the autonomous entity. Autonomy is not peace, even when successful, for finally to have murdered everyone who opposes me is not to have brought peace.

In contrast, peace is justice for and dedication to the Other. As a consequence, those who are in the flesh and have no breath are powerless to be in a positive relation to God, for that relation requires living in peace, not satisfying his whims. Though those whose being is in the flesh would rid themselves of it if they could, murder is in their hearts, for the only being that ultimately matters is their own. But to please God is to be just, as he is just. It is to be accommodated to his character, the character of the Paraclete, not the murderer.

Verse Nine

> [9]You, however, are not in the flesh, but in the Spirit—if the Spirit of God dwells in you. If anyone does not have the Spirit of Christ, that person is not his.

The possibility of heteronomous life, obedience to the law, righteousness, is not a pie-in-the-sky possibility. It is not something we must wait for the eternities to inherit. Those whose autonomy has been disrupted by the sacrifice of Jesus Christ, by the offering without demand, now find themselves under the law of heteronomy, open to the Other, breathing and, therefore, capable of justice—as long as they remain exposed to the Other, as long as they allow their lungs to turn outward to the breath of God. The breath of the autonomous is only their own; they breathe nothing more than their own flesh and, therefore, they die. But those who live heteronomously, those who have been interrupted by the sacrifice of Jesus Christ and the influx of the Spirit—who have been converted—are interpenetrated by the breath of the Other. The movement of their diaphragm is not an autonomous act.[16] It is the individual's response to another, to *the* Other. Breathing happens between the inner and the outer, not merely as a matter of one or the other.

Verses Ten and Eleven

> [10]If, then, Christ is in you, the body is dead because of sin, but the Spirit is life because of justice. [11]If the Spirit of the One who raised Jesus from death dwells in you, then he who raised Christ from death will make your mortal bodies alive by his Spirit which dwells in you.

If we have received the breath of God through Jesus Christ, we have been resurrected, here and now. We await a second, final resurrection to immortal bodies, but the most important resurrection, spiritual resurrection, has already occurred. It has brought our bodies to life in this life so that we may be just.

If God has breathed into us through his Son, Jesus Christ, then we become like Christ, the new Adam, the Unique One.[17] Heteronomy makes our individuality possible, for autonomous individuality is nihilism, death. Only if there is another can individuality make sense. The mortal resurrection brought about by conversion is a resurrection to life and individuality as well as community; it is a destruction of death and autonomy and a foreshadowing of the resurrection that is to come.

Verses Twelve and Thirteen

> [12]Therefore, fellow saints, we have an obligation—but not to the flesh, to live according to the flesh; [13]for if you live

---

16. Note that *phronēsis* ("prudence" or "good judgment") is from *phrēn* ("diaphragm"). See Henry George Liddell and Robert Scott, comps. *A Greek-English Lexicon* (1843; repr., Oxford: Clarendon, 1996), s.v. θρήν.

17. John Bowker translates Genesis 3:22 as "He [Adam] is become like the unique One among us." John Bowker, *The Targums and Rabbinic Literature* (Cambridge: Cambridge University Press, 1969), 117–18.

according to the flesh, you are condemned to die, but if you
kill the deeds of the body by the Spirit, you will live.

Mortal resurrection creates an obligation in us, the obligation to
justice. But that is not an obligation to ourselves and our autonomy,
since our autonomy is dead. Neither is it an obligation to some exterior autonomy. We are obliged by our very being to be just to those
who stand before us. We are obliged to expose ourselves to their needs
and to work to satisfy those needs. The Other gives me my breath, the
breath upon which I draw for my life, so it is the breath which I must
exhale. To have received the Spirit of God is to be obligated, to give as
the Spirit gave to a brother or sister, to one who also needs the breath
of life.

Autonomy creates no real obligation; ultimately obligation to self
makes no real sense. As a result, those for whom life is a matter of
body but not of breathing are always at the moment of death. Ironically, though they fear death more than anything and do everything
to prevent it, they are always dying and, so, unable to live or to give
life. Sophoclean heroism, recognition of the imminence of death and
bravery in the face of it, is the only alternative for the constantly dying.
But the autonomy of the body is destroyed by inspiration; the breath
of the Other kills death and resurrects us; those who breathe in the
breath of life live and give life.

Verse Fourteen

[14]All who are led by the Spirit of God, are the sons of God.

The answer to the contradiction between our finitude and the infinity of the law is found in the Spirit. But how can one be led by a
breath? There is nothing to see; how can we follow? Philosophy has
constantly demanded and continues to demand vision: we must see
the truth, we must behold it. But the gaze is the work of autonomy.
Vision converts the exterior into the interior. It takes a position of
superiority to what is seen and masters it. The eye is an extension of

the hand; but the breath is an infusion through the nose and mouth. If we are autonomous, we cannot be led by a breath, for there is nothing to see, so we must constantly fail as we try to do good. Our own light does not reach far enough for us to see, and the Other gives not light, but breath. In the absence of light, what can we do? We can be led by that breath if we inhale.

The command of the Other, a command to justice, is a breath we can receive, as does the Son, and if we do, then we are also sons of God: we do the same thing that he does. (The point is not about the gender of God's offspring, but their imitation of the Son.) To be Christlike is to hear and to breathe. It is to respond by offering oneself to justice, not merely to submit.

Verse Fifteen

> [15]You did not receive a spirit of slavery that caused you to fear again; instead you received a spirit of adoption, by which we cry out, "Abba! Father."

The breath of life does not subjugate us. We are not simply subsumed into the will of God and his supposedly more primordial autonomy. There is nothing to fear because, having opened ourselves to the breath of God, we are not protecting our autonomy. Our resurrection in and through Christ makes us sons—children—of God. The Father breathes into our dead, Adamic bodies and makes us his children. Though we were outside of the divine family ties in alienating autonomy, we are, once again, part of a family and not merely on our own. We obey because we are obliged to obey by our openness to the Other in an eternal family, not because we are subjected but because we love. Our obedience is a matter of our parentage and our filiation.

Verses Sixteen and Seventeen

> [16]The Spirit himself bears witness with our spirit, that we are the children of God. [17]But if we are children, then we are heirs:

heirs of God, heirs with Christ—provided that we suffer with him so we may also be glorified with him.

The Spirit breathes into us the knowledge that we are part of a divine family, a group of at least three that immediately spreads out to infinity. Our inhalation of the breath of life is the knowledge that we live with others in fraternity and sorority.

If we continue to breathe, we become as the Son of God; we become the children of God. With Christ, we inherit what the Father has to give: "And he that receiveth my Father receiveth my Father's kingdom; therefore all that my Father hath shall be given unto him" (Doctrine and Covenants 84:38). We are accustomed to the promise of the glory we are to inherit: power, authority, honor. In noticing these, however, we often overlook the rest of that inheritance. We often forget that to inherit the glory of God is also to inherit suffering. Only the dead, the absolutely dead, do not suffer. Those who live and breathe must suffer with Christ—be exposed with Christ—or deny him.

The suffering of Christ is unjust suffering. It is not deserved or even explicable. Christ's suffering is the concomitant obverse of the fact that he has poured himself out into the lives and bodies of others in order to be just and to bring justice about (see Philippians 2:7). His mercy is his justice, a justice that mercifully obligates us to justice by exposing itself to injustice. By his mercy and justice, he disrupts the agony of our autonomy. He calls us to justice by suffering unjustly.

We find autonomy, life in the Absolute, appealing because it seems to hide us from exposure and suffering. But the avoidance of suffering to be found in autonomy is unavoidably agonistic because it is unavoidably egoistic. It is agony. Avoiding suffering brings us the agony described in Romans 7, and it inflicts agony on those who are other than ourselves. When we choose to avoid suffering, we choose to suffer death and agony, and we choose to inflict injustice. If we breathe in the breath of life, we cannot forget that God himself suffered and continues to suffer. His suffering—his allowing rather than determining—is his glory.

Jesus's suffering injustice for justice is his glory, but Moses 1:5 and 1:39 indicate that his work is also his glory. The autonomous individual conceives of work as that which is to be completed, as something to be finished and then encompassed or left behind. The autonomous individual conceives of her existence as a work to be accomplished and is frustrated that, given her finitude, its only completion is death. She cannot perfect herself, and so she assumes that perfection is impossible—"at least in this life," as they say. For the autonomous individual, the point is to get to the point where one needs no more to work, where everything that needs to be done has been done. In other words, though she would never describe it in these terms, the autonomous individual desires death.

Although already dead—because unbreathing—the autonomous individual seeks death by seeking to bring an end to time. He seeks to be contemporaneous with himself and his works. Since he is autonomous, undisturbed by the Other, he would give his works to no one but himself. He would have everything fit into one spherical and systematic ball of being, of which he is the identity. The living God, however, not only does not renounce work, he affirms it. There is no completion of the work of God, just as and for the same reason that there is no end to his glory. For God, something always remains to be done. He has never finished exhaling. He can never have been exposed to us and the possibility of our injustice enough. Rather than living in the already over, God lives in the "not yet," where there is still time, where it is still possible to act. Only in the not yet does justice remain a possibility, and only in the not yet does our obligation to bring about justice make sense. Unlike the autonomous, for the heteronomous, work is a matter of grace, the gift to the Other, the breath of life.

God's mercy is his justice. His work is his glory. His glory is his suffering. His suffering is his grace. His grace is his Spirit.

Index

Neal A. Maxwell Institute
for Religious Scholarship

Brigham Young University's Neal A. Maxwell Institute for Religious Scholarship is devoted to the study of texts, particularly religious texts. Our primary area of emphasis is Latter-day Saint scripture. We bring together scholars from a variety of backgrounds and disciplines to study these writings, thus fostering a useful cross-fertilization of approaches and disciplinary insights.

The Maxwell Institute fosters scholarship on Latter-day Saint scripture, as well as on other inspired writings that have come forth as a result of the Restoration. Scriptural and related studies are made available in books and other formats and in three of our periodicals—the *Journal of the Book of Mormon and Other Restoration Scripture*, *Studies in the Bible and Antiquity*, and the *FARMS Review*.

The Maxwell Institute pursues and supports the study of religious and other texts from the ancient world, through late antiquity, and on into the medieval period. A major emphasis of our Center for the Preservation of Ancient Religious Texts is research on the Bible in antiquity, centering on the reception of the Bible in early Christian and Jewish tradition. The Institute's Middle Eastern Texts Initiative publishes bilingual editions, in three separate series, of the principal works of some of the greatest Muslim, Christian, and Jewish thinkers.

Our mission reaches over our own walls into the BYU academic community and beyond. We sponsor conferences and other public events, provide research grants, and support interdisciplinary research and publications. All of this work is made possible because of generous support from major contributors.